SIR JOHN SCOT
LORD SCOTSTARVIT

His Life and Times

Scotstarvit Tower

SIR JOHN SCOT
LORD SCOTSTARVIT

His Life and Times

by

T. G. SNODDY

Printed by
T. AND A. CONSTABLE
EDINBURGH

SBN 9oo897 oi 5

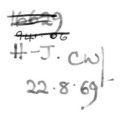

CONTENTS

LIST OF ILLUSTRATIONS

PREFACE

Sir John Scot, a descendant of the House of Buccleuch, Director of Chancery, Lord of Session, and Privy Councillor; he commands attention by his positive career as a statesman, scholar, and patriot. He gave noteworthy service in the patronage of letters. To him we owe the first collected editions of the poems of William Drummond and Arthur Johnston, and the *Delitiae Poetarum Scotorum*, the cream of Scottish Latinity in verse. He was responsible also for the first Atlas of Scotland composed of the maps of Timothy Pont and printed in his celebrated European series by the publisher Blaeu.

It has been said with some truth that from Duns Scotus until the advent of Sir Walter no name of Scot was more highly reputed than his in the learned circles of Europe. Domiciled in his primitive Tower of Scotstarvit he lived intellectually—and by actual intercourse—in the broad world of European culture.

When the Court moved to England in the reign of James, and of Charles, and the Privy Council exercised unusual powers as an official executive, he shared largely in its responsibility and continued at the centre of the national life until the establishment of the Cromwellian rule in 1650.

For the student of history the account of this little-publicised career sheds its peculiar light on the manner of government and the familiar converse of monarch and statesmen in that age. The practical effect of the bond of kinship and the influence of feudal relationship can also be clearly discerned. It was against the entrenched force of hereditary lordship that the land-owning gentry fought for civil rights in the enjoyment and use of their possessions. The appearance on the political scene of 900 landed petitioners engaging Sir John Scot to pursue their cause before Parliament in 1648, illustrates the organisation of a new social movement destined to assault ancient privilege and to lead in time to a state of greater freedom and equity.

Sir John was particularly involved in the proceedings arising from Charles's autocratic action in changing the Session and revoking the grant and disposition of Church properties. His debate

7

at the Palace of Whitehall with the Earl of Haddington, under the presidency of the Duke of Buckingham, and later in the King's presence, must remain as a unique event in Scottish history.

Notice is also taken of Scotstarvit's brief biographies of Scottish statesmen, perused and commended by Carlyle, where the lives of earlier and contemporary figures are appraised under the severe rule of Calvinistic propriety.

In the present work the author has freely consulted the official records, as must be evident throughout. These are no dry-as-dust depositories; they are often alive with action and humanity, and convey in the script of clerk or scribe the sound of early speech and the quaint pattern of native idioms.

In it all Sir John appears as a faithful representative of his time; dutiful in office, fired with a zeal for learning, steadfast in the covenanted faith, testy of his honour, acquisitive of worldly gain, but benevolent in good causes. A resolute individualist and commoner he echoes in his patriotic convictions the sense of Scotland's ancient integrity and the sturdy courage and independence of his fellow-countrymen.

CHAPTER I

EARLY LIFE, EDUCATION AND FAMILY

Among the hills of Fife that fringe the southern side of the lovely valley called the Howe, and not far from the market town of Cupar, the visitor may catch sight of a square and quaintly-topped tower. It stands by an old grass-grown highway on a crest of the hill above the river Eden near the lonely village of Chance Inn. This is the ancient house or castle called Scotstarvit.

When you approach it you find a tower sixty feet high with a small cap-house on its top. The building has a square abutment on one side with a doorway in the angle, and the only break in the structure is above where the moulded corbels project to support the parapet. Behind the parapet runs a roof-walk which allowed the inhabitants to take the air and commands much of the surrounding scenery. From it can be seen the full extent of the Howe backed by the graceful Lomond peaks, and to the north the mountainous outline of the Grampians. To the south and close at hand lies the small picturesque town of Ceres, and farther south the waters of the Firth of Forth spread over to the Lothian coast.

The abutment that has been mentioned carries up a circular stairway to four landings, and allows the single chamber of each storey to have the full scope of the main building. Each is a large roomy apartment. Two are roofed with stone arches and two originally had joists: there is evidence that one was divided with wooden screens in the days of its use. The small windows are deeply embrasured in the thick walls and have been fitted with stone seats. At the top of the tower the stairway emerges on the roof-walk in a small and prettily decorated stone turret, and as you step out of the doorway and inspect its lintel you find a panel bearing a coat-of-arms flanked with the initials S.I.S. and D.A.D., and the date 1627.

These letters signify Sir John Scot and his first wife, Dame Anne Drummond, a sister of the poet William Drummond. It might seem that the armorial panel is somewhat large in proportion

9

to the doorway, and this perhaps betrays something of the exuberant qualities of the Laird of Tarvit. In this it is assisted by a handsome stone fireplace which was installed in the study at the same date, and was decorated with the thistle, the rose, and fleur-de-lis, and with the design of a flambeau in the centre of the pediment, all cut in relief. The date is repeated on the fireplace, and the broad lintel contains the coat of arms of both parties with their initials.[1] Here too in the centre is a scroll with the inscription SPE EXSPECTO, a motto of hope well suited to the temperament and ambitions of the owner. These prominent and floriated efforts suggest that Sir John Scot was an energetic and assertive man with definite cultural interests, and that he believed in providing posterity with historical memorials of his existence and activities.

As we cannot imagine him doing anything devoid of strong personal opinion or taste, we may assume that the prominence of the thistle pays tribute to his patriotic zeal as a Scotsman, while the symbols of England and France may indicate those wider sympathies and loyalties which were a marked feature of his connections with the south and with the Continent, and of the variety and nature of his numerous interests, projects, and doings.

These two architectural features—the panel and the fire-place—have some bearing on the date of the tower. The estate of Tarvit belonged in 1475 to the family of Inglis, and was known as Inglis-Tarvit. There was at that time a "Turris de Tarvet", or house constructed in the ancient fashion of a tower. As a charter of 1550 contains no similar reference it may be assumed that the old edifice had fallen into disuse. But in 1579 there is evidence of a tower, and in a petition of Sir John Scot to Parliament in 1621 "the tower" is included in the description of the property: he is invested in the Lands and Barony of Scotstarvit, "comprehending the barony of Tarvett with the tower, fortalice, manor place",[2] etc.

As it was in 1611 that the estate was purchased from the family of Inglis,[3] it is hardly likely that the new laird, then a young man of twenty five years, would set about constructing another residence where a comparatively recent one already existed.[4]

How then are we to account for the prominent memorial date of 1627? Possibly it was a feature introduced at that time by the

[1] Note No. 1, p. 221.
[2] Act. Parl. Scot., IV, p. 678.
[3] Reg. Gt. Seal of Scot., VII, 588.
[4] Note No. 2, p. 221.

owner to signify the incorporation of his various lands into the Barony of Scotstarvit. The Register of the Great Seal of Scotland has the following entry:

"At Holyroodhouse 30th July 1626. The King confirms to Sir John Scot of Scotstarvit, Director of Chancery, one of the Lords of Secret Council, and to his heirs male, the lands and barony of Scotstarvit, comprehending the lands and barony of Tarvit, with tower, manor, etc. in the parish of Ceres, and other lands (here a list of his estates follows) all incorporated in the barony of Scotstarvit: Tarvit the principal dwelling.[1]"

As this Act was made in his favour in the latter part of 1626 it seems probable that the memorials would be prepared and erected in the following year. Moreover there are signs that they have been intruded in the earlier masonry.[2] To the foregoing the following considerations may be added.

By 1627 Sir John Scot was fairly settled in his important and successful career, and in this year his brilliant brother-in-law, William Drummond, already widely acknowledged as a poet, returned home after a somewhat protracted continental sojourn and made his munificent gift of five hundred rare volumes to the University of Edinburgh. Renewed association with Drummond at Scotstarvit may have added its prompting to celebrate the family connection in the memorials so definitely inscribed and dated. And indeed other events of a national kind occurring then, and of interest to Sir John as a Privy Councillor and a landowner, may have stimulated him to regard 1627 as a memorable year.

Here, then, in the dignified and happily situated Fife keep which caught his fancy in 1611 we find him comfortably installed, and it was his principal dwelling outside of Edinburgh until the far advanced year of 1670.

Sir John Scot, who was born in 1585, was a son of Robert Scot of Knightspottie in Perthshire. His mother was Margaret Acheson of Gosford, of the family of the Earls of Gosford.[3] Even genealogically considered he is an interesting individual both in what he inherited and what he bequeathed, for he was descended from the house of Buccleuch, and he founded a family which was not only numerous but in various instances gifted and distinguished. By his direct descendant, Major-General John

---

[1] Sir John also had a residence at Thirdpart in the parish of Kilrenny.
[2] Note No. 3, p. 221.
[3] Nisbet's *Heraldry* (1722), App. II, p. 292.

Scott of Balcomie in Fife, the strain ran on through several families eminent in Scotland and England. The famous Earl of Mansfield, Lord Chief Justice of England, was a great-great-grandson of Sir John Scot. The Duke of Portland is the present head of the family.[1]

It is questionable however if any offspring of his clan ever displayed more fighting spirit than Sir John, or if any member of his house either before or after him evinced interests so pronounced and original, or possessed in greater measure his capacity to be alive and active in many ways. Seldom, too, can Scotland have had a more benevolent and public-spirited patriot.

The immediate ancestor of the family was Sir David Scot of Buccleuch representing the eleventh generation of that house in a direct male line. He lived in the reigns of King James II and James III and married a daughter of Thomas, Lord Somerville. There were two sons, David and Robert, from the latter of whom the Scots of Scotstarvit are descended. Robert, who was designated by the titles of Allanhaugh and Whitchester, had three sons, Robert, Alexander, and James, and it was the second of these, later Sir Alexander, who carried on the line of the family.[2]

There is a significant note about the above James Scot. He was bred to the church and became provost of Corstorphine, and being a man of unusual learning and integrity he was made Clerk to the Treasury by King James V, and was afterwards appointed a senator of the College of Justice on the spiritual side.[3]

Sir Alexander was bred to the law, and James V appointed him Vice-Register in 1534.[4] He died untimely leaving one son Robert, and it is of no little interest to learn that this excellent person, who was the grandfather of Sir John Scot and became his guardian, was carefully tutored and educated by his gifted uncle, the provost and senator.[5]

Robert Scot followed what had become a family tradition, he studied law, and became so eminent in his profession that in due course he was chosen a Clerk of Session: a note speaks of him as "ane of the scribes of the College".[6] On the death of the Clerk

---

[1] Note No. 4, p. 221.
[2] Nisbet's *Heraldry*, App. II, p. 291.
[3] Douglas's *Baronage*, p. 221.
[4] Rogers, *The Staggering State of Scots Statesmen*, p. 1.
[5] Nisbet's *Heraldry*, App. II, p. 292.
[6] Reg. Gt. Seal of Scot., IV, 2863.

Register he, as the oldest clerk, was called on to succeed to that office but he declined in favour of Alexander Hay, who afterwards resigned the Directorship of Chancery on his behalf. This office Robert Scot assumed in 1579.[1] Of this devoted and worthy man two matters of personal interest are noted. First, that he firmly declined the offer of James VI to make him a Lord of Session, saying "that upon no terms would he be a Lord";[2] and second, that at his death he was eulogised by the poet, Alexander Montgomery.

> "Good Robert Scot, since thou art gone to God,
> Chief of our sovereign College Justice Clerks,
> Who while thou liv'dst for honesty was odd,
> As writ bears witness of thy worthy works;
> So faithful, formal, and so frank and free
> Shall never use that office after thee."[3, 4]

This individual, favoured by his sovereign and eminent in office, married as his second wife Elizabeth Scot, a widow with two sons, one of whom was Sir William Scott of Ardross. By the marriage there were two sons and one daughter. The older son, also named Robert, was the father of Sir John Scot. The younger was James of Vogrie; the daughter married the heir apparent of Andrew Hope-Pringle of Smailholm and Galashiels.

Robert Scot, the Director of Chancery, is credited with the acquirement of considerable estates. At least four charters under the Great Seal denote his acquisition of lands with the confirmation of James VI. In title he was designated as of Knightspottie in the parish of Dunbarney in Perthshire, a designation assumed also by his son Robert and, briefly in his early career, by Sir John Scot. As Sir John's father died prematurely, he became not only the heir but the ward of his grandfather.

The final history of the aged Director is that in 1585 he transferred his office to his son Robert, wisely reserving to himself the survivance by a charter under the Great Seal.[5] Robert dying three years later, the Directorship reverted to his father. The latter died in 1592, having resigned his office to his stepson,

---

[1] Reg. Gt. Seal of Scot., IV, 801. First entry 6th November 1579.
[2] *The Staggering State* (1754), p. 120.
[3] *Poems*. Edited by James Cranstoun, LL.D., p. 221.
[4] Note No. 5, p. 221.
[5] Reg. Gt. Seal of Scot., V, 304.

William Scott of Ardross, who accepted an obligation to retire in favour of the youthful John Scot as soon as he came of age.[1]

It would appear, therefore, from this genealogical record that the future Senator and Privy Councillor, while derived from an adventurous ancestry, had inherited the law as a second nature, and was born into a world of writs, testaments, and charters, into which fate had also whimsically tossed the example and memory of a legal grandsire who "for his honesty was odd".

This hopeful descendant of high family, who succeeded to his grandfather's estate at the age of seven, became in due course a St Andrews student, and must have matriculated at St Leonard's College in the year 1600, for when enrolling in 1603 he subscribes himself as, "Johannes Scotus, cursus sui anno tertio". He graduated in 1605, having no doubt qualified in the course of Philosophy and having also studied Law.[2]

It is of interest to note that he would share the benefit of the reformation which had lately been instituted in the University's teaching system. Under the old regime there was no professorial specialisation in a subject, each regent taking the same class of students through the whole four years' course. But in 1579 the Commissioners drew up a new system, and in order that "the youth might attain unto perfect knowledge of humanity and true philosophy", it was ordained that St Leonard's and St Salvator's should have, besides the Principal, four ordinary professors each confined to his own subject. In the curriculum both Latin and Greek were included, and these languages supplied very largely the medium of instruction.[3]

James Melville tells us in his *Diary* that in his third and fourth year he studied law, the teacher being William Skene the judge of the Commissary Court. Under the new arrangement there was a permanent lecturer who read four lessons weekly at which all who were preparing for the profession of Law attended.

As John Scot was designed for this profession and afterwards exercised his calling with skill and success, we must assume that his training was complete. On this point Nisbet says that after

[1] Wm. Scott, Director of Chancery 20th November 1589. Reg. Gt. Seal of Scot., V, 588.

[2] University of St Andrews, Matriculation Roll, Acta Rectorum. III (The muniments U.Y. 305).

[3] *A Source Book of Scottish History*, Edited by Professor Wm. Croft Dickinson and Dr Gordon Donaldson, III, pp. 412-417.

William Drummond of Hawthornden
1585-1649
Reproduced by permission of the Scottish National Portrait Gallery

concluding the Course of Philosophy he proceeded to study not only the civil and canon law but also the municipal law of the kingdom, and that he came to understand the Constitution as fully as, if not more fully than, any man of his time.[1] His instructor may have been the celebrated William Welwood.

In 1606 he achieved his majority and in the same year he may have been admitted an advocate,[2] but it was not until 1611 that he assumed the post which we must always associate with him, namely as Director of Chancery.[3]

There is some doubt as to whether after graduation and his admission to the Bar Scot travelled abroad, the years involved being 1606 to 1611, but it is most likely that he did. Dr Rogers, in his short sketch of Scotstarvit's career, says that after graduation he proceeded to a continental university to study classical learning. This was the regular habit of that day, and we hear of Drummond, the poet, journeying between Edinburgh and France in 1606 and in subsequent years when studying law at Paris and Bourges.

We accept the probability further because otherwise it is difficult to account for Sir John's acquaintance with various continental scholars with whom he afterwards maintained a long friendship and correspondence.[4] This connection was marked by intercourse and visitation, which would no doubt be mutual, and overseas scholars were welcomed as guests at Scotstarvit Tower: the establishment of an earlier acquaintanceship is to be assumed. To quote but one instance, it is noticeable that Caspar Barlaeus of Antwerp, Logic professor at Leyden and afterwards professor of Philosophy and Rhetoric at Amsterdam, who is frequently mentioned, was practically of his own age, being born in 1584.[5] They may have met originally when studying in the same university. Scot, however, was at home in 1608, for by the middle of that year he was married to Anne Drummond, and the parochial baptismal registers of Edinburgh show that he was then definitely committed to a life of domestic responsibility.

During these earlier years he must have been imbibing, not only from his studies but from the social experience of his family

---

[1] Nisbet's *Heraldry*, II, p. 293.
[2] Note No. 6, p. 221.
[3] Reg. Gt. Seal of Scot., VII, 168.
[4] *Letters from learned men to Scotstarvet.* Adv. M.S. 17.1.9.
[5] *Nouvelle Biographie Generale* (1855), IV, p. 143.

relationships, that acquaintance with letters and life which permitted him while still young to enter public service and high office. The professional status which he achieved in 1606, along with his crown appointment at the Chancery in 1611, might have sufficed for less aspiring natures but they proved to be initial trophies to one who appeared to be ambitious of preferment from the first, and who for almost fifty years was active in securing honourable place in our country, and in effecting outstanding public services for his countrymen.

Scot was a loyal and indeed an affectionate pupil of St Leonard's College, and we assume that it was his early residence at St Andrews which gave him a love of Fife, and led to the acquirement of his estates and his country seats there.

When we visit the excellently preserved tower it is of the scholar that we think. Here in the library he must have studied and planned his many liberal and original projects. The tradition of his culture lingered long and Nisbet reports that men of letters resorted to him from all quarters, "so that his house became a kind of college."[1]

To Scotstarvit came William Drummond in 1627. Sage in his biography of the poet says that "after his long stay abroad he again returned to Scotland where there were great heart-burnings, feuds and animosities. This made the retirement which he so passionately loved very necessary, and he went and stayed some while with his brother-in-law, Sir John Scot of Scotstarvit, a man of excellent learning and good conversation."[2]

According to tradition it was here that Drummond composed his *Polemo-Middinia*, a burlesque poem in which the dog-Latin scarcely veils the use of a homely Scots diction. Sage remarks of this piece, "It is reprinted here (in Edinburgh) almost every year."[3,4]

The subject was a quarrel which took place between Cunningham of Barns and Scot whose estate of Thirdpart adjoined Barns. The dispute was carried to the Privy Council, and Sir John, a newly elected Councillor, found himself called upon to answer charges of unruly trespass by his servants, and an act of violence

[1] Nisbet's *Heraldry*, II, p. 293.
[2] *The Works of William Drummond of Hawthornden*, edited by Bishop Sage and Thomas Ruddiman, 1711, p. iv. John Sage was born at Creich, Fife, 1652. Died 1711.
[3] *Ibid.* p. v.
[4] Note No. 7, p. 221.

by himself. The charge said that, "Sir John Scot convocatit ten men armed with swords, staffs, stangs, and other armour, and came in a braggin manner and cast down Cunningham's stank dyke".[1] Scot on his oath denied the accusation and was assoilzied from the charge, and somehow the dispute was satisfactorily settled.[2]

Of Sir John's domestic state it may be reported that he was married three times and had nineteen children. The facts pertaining to the first partnership, namely with Dame Anne Drummond, are contained in the old parochial registers of Edinburgh and give us the dates of baptisms.[3] The date of the marriage, which would be entered in the register of the parish of Lasswade, is not available as it was the year 1617 when the existing record commenced; but it can be seen from the baptismal register that the year would probably be 1608.

The first entry reads:

"14th May 1609, Mr John Scot of Knichtspotie and Anna Drummond, maried, a son named Robert. Witnesses Mr Robert Scot, minister; Laurence Scot, advocat."

The register has particulars of sixteen children. The father is designated firstly of Knightspottie, then of Caiplie, and finally of Scotstarvit. In three if not four instances the duplication of names shows that some of the children died in infancy. The fact that all were baptised in Edinburgh indicates that the domestic life centred there. Dame Anna, after almost thirty years of wedded life, died in May 1636 or 1637. Her Testament was recorded in August of the latter year in the Commissariot of Edinburgh.[4]

Sir John married as his second wife Elizabeth Melville, daughter of James Melville, the laird of Hallhill,[5] and as they had a child, Elizabeth, baptised on 2nd October 1640, it may be assumed that the wedding took place in 1638 or 1639. A second child, George, was baptised on 7th April 1643, when James Melville the grandfather was present. These baptisms are recorded in the parochial register of Kinghorn, the parish in which Sir John was an elder.[6]

[1] Note No. 8, p. 221.
[2] Reg. P.C. 1619-1622, pp. 716-718.
[3] Parochial Registers of Edinburgh: Baptisms. Ref. No. 685. Vols. I, II, III, IV.
[4] Register of Testaments, Vol. II, Part II, p. 119.
[5] James Melville, son of Sir James the courtier and diarist who died in 1617.
[6] Ref. No. 439, Vol. I (pages not numbered).

The third marriage was to Eupham Monypenny, daughter of the laird of Pitmilly and widow of William Rigg of Aithernie.[1] These are Fife estates. It is probable that the wedding took place in 1647, and there was one son, Walter Scot of Edenshead. When Scotstarvit's Testament was recorded in the Commissariot of Edinburgh on 11th February 1671, it was made and given up by Sir Walter Scot of Letham, son lawful and only executor dative, the youngest of the family: Letham had been purchased by his father prior to 1665. In 1634 Sir John provisionally secured his son James to be his successor in the office of Director of Chancery. James was knighted by Charles I and died in 1650.[2]

Sir John Scot died, probably at Scotstarvit, in 1670, and his age was 84 years. He had already during his lifetime disposed of most of his property to his family. We have no definite note of the place of burial, but he had a right of sepulture in the parish church at Kinghorn, as the following Kirk Session minute of 17th May 1642 shows: "The Kirk Session assigned to Sir John Scot of Scotstarvit, and his wife and children, for sepulture in the south-east part of the church, extending in length sixteen feet from the east end westward, and fifteen feet of breadth from the south wall to the partition wall of the choir."[3] An easterly portion of this building which stands close to the shore still exists, and in it the mortal remains of the seventeenth-century statesman and patriot may rest.[4]

[1] The Primate of St Andrews gave Pitmilly (Petmullin) to Richard Monipenny in the year 1211. Sibbald's *Hist. of Fife and Kinross* (Ed. 1843), part IV, p. 348.

[2] *The Staggering State* (1754) p. 162.

[3] *Extracts from Minutes of the Kirk Session of Kinghorn*, Crawford, Kirkcaldy (1813), pp. 41-42.

[4] Note No. 9, p. 221.

CHAPTER II

HONOURS AND OFFICE IN A SCENE
OF CONFLICT

An outstanding event of a ceremonial kind occurred in Scotland in 1617. This was the visit north after an absence of almost fourteen years of James VI. The King came, he said, "because of his great and natural longing and salmond-like instinct to see his native soil".[1]

Sanderson, the English divine, makes a flattering error in reading "Solomon-like" for "salmond-like", not perhaps being so well-versed in the ways of salmon as the Scottish King.[2] James was always ready to confess a special devotion to his homeland and was partial to a homely phrase. His playful familiarity in addressing his countrymen was well exhibited at this time when, Parliament being convened to hear him, he wittily commented on the national change in social manners by saying that "the Scots had learned of the English to drink healths, to wear coaches and gay clothes, to take tobacco, and to speak neither Scottish nor English".[3]

The occasion of the visit was accepted as one of public joy and congratulation, and many official bodies offered to the King their tributes of delight and honour. Calderwood relates that when James came to the Palace of Holyroodhouse "the professors and students of the College of Edinburgh presented to him some poems made to his praise and in signe of welcome".[4] The poets were busy, and Drummond produced his "Forth Feasting: A Panegyric to the King's Most Excellent Majesty."[5]

The best that Scot could do in this line was to give the utmost

---

[1] Reg. P.C. 1616-1619, p. 685.
[2] *Lives and Reigns of Mary Queen of Scots and James VI* (1656), p. 451.
[3] Reg. P.C. 1616-1619, p. 157 footnote.
[4] Calderwood's *History of the Kirk of Scotland* (Wodrow Soc.), VII, p. 246.
[5] Reg. P.C. 1616-1619, footnote, p. 136.

publicity to a congratulatory poem in Latin addressed to "The Serene and most invincible Monarch" by John Scott, his youthful cousin. This poem, called "Hodaeporicon", appeared in *The Muse's Welcome* in 1618 and in the forefront of Scot's own Latin verse which was published by Andrew Hart in 1619. That he had attracted the King's attention was however proved, for during the visit James is said to have conferred with him with great satisfaction on certain aspects of the Constitution,[1] and he received the honour of knighthood.[2] He was now thirty-two years old and was fully launched on a career of influence and position. In the worldly race he had outstripped many others, including his gifted brother-in-law.

In assessing the forces which operated in his favour we cannot omit the part played by family connections and interests. The tradition of high service for the Crown which existed among his antecedents is illustrated by the King's personal and intimate knowledge of his grandfather. It is also clear that the members of the clan stuck together and gave their support in the affairs of business and office. We have a glimpse of what race may have meant to him in the fact that his cautioners in a loan of £1000 Scots which he received in 1621 from William Dick, a wealthy merchant and Provost of Edinburgh, were Walter, Earl of Buccleuch, Lord Scot of Whitchester, Captain William Scott, and John Scott of Sintoun;[3] when his first child was baptised the witnesses were both Scots, a minister and an advocate.

Sir John was a trusted and intimate counsellor in the affairs of the Buccleuch family, his close relationship to the ducal line being clearly recognised. Sir William Fraser makes a comment on the failure of the direct male line by the death of Francis the second Earl in 1651. He says that there remained some uncertainty as to the person with whom the male representation should rest, and he reports that when Sir Walter Scott came to study the question he judged that the honour of male chiefship fell to Sir John Scot of Scotstarvit.[4, 5]

Walter the first Earl went with his regiment to Holland in the expedition of 1627 and on his temporary return in 1629 he executed

[1] Nisbet's *Heraldry*, II, p. 293.
[2] Reg. P.C. 1616-1619, footnote, p. 831.
[3] Roger, *The Staggering State* (1772), p. 21.
[4] *The Scotts of Buccleuch* (1878) Sir Wm. Fraser, I, p. lxxxiii.
[5] Note No. 10, p. 221.

a commission in favour of his Countess, Lady Mary Hay, and a number of his kinsmen, all Scotts, among whom the first-named was Sir John, followed by Walter of Harden. Included was Laurence the advocate of Harperrig who infrequently appears in Scot's domestic history. Authority was committed to them to attend to all business of lands, courts, and accounts. Buccleuch was back in Scotland in the autumn and winter of 1632-33, and in January of the latter year before returning to the wars he made his testament in which he appointed as tutors to his children five relations, Sir John always to be one of the number.

The Earl having died late in 1633 Balfour reports that at his funeral, the mourners "marching" from Branxholm to the church at Hawick, Scotstarvit "carried the defunct's coronett overlaid with cipress on a velvet cusheon".[1]

Sir John travelled to London in 1634 and also in 1655,[2, 3] in connection with estate affairs, and in 1659 he had trouble with Kirkcaldy Presbytery over the marriage of the youthful Countess. During this difficult period an unusual device had been contrived for guarding the privacy of the Buccleuch charter chests. This was achieved by having three different sets of keys. Sir John Scot had custody of "the hanging locks". Patrick Scott of Langshaw kept the keys of the actual kists: these were laid in the shuttle of a cabinet and the key of the shuttle was given to Sir William Scott of Harden.[4] This doubtless secured the ancient writs from unwarrantable inspection and at the same time satisfied family honour.

It will be seen that the laird of Scotstarvit was no solitary and unsupported careerist: he was linked to and aided by a family dynasty widely ramified in Scottish society. But, as in the case of his grandparent, individual merit and character now brought him into an official position which it was beyond the power of mere social status to accomplish. The following is a brief outline of his promotion to office before and after the Revolution of 1638.

On the 14th March 1622, he was appointed a Privy Councillor

---

[1] *The Scotts of Buccleuch*, I, p. 256. Quoted from The *Annals*. (At this time he made out a catalogue of the Earl's library, 12,000 volumes), p. 266.

[2] *Ibid.*, I, p. 281, p. 331.

[3] Note No. 11, p. 221.

[4] *The Scotts of Buccleuch*, I, p. 411.

by the King's warrant,[1] and on January 1629 he was made an Extraordinary Lord in the Court of Session.[2] The appointment in this subordinate class was withdrawn in November 1630 and Sir John Hamilton took office in his place.[3] A curious light is thrown on this by Traquair in a letter to Earl Morton of date 3rd February 1629. He says: "We marveled much at Sir John Scot getting Sir Andro Kers place in Session, but the Lord Monteith assured us it is for the interim, untill he speak with the King".[4]

Menteith apparently accomplished his design, but Sir John's claims must have been insistent, for in July 1632, he succeeded Sir Alexander Morrison of Prestongrange as a Lord Ordinary, and took his seat as Lord Scotstarvit.[5] When Charles appointed a Court of High Commission in October 1634, his name was included in the warrant. After the Revolution, Parliament re-constituted the Privy Council in 1641 and Scot was not a member, but this was probably a matter of little moment as he had already been appointed to the Committee of Estates, which in the current difficulties was formed to become a State Executive.

This powerful body, instituted in June 1640, consisted of thirty-nine members drawn in equal proportion from each of the Estates, and was given "Full power, warrant, and commission to do, order, direct, act, and put in execution everything necessary, expedient, and incumbent, as well for the preservation and maintenance of the armies, as for the ordering of the country and whole body and inhabitants thereof: without prejudice to the College of Justice".[6] In November 1641 Charles approved the Committee: "They have behaved themselves as good Christians, loyal subjects, and well-deserving patriots."[7, 8]

We have some indication that Sir John participated actively in its decisions and doings. Among the collected papers of the Atholl and Tullibardine families are three letters sent to the Earl of Atholl in March 1641, which show that although the Committee nominally consisted of thirty-nine members it acted at times, if not

---

[1] Reg. P.C. 1619-1622, p. 702.
[2] Brunton and Haig, p. 280.
[3] *Ibid.*
[4] *Trew Relation of Menteith's Affair,* attached letters, Nat. Lib. 6.234(10) 56.
[5] Brunton and Haig, p. 280.
[6] Acts Parl. Scot., V, p. 282.
[7] *Ibid.,* p. 390.
[8] Note No. 12, p. 221.

consistently, through a very small powerful minority.[1] The first letter asks Atholl to compear and give evidence that he has renounced the Cumbernauld Band.[2] The sederunt authorising the summons, reads: Balmerino, Cupar, Napier, Murray, Richard Maxwell, Craighall (the Advocate) Scottistarvett, Thomas Paterson, Edward Edgar.

The other letters, one of which requested the Earl's assistance to improve public affairs in the Presbytery of Dunkeld, were sent in the name of, Balmerino, Cupar, Caprintoun, Scottistarvett, G. Hamilton, Murray, Jaffray, and Craighall.

In the same month of November 1641 Scotstarvit was reappointed one of the fifteen Ordinary Lords of Session and Senators of the College of Justice:[3] in July 1644 he became a Commissioner of Exchequer (one of fourteen) to assist the Treasurer, John Earl of Crawford and Lindsay,[4] and in April 1648 he was nominated to the Committee of War for the Sheriffdom of Edinburgh, where the Convenership was in the hands of Johnston of Warriston.[5]

Scot's importance during the revolution decade, and probably also his peculiar standing in the sphere of letters and culture, is illustrated by the fact that when he made a visit to the Netherlands in 1645 in connection with the publication by Blaeu of the maps of Timothy Pont, his journey was put on the footing of an affair of State, and Parliament after its successful accomplishment ordered the President to subscribe a letter to be sent to "The Estates and Admirall of Zeeland expressing their thanks for the kindness shown to Sir John Scot in his recent visit".[6]

Throughout these and the succeeding years up to 1650 he was one of that small group of statesmen responsible for the government of the country, and we have a significant glimpse of him when he appears at a difficult juncture on an embassy sent to Cromwell's headquarters to negotiate concerning the surrender of Berwick and Carlisle in September 1648.

The situation prior to this was that the Duke of Hamilton and the Moderate party had ousted from government the strict

---

[1] *Chronicles of the Families of Atholl and Tullibardine*, I, p. 110.
[2] Note No. 13, p. 221.
[3] Acts Parl. Scot., V, p. 389.
[4] *Ibid.*, VI, p. 235.
[5] *Ibid.*, VI, (Part II), p. 30.
[6] Balfour's *Annals*, III, p. 351.

Covenanters led by Argyll, and late in 1647 had compromised on Episcopacy with Charles in a pact called "The Engagement".[1] Hamilton thereafter led an army into England on the King's behalf and was defeated by the Parliamentary forces near Preston. The date was 17th August 1648, and on 18th September Cromwell was in communication with Loudon the Chancellor and the Covenanting party to the following effect:

"Letter from the Lt. General of date 18th September 1648, at Cheswick near Berwick, directed to Loudon the Chancellor, To be communicated to the Noblemen, Gentlemen, and Burgesses now in arms[2] who dissented in Parliament from the late Engagement against the Kingdom of England." The letter was addressed in the terms of a friendly ally, and in response to it a commission was sent by the Committee of Estates and reached Mordington on 22nd September. An official notice arriving then or earlier intimated to the General that certain "influential persons" were being sent to order the giving up of Berwick and Carlisle instantly. These "influential persons" when they came comprised, "the Marquis of Argyle, the Lord Elcho, Sir John Scot, and others".[3] Sir John has reported that in the Parliament of 1647 he presented the protest of the Gentry against the Engagement which probably accounts for his presence on the delegation.[4] His political position is thus made clear and he must now have made some manner of acquaintance with the future Protector, in whose hands his life and fortune were soon to be placed.

The change in the English situation had in turn involved the Covenanting party in conflict with the English leaders. Following upon the execution of Charles in 1649 and the establishment of a Commonwealth, the Covenanters proclaimed Charles II King, and agreed to support his claim to the English throne in return for his acceptance of the Covenant. But the defeat of David Leslie at Dunbar on 3rd September 1650 shattered the government of Argyll and released the King to act on his own initiative. The Moderates were brought back to power and in the reconstituted

---

[1] Acts Parl. Scot., VI, part ii, pp. 17-18.

[2] Note No. 14, p. 222.

[3] *Letters and Speeches of Cromwell*. Carlyle (Everyman Lib. 1907), I, pp. 304-307. Carlyle makes a characteristic comment on Scotstarvit, pp. 70-71.

[4] *The Staggering State* (1754), pp. 99, 101. Cal. State Papers, Domestic, 1654, p. 158.

Committee of Estates Sir John Scot with others was significantly omitted. In exactly a year's time the battle of Worcester was decisive, and Scotland fell to Cromwell and the ten years Occupation.

It scarcely needs to be said that Scot was an avowed Covenanter who stood with Argyll and the leaders of the Kirk. On 30th April 1638 he had signed the National Covenant at the parish church of Ceres,[1] and Principal Baillie says that in November of the same year he, along with the Lords Durie, Craighall, and Inverteil, "did peremptorlie refuse" when the King's Commissioner (the Marquis of Hamilton) went to the Tolbooth and moved them to subscribe the King's Covenant.[2] At this time the Lords in question sought to secure their position by pointing out that the terms of the latter were not in harmony with the Confession of King James of 1581.[3] But Sir John with characteristic thoroughness proceeded further, for he took steps to secure a copy of James's Confession and was so successful that he unearthed the original, which is now lodged in the National Library of Scotland and bears the following endorsation:

"Covenant subscryved by King James of worthie memorie and his household, 28 January 1580. Sent from Somer in France by Monsieur — to my Lord Scottistarbett in August 1641."

The document, a valuable one both intrinsically and historically, must have formed an item of curious interest to the Covenanters during the rule of Parliament. Peterkin in his *Records of the Kirk* says that it was delivered to the Church of Scotland by Sir John Scot in 1646, when the General Assembly minutes its appreciation and thanks.[4]

It is highly probable that the document in question was obtained through the instrumentality of Mark Duncan (or his family) Professor of Philosophy and finally Principal of the Protestant University of Saumur. In August 1639 he wrote to Sir John in an effort to obtain a certificate of nobility so as to relieve him of a certain burden of taxation. Also, among the Letters of Learned Men to Sir John Scot, there is one written by a son of Professor Duncan from London in October 1641, expressing gratitude for many favours received.

[1] The Statistical Account (1845), p. 523.
[2] Baillie's *Journal* I, p. 111.
[3] Signed by James VI in 1580 and by persons of all ranks in 1581, with a band and renewal in 1589. Adv. M.S. 20.6.12.
[4] Note No. 15, p. 222.

Scot blamed the troubles of the country on the mutual rivalry of Hamilton and Argyll: "By their factions this kingdom has become a prey and a conquest to the English nation."[1] He has nothing further to say of Argyll, but he charges Hamilton with effecting the Engagement, "which has been the chief ground of the English invasion and overthrow of this land".[2]

Hamilton must not be too severely criticised. Answering a charge of inconsistency (inasmuch as he had signed the National Covenant) he declared:

"If my life could procure the peace of this torn Church and Kingdome, to the contentment of my royal Master and the comfort of his distracted subjects, it is the sacrifice in which I would most glorie, and which I would most sincerely offer up to God, my King, and Country."[3]

In *The Staggering State* the aged statesman thus briefly sums up his official career, speaking of himself in the third person.

"Sir John was a counsellor to King James and King Charles I, and Lord of Exchequer and a Lord of Session. Albeit he was possessor of the place of Chancery above forty years, and doer of great services to the king and country, yet, by the power and malice of his enemies, he has been at last thrust out of the said places in his old age, and likewise fined in £500 sterling, and one altogether unskilled placed to be director. He had been a counsellor since the year of God 1620, and for his majesty's and predecessor's service had been twenty-four times at London, being 14,400 miles, and twice in the Low Countries for printing the Scots poets and the Atlas; and paid to John Blaeu a hundred double pieces for printing of the poets."[4]

This note it should be observed refers only to the official aspect of his life and to the treatment he received after his long service to king and country. That he is not complaining against Cromwell's judges is shown by his reference to old age, and in particular by the quoted figure of the fine. The latter is the fine exacted at the Restoration, and at that date he was seventy-five years old. Although he was supplanted in office by Jaffray

---

[1] *The Staggering State*, p. 7.

[2] *Ibid.*, p. 99.

[3] Pamphlets dealing with the preparing and signing of the Covenant in 1638. Nat. Lib., 1. 234.

[4] *The Staggering State* (1754), p. 163. There is a curious disparity of two years in several instances. The year of his appointment was 1622.

26

in 1652 Sir John ignores this, treating it possibly as an accident of war, and in any case it had already been officially acknowledged as a mistake. His concern in the above statement is not with the blundering action of the usurpers, but with the alleged injustice done him by his own king and state. Equally, in his reckoning of the London and Continental visits, he is referring to journeys of a public and official character and taking no account of private movements.

Nevertheless, although he was a faithful servant of his king and homeland and acted conscientiously in the tangle of policies which marked the revolutionary period, yet when the Commonwealth had settled its rule in Scotland so that no man could see its early or eventual cessation, he submitted proffers of service to Cromwell which were placed on record, and certainly stood him in ill stead when the monarchy was unexpectedly and swiftly restored.

CHAPTER III

PUBLIC DISAPPOINTMENTS

By the year 1651 the situation was that a neighbouring Power had subjugated Scotland, suppressing its Parliament and later its chief Church Court, and disposing of all the offices of its administrative life as it judged to be best.[1] It was scarcely to be expected that a statesman who had held office at the Chancery, in the Privy Council, the Exchequer, and the powerful Committee of Estates, and appeared to have shared the official policies which brought about the conflict, would be spared from retribution by the victorious enemy.

In March 1652, Alexander Jaffray was given the post of Director of Chancery,[2] and Scot also lost his place as a Lord of Session and was charged with a fine of £1,500.[3] In the following year the Scottish Treasury was ordered to pay Jaffray this precise sum.[4]

The above-named person, sometime Provost of Aberdeen, had from 1644 represented Aberdeen in Parliament and during Argyll's ascendancy was also a member of the Committee of Estates. He was taken prisoner at the battle of Dunbar and while imprisoned had much intercourse with Cromwell, who gained his confidence and arranged for his discharge, which took effect in June 1651. Not only did Jaffray supplant at the Chancery his former colleague but with four others, all selected by Cromwell, he sat in the "Little" or "Barebones Parliament" of 1653.[5]

The descendant of the House of Buccleuch was, however, far from tamely accepting the situation as it left him in 1652. Indeed before the Judges reached their decision he was already presenting

[1] The two countries were constituted a single Commonwealth in December 1651. Cal. State Papers, 1654, p. 90. The General Assembly was dismissed by English troops in 1653. Baillie's *Journal* III, p. 225.

[2] *Dict. Nat. Biog.*, X, p. 564.

[3] Cal. State Papers, 1653-4, p. 382.

[4] *Ibid.*, 1655, p. 71.

[5] *Dict. Nat. Biog.*, X, p. 564. Jaffray was one of those sent by the General Assembly to treat with Charles II at the Hague in 1649, and in the following year the Estates sent him on a similar errand to Breda.

his case in influential places in the executive sphere of the Common-wealth, and during almost the whole ten years of the Occupation he was continually making determined attempts to regain his lost offices and obtain a remission of his fine. Although he certainly made headway in correcting the erroneous estimate of his standing as Director of Chancery, yet the promise of reinstate-ment was not realised. But he was fully successful in his quest for relief from any financial exaction. Perhaps indeed he was too successful—from the Restoration point of view—in rehabilitating himself in the good graces of the Protector and his Council.

The earliest documentary news we have of his efforts comes from a letter written on his behalf by Cromwell's adjutant, Colonel Robert Lilburne, brother of the remarkable political agitator, John Lilburne. It is dated Dalkeith, 14th February 1653, and raises the question of the publication of Blaeu's Atlas, apparently with a view to seeking protection against the possible piracy of publica-tion rights. At the close it deftly reports that Sir John "hath somewhat else" to submit for consideration. It is noticeable that the letter says, "This Bearer", which indicates that the dis-possessed Director of Chancery aimed at a personal interview with Cromwell, which he probably achieved early in the succeeding year. The following is the text of Colonel Lilburne's letter:

"May it please your Highnesse: This Bearer, Sir John Scot, having made a great progresse in drawing and causing to be drawne an exact mappe of Scotlande which hath cost him almost 20 yeares paines,[1] and for that it is now printed at Amsterdam, and the printer having been at extraordinary charges in perfecting the same, and being doubtful (if it come to be sold in publique before he have some assurance that no other person for some certaine time shall print it) that it will be a great damage to him, the said Sir John hath prevailed with me to recommend it to your High-nesse; which I have rather presumed (to do) because having seene severall of the copies I finde the said mappes might be very useful to the army: which I humbly leave to your Highnesse's better judgement and a further accompt from Sir John himself, who also hath somewhat else to lay before your Highnesse. I remain your Highnesse's most humble, servant. R. L., Dalkeith, 14 Feb. 1653."

Further light is thrown on these matters by two petitions which he submitted to Cromwell when he (Scot) was in London in 1654.

[1] Note No. 16, p. 222.

The first letter, couched as if it were his initial approach, reads as follows.

"Petition of Sir John Scot of Scottistarvet to the Protector.

"I am lineally descended from those who have constantly and dutifully served as clerks of the Rolls, lords of Session, clerks of Council and Exchequer, and directors of Chancery, from 1502 to your coming to Scotland. I have myself been 30 years a councillor, 20 a judge, and 40 a director of the Chancery office without reproach, and Lord St John promised me a hearing before my places were disposed of.

"I have not contravened any of your proclamations, yet am I dispossessed, not only of those places of Council, Session, and Exchequer, which I held by the Prince's letters and which could be taken away at the will of the superior power, but of my Chancery office, which being by grant under the Great Seal can only be taken away by (because of) treason or forfeiture. And the arrears of my fees are detained.

"I beg restoration to my places as judge in the Session and director of the Chancery, and a warrant to recover my past arrears."[1]

The Lord St John who is mentioned was Oliver St John, made Solicitor General by Charles in 1640 and now Lord Chief Justice of Common Pleas in the Commonwealth. He gained distinction by his defence of John Hampden and married as his second wife a favourite cousin of Cromwell.[2] St John was one of eight judges commissioned in October 1651 to settle the civil government of Scotland.[3] As he arrived in Edinburgh in January 1652 and the judges completed their task by May, this would give Scotstarvit opportunity for consultation, but as noted it was in March during this visit that Jaffray's appointment to the Chancery was made.

To Scot's petition there was no immediate response, but he persisted in his suit and finally made a decided and favourable impression on the Protector.

His second Petition was linked directly with the official intimation of the fine already mentioned. This was involved in "The Ordinance of Pardon and Grace to the People of Scotland", shortly called "The Act of Grace", which was announced by

[1] Cal. State Papers, 1654, p. 158.
[2] Note No. 17, p. 222.
[3] Cal. State Papers, 1651, p. 489.

the Council of State at Whitehall on 12th April, 1654.[1] It read thus:

"His Highness, the Lord Protector of the Commonwealth of England, Scotland, and Ireland, being desirous that the mercies which it hath pleased God to give to this nation should be improved, and the people of Scotland be made equal sharers, therefore they are acquitted and discharged from all forfeitures, except" etc.

The exceptions are then listed and Sir John Scot is among them, his offence being charged with a fine of £1,500. Sir John protested almost forthwith, his letter being quoted immediately after the other in the State Papers He has now not only the deprivation of his official posts to complain of but the threatened financial penalty. It will be seen with what determination he endeavours to meet these, and how openly he speaks of "those who formerly did him ill offices", and who are apparently seeking to inflict further punishment.

"Petition of Sir John Scot to the Protector.

"I came here a month since to procure your favour for the printing in Holland by John Blaw of maps of Scotland and Ireland. I also showed my wrongs in being deprived of my offices in Scotland, and I think those who formerly did me ill offices have now got my name inserted in the Act of Grace for payment of £1,500 fine, though I have been a constant opposer of malignancy, and in 1648 was president of the committee of gentry who protested against that unlawful Engagement in the very face of Parliament. I beg discharge from my fine and reference to the Council about my places. With references accordingly, 29th April 1654."[2]

The date of this appeal suggests that the first was made at the end of March, but the reference to maps (not actually mentioned in the earlier petition) would indicate that Sir John had a personal interview where he presented Colonel Lilburne's letter and included all he had at that stage to say: "I also shewed my wrongs".

It will be noticed that the print concludes by saying: "With references accordingly", and these are to be found in two statements which are annexed to the second petition. One reads like the official summary of a more extended statement, and the other supplies certification (somewhat startling in respect of the testifiers)

[1] Cal. State Papers, 1654, p. 90. Proclaimed at the Mercat Cross, Edinburgh, 5th May 1654. Nicoll's *Diary*, p. 125.
[2] *Ibid.*, 1654, p. 158.

that he publicly opposed the policy of the Moderates in the invasion of England and was free from any taint of malignancy. His private life was quiet and law-abiding.

"I. Statement in detail of the offices held by his ancestors and himself. His grandchild, James Scott, holds the baronies of Tarvet and Caiplie, and most of his lands and monies are divided among his children, he relying on the profits of his office. He has not been a Member of Parliament or Committee since 1644. His houses at Inchkeith[1] and Shank were demolished by the soldiers. His losses of fees and office nearly equal the fine laid upon him, and the detention of the arrears is contrary to law.

"II. Certificate by Patrick Gillespie and John Livingston that he protested against the invading of England in 1648, never abetted any malignant design, and behaved peaceably in a private station. 28th April, 1654."[2]

The foregoing date was little more than a fortnight after the issue of the Act of Grace and shows that being on the spot he lost no time in pressing his claim in respect of the various wrongs done to him.

It is a somewhat intriguing fact that the names of Patrick Gillespie and John Livingston should appear underwriting the character and professions of Lord Scotstarvit, for the persons referred to were champions of the more extreme Covenanting principle and were men of exceptional ability and mark in their day, although of widely different temperament and mode of life.

Patrick Gillespie of Kirkcaldy was the younger brother of the more famous George, and proved to be a churchman whose political animus against Royalists and Prelacy led him finally into the camp of Cromwell. In May 1648 he was settled in the Outer High Kirk, Glasgow. After the Engagement and the concordat with Charles, and during the effort to organise the national resources to meet the threat of the Parliamentary forces from the south, when for this purpose the main tide of opinion in the Church Courts favoured a policy of leniency towards, and even of co-operation with, Moderates and Episcopalians, Gillespie led the Protesters in opposition, and his conduct finally brought about his deposition by the General Assembly in July 1651.[3]

[1] Scot acquired the island of Inchkeith in 1649. *Statistical Account* (1845), p. 820.
[2] Cal. State Papers, 1654, p. 159.
[3] Nicoll's *Diary* (Bannatyne Club), p. 54.

Under the patronage of the Occupation authority he was appointed Principal of Glasgow University early in 1653 and is said to have worked successfully for its enlargement and the increase of its endowments.[1] In the following year he was called to London where he took counsel with Cromwell and preached before him in his rich, rarely cut, velvet cassock.[2] In October 1655 when conducting worship in St Giles he startled the congregation by praying for the Lord Protector, being the first minister who did so openly in Scotland.[3] At the Restoration he was the object of the King's severest displeasure, being indicted for treason, and was exceedingly fortunate to escape with his life.

It has been said of him: "his superior abilities, fluent delivery, and popular manners made him at one time a man of great personal influence. He was however ambitious, domineering, and extravagant, so that no bishop in Scotland had ever lived at so high a rate."[4]

John Livingston, a very able but contemplative and scholarly man, a moving preacher of evangelical truth and noted for his piety, was licensed in 1625 after a studentship at St Andrews, and early revealed his principle by refusing—because of his objection to the Articles of Perth—several tempting presentations. He went to Ireland in 1630 and was ordained at the hands of Andrew Knox Bishop of Raphoe and some Scottish ministers. In 1638 he was back in Scotland and not only signed the National Covenant but was sent to London to obtain the signature of Scottish noblemen at Court.[5]

Livingston, who is associated with the charges of Stranraer and Ancrum, greatly impressed his contemporary churchmen, and was one of those appointed to negotiate with Charles at Breda in 1650. He, however, distrusted Charles and was opposed to the Scone coronation and the conduct of the government. Like Gillespie he was a Protester, and like him he preached before Cromwell in London in 1654. On that occasion he prayed for the Royal House and implored mercy for those who had usurped its authority! At the Restoration he refused to take the Oath of Allegiance before the Privy Council but was mildly dealt with and

[1] Nicoll's *Diary*, p. 108.
[2] *Dict. Nat. Biog.*, VII, p. 1241.
[3] Nicoll's *Diary*, p. 162.
[4] Note No. 18, p. 222.
[5] *Dict. Nat. Biog.*, XXXIII, p. 402.

retired to Rotterdam, where he died in 1672. Livingston, said to be of high descent, was held in wide respect, being "modest in manner, sweet in temper, and of retired and contemplative habits". In his moderation he deplored the division which had torn the Church asunder.[1]

It may be regarded as a significant thing that Sir John Scot should have the support of two ministers whose ecclesiastical and political complexion has been indicated.

Whether it were chance or policy that brought all three together in London at that time, and whatever the nature of the relationship, it is undoubted that for his purpose he could have found no stronger advocates; and it is clear that in gaining their assistance the Scottish lawyer had not parted with his natural sagacity or his professional diplomacy. Here, however, for the remedying of his present ills he took certain critical steps which in the end were difficult to reconcile with loyalty to the banished sovereign, and may have gained the disfavour of the King.

It is a year later that we find his affairs raised again under the Proceedings of the State Council sitting at Whitehall. On 9th March 1655, Colonel Jones submits a list of the Scottish nobility and gentry who are lying under fine, and reports the respective fines which are continued upon them according to a certificate from the Scottish Commissioners.

The business reveals that these exceptional cases are having favour extended to them under recommendation of the Scottish Committee, and it is probable that the process of consideration has been occupying the intervening time. The list—twenty-seven in all—is given, and the original fines range from £3,000 to £1,000. In almost all cases a reduced figure is recommended. Sir John Scot's fine of £1,500 is set in the recommendation of reduction at £500.[2]

It so happens that under the Day's Proceedings of the above date there are three specific references to our subject, showing that the Commissioners in their sittings reduced the figure further to £300 and then resolved to continue consideration because the case was "particular". On 19th March they decided that the proposed fine of £300 imposed on "Sir John Scot of Scottistarbitt be discharged and taken off in consideration of his pains and service".

[1] Note No. 19, p. 222.
[2] Cal. State Papers, 1655, p. 71.

On 17th July, after application had been made to Parliament, the fines laid on him and five others were "absolutely discharged and their estates freed therefrom".[1] The foregoing record corrects the long-standing errors that have been made concerning his penalty under the Commonwealth.

Having achieved this success Sir John now bent all his powers in an effort to be reinstalled as Director of Chancery. It is a matter of interest bearing upon the public circulation of ephemeral papers in that day that the story of Scotstarvit's supreme effort, with its note of personal appeal and persuasion, is found in a pamphlet which carries a head-line suggesting a cause of no little general interest, namely, *Sir John Scot's Humble Address to the Protector.*

This print has evidently been extracted bodily from a collection of pamphlets, and although separately and carefully printed it supplies no date as to its original publication, but there is internal evidence that it was composed in the latter part of 1655. In the Introduction there are some sentiments of a political character which if they came to the Royal notice at the Restoration would certainly ensure that Sir John Scot if reseated at the Chancery at this juncture would be unseated then. It is thus presented.

"To His Highness, Protector of the Commonwealth of England, Scotland and Ireland and the Dominions thereunto belonging, The Humble Address of Sir John Scot of Scottistarvet.

"May it please your Highness.

"The free access which you are pleased to give to all strangers, and the speedy satisfaction that you afford to their grievances, emboldens me to present these papers to your Highness.

"My Lord, I had possession of an office in Edinburgh called the Directorie of the Chancery granted to my ancestors, and after them to me and my Son for our lives under the great Seal of Scotland. The grounds and reasons of my being put out I do here humbly submit to your Highness; which I have the rather done partly that I might conceal no occasion for your Highness to shew your Justice in deciding the cause of the innocent, and partly out of an Ambition to be employed among the rest of my Countrymen in your Highness' service, counting it the chiefest happiness of me and my family that I have some title and claim to so great an honour."[2]

[1] Cal. State Papers, 1655, pp. 72, 86, 117, 247.
[2] Collection of Pamphlets in the Nat. Lib., 5.1540 (14).

After this introduction he proceeds to support his case and relates the history of his Petitions. It is unnecessary to recount in full his detailed and persuasive statement. His main contention is that the English commissioners sent to order and settle Scottish affairs had erred in assuming the Chancery office to be subservient to the Court of Justice. In proof he advances fourteen Reasons based on ancient and established law and practice showing the separate character of the Chancery and the independence of the Director.

Finally he appeals to the law of the Commonwealth itself, which in the Act of 28th October 1651, permitted all who had carried themselves soberly and were guiltless of anything that moved war, to enjoy their liberties and estates, "whereof no doubt my office is a part". Moreover the Act of Council freeing him from his fine had declared him capable of all favour as one found by his Highness to have done good service.[1]

This Address so supported was submitted by the Protector to competent judges, who found Scotstarvit wrongly deprived of office, and it appears that only the unexpected death of Cromwell denied him the reinstatement he sought so long.[2]

The last we hear of Sir John's efforts, which makes plain the foregoing and contains a reference to four earlier attempts, was undertaken on his behalf by no less a person than the secretive and astute General Monk. We find that the military commander wrote Secretary Thurloe in October 1658, a month after Cromwell's decease, and strongly pleaded Scot's case, although with the insertion of a peculiar qualification. The following is the letter, dated Dalkeith, 1st October 1658.

"My Lord,

"Sir John Scott of Scottis-Tarrvit, having gift of the late king under the great seal for the place of director of Chancery in Scotland for life, and the said place being disposed of by the Commissioners from the Parliament in the year 1651, he made four several addresses to his late highness (Cromwell), at the last whereof it was found by the Commissioners of the great seal, Sir Thomas Widdrington, the Lord Montague, the Lord Whitlock, and Colonel Sydenham, to whom his highness referred the cognition thereof, that they found no cause why he should have

[1] Cal. State Papers, 1651, p. 90.
[2] Ibid., 1655, p. 86.

36

been displaced out of office, the same being only ministerial (administrative). But upon his last petition, seeking to be restored, his highness would give no determined answer till he had advised with his Council; the cause whereof was that he had made a gift of the same to one Alexander Jaffray, not having understood of Sir John Scott his right thereto. And now Mr Jaffray being very sick, Sir John and myself make it our request unto you that your lordship will be pleased to stand his friend to his highness (Richard Cromwell) that in case Mr Jaffray should die, his highness will not dispose of the said place of director of the Chancery till he hath heard Sir John Scott speak for himself. I crave your Lordship's pardon for giving you this trouble, and remain,

Your Lordship's most humble servant,
George Monck."[1]

It is clear that important admissions had already been made—the Protector himself confessing to a misunderstanding—but the disturbance of the times and the dissension which followed upon Richard Cromwell's succession must have pushed the matter out of sight. And in any case Alexander Jaffray, whose immediate death would seem to have been expected, lived on until 1673. Thurloe's answer, if he made one, has not been preserved, and it seems likely that his Highness did not hear "Sir John Scott speak for himself". At the Restoration his case was no better: the Chancery post was given to Sir William Kerr, son of Lord Lothian, who, Sir John said with biting humour, "danced him out of his office, being a dexterous dancer".[2] Kerr was popularly celebrated as a swordsman and dancer.

Robert Baillie, one of the five commissioners sent to the Westminster Assembly in 1643-1648, whose Letters and Diary are of much historical importance, has a striking reference to Sir John, made in 1662. It is expressed in a curiously cool and detached mood about one whom he had once called "Our good friend Sir John Scot".[3] The note is remarkable also for the harshness of its reference to Milton amongst others, and in the fact that it links the adverse fortune of Scotstarvit with that of Loudoun and Lothian, the former Chancellor, and Secretary, respectively, and with all "the maleficent crew" in England.

[1] Thurloe's *State Papers*, VII, p. 421.
[2] *The Staggering State* (1754), p. 163.
[3] Baillie's *Journal* I, p. 370.

37

Baillie, it is appropriate to remember, was one of the commissioners sent to Holland in 1650 for the purpose of inviting Charles II to Scotland and of settling the terms of his active resumption of sovereignty. He died in August 1662, his death being probably hastened by mortification at the King's reimposition of Episcopacy soon after his return. Part of the passage, which was penned just after the landing of Charles at Dover, may be transcribed. Baillie wrote as an eye-witness of the events and betrays the extravagance of loyalty which affected all but the shrewdest heads in Scotland at that juncture of history.

"He (the King) pressed the Houses to haste the Bill of Indemnity. They excepted a very few from it, scarce a dozen, in which the people had much more satisfaction than he, for he could have been induced to pardon all. But it was the justice of God that brought Peters, Harrison, and others to a shameful death: to hang up the bones of Oliver, Bradshaw, Ireton and Pride on the gibbet at Tiburne; to disgrace the two Godwins, blind Milton,[1] Owen, Sterrie, Lockyer and others of that maleficent crew."

He proceeds:

"The most of our (Scottish) nobles, with very many of our gentry, ran up to Whitehall: all were made welcome. Old places were restored to Crawford, Cassilis, and others. No wonder the Chancellor's and Secretary's places were taken from Loudoun and Lothian, yet with recompense enough to them both, whom some thought deserved little. Loudoun had his pension of a thousand pounds and gift of amnesties continued. Lothian got his second son Director of Chancellary, which Sir John Scot was not thought to deserve."[2]

In his Memoirs Sir John is cautious in his references to Royalty. All he has to say about the conduct of Charles II is that "his return has not had the success expected by the Kingdom of Scotland", an observation which in the circumstances is noticeably restrained.[3] In May 1662 the Rescissory Act of the Scottish Parliament annulled the legislation of the last twenty years.

At this juncture zealot and moderate were alike confounded and

---

[1] Note No. 20, p. 222.

[2] Louden: John Campbell of Lawers, Chancellor, 1641. Lothian: Sir William Kerr, Secretary, 1644. Baillie's *Journal*, III, p. 433.

[3] *The Staggering State* (1754), p. 107.

Bishop Burnet says that "all possible security for the future was shaken".[1] Argyll, whose Presbyterian zeal had humiliated the King, and to whose variance with Hamilton Sir John largely attributed the country's woes, went to the block convicted of a treasonable correspondence with Monk.

In 1651 Sir John Scot might have been regarded as elderly: he was sixty-five. But, as may be judged from his interests and the length of his days, he was a vigorous and fit man who had little thought of retiring from active life.

Now, however, in 1661, he was seventy-five years old, and although he lived for nine more years there is no evidence of any fresh activities. If we imagine a robust old man—as we are justified in doing—he may still have entertained scholars in the high study of his ancient tower and regaled them with a septuagenarian's memories and anecdotes.

In the large collection of "Letters from learned men to Scotstarvit" in the National Library, representing at least fifty correspondents, most of whom were Continental, there are letters dated as late as 1660, 1665, and 1667, the latter just three years before his death.[2] But at his advanced age he must have largely outlived his friends and lost the keen scent which formerly set him in pursuit of so many literary and liberal adventures.

There were however still domestic events of importance. For example, a note of 29th April 1662 reads, "The Lady Scotstarvit, younger, married to the Laird of Erdlee, surnamed Preston. The marriage feast stood at Tarvit."[3] This was probably Elizabeth, born in 1640.

It is of interest that Janet, daughter of Anne Drummond, is the only member of the family who is reported to have inherited the father's scholarly habits and endowments. Nisbet says she remained unmarried, and presumably resided at the ancestral home.[4]

It was now, we believe, that Sir John finally retired and filled in the lapses of trivial occupation by musing over the figures and movements of other days. And it is probable that in the quiet study of his remote house, given up to a strain of aged preoccupation, he began to trace in the numerous instances of the families

---

[1] Burnet's *Hist. of Scot.*, I, p. 93.
[2] ADV. MS. 17.1.9.
[3] *New Stat. Account*, IX, p. 524.
[4] Nisbet's *Heraldry*, III, p. 293.

whose record he had knowledge of, the vexing pattern of misfortune and retribution following upon the doubtful acquisition of power and wealth. This he set down in *The Staggering State of Scots Statesmen*, a memoir which may, at the most, have been intended for private circulation amongst his family and intimate friends.

CHAPTER IV

CULTURAL INTERESTS AND PROJECTS

Professor P. Hume Brown in describing the state of the national literature in the late sixteenth century, says with reference to James VI: "though himself a lover of learning, and in his own way a man of letters, the reign of James was not a blossoming period in Scottish literature. The turmoil in which the nation lived, the constant preoccupation of men's minds with the burning questions of the hour, and the narrow view of life involved in the prevailing type of religion, may account for the failure of great creative genius."[1]

It is however refreshing and instructive amid the calamitous times that prevailed to find how the spirit of poetry and culture, if it did not flourish conspicuously, at least survived; and it is a fact that in respect of these interests Sir John Scot was a liberal patron and promoter, and to some extent a personal exponent.

At the opening of the seventeenth century it was not only the strictness of religion that influenced the state of literature. The native spirit and mode of expression were being affected also by new models and by the change that was creeping over both the spoken and the written word. The union of the crowns and the presence of the Court at Whitehall had alienating effects, and the King himself is reported to have adopted southern English almost as soon as he arrived in London.[2]

The consequent decline from Scottish themes and diction was illustrated in two ways. On the one hand by the courtly school who wrote verse in English, and on the other by a large group of poets who composed chiefly moral and elegiac verse in Latin. Latinity was the chief delight of the scholarship of the age, its best exponent being George Buchanan. His perfect command of the Latin language, coupled with his real gifts of poetry and original thought, had maintained the classical tradition in full force and

[1] *Hist. of Scot.*, Hume Brown, II, p. 220.
[2] Reg. P.C. 1607-1610, pp. lxxii-lxxiii. Hume Brown links James with the school of Courtier poets.

had fanned among his compatriots that zeal for humanism which was then widespread on the Continent.[1]

It happened in this situation in 1608 that Blaeu, the Dutch publisher, perceiving the harvest that might be reaped in the publication to the schools and learned circles of Europe of the wealth of existing classical verse, began his issue of the same in a challenging series of national collections. It was Sir John Scot who for his country's sake felt the call to present to the world Scotland's contribution, and when the collection—briefly called *Delitiae Poetarum Scotorum*—appeared in 1637, it was made plain that if Scotland had few poets to sound a native wood-note she had many who were well-schooled in grave and elegant and witty Latin versification.

Scot himself was early active as a versifier. There is a Latin piece belonging to his eighteenth year when he was a student at St Andrews. To the *Delitiae Poetarum Scotorum* he contributed a number of poems, one of which we have in a translation made by his friend Drummond. On examination it is found to be a collection of epigrams, which although cleverly balanced contains little of the spirit of poetry. Its theme is the vanity of human existence, and it contains in brief what Dr Johnson did so well a century later in his famous satire.[2]

> "What course of life should wretched mortals take?
> In books hard questions large contention make.
> Care dwells in houses, labour in the field.
> Tumultuous seas affrighting dangers yield.
> In foreign lands thou never can be blest,
> If rich, thou art in fear, if poor, distrest.
> In wedlock frequent discontentments swell,
> Unmarried persons as in deserts dwell.
> How many troubles are with children born?
> Yet he who wants them counts himself forlorn.
> Young men are wanton and of wisdom void,
> Grey hairs are cold, unfit to be employed.
> Who would not one of these two offers try—
> Not to be born, or, being born, to die."[3, 4]

[1] Note No. 21, p. 222.
[2] *The Vanity of Human Wishes.*
[3] Drummond's Works, Sage's edit. 1711. The Poems, p. 43.
[4] Note No. 22, p. 222.

It seems that Sir John held the patronage of letters but not the patent. In patronage he was supreme. No Scotsman of his day compares with him in his zeal for the promotion of liberal interests in national art; and in respect of his collection of the poets, and Blaeu's publication of the maps of Timothy Pont, he effected two productions which are of permanent historical value to this country.

The first venture we hear of in this connection was a book of Latin poems addressed to his friends by John Scott, a youthful cousin on his father's side.

He was a son of Sir William Scott whom we have already introduced in a reference to the Directorship of Chancery. Sir William Scott's first wife was Elizabeth Hamilton, a daughter of Thomas Hamilton of Priestfield and sister to the Earl of Haddington. John Scott *adolescens* was a son of this marriage. There is a note about him in *The Staggering State* which says that he was author of a poesy to King James which was printed in the *Scots Poets*; being very learned his father sent him to Rochelle to profess humanity, and he died there of the plague.[1]

The book produced under the name of this promising youth was published at the shop of Andrew Hart in the High Street, Edinburgh, in 1619. Sir John was thirty-three years old, and the evidence makes it clear that he supervised the work, writing an introduction in which he quotes Seneca and airs his Greek, and contributing items to it.

But the main interest lies in the taste with which the book has been printed, decorated, and bound. The calf-skin covers are tooled and grained in gold; the pages have decorative borders, and each poem is divided from the other with scrolls and ornate bands in various styles. Over the preface there is an artistic panel in which the Thistle and the Rose flourish together. In fact there is much of the virtuosity which was afterwards exhibited so delightfully in the fire-place at Scotstarvit Tower. The volume, which was dedicated to the Earl of Haddington, the poet's uncle, must be a singular example of the printer's and bookbinder's art in that day in Scotland.[2]

Hart as a publisher had a short but impressive record. Besides first editions of poems by Drummond and plays by Sir William

---

[1] *The Staggering State*, p. 162.
[2] *Schediasmata Miscellanea.* Nat Lib., L.C. 593 (1).

Alexander, with Napier's epoch-making book on Logarithms, we find him bringing out fresh editions of works by George Buchanan, Sir Francis Bacon, Sir David Lyndsay, and Alexander Montgomery. Between 1610 and 1621, in which latter year he died, he published at least eighty-one works. Under the year 1619 is set John Scott's *Hodaeporicon* which must have been published independently of *The Muse's Welcome*, a collection of congratulatory poems presented to James in 1617, and also produced by Andrew Hart.[1,2]

In chronological order Sir John's next literary project was the *Delitiae Poetarum Scotorum*. It was published at Amsterdam in 1637 and paid for by him in a hundred double pieces of gold. The gold this time was in the price of production and not in the decoration of the work. Here we reach the story of Scot's collaboration with the distinguished poet, Arthur Johnston.

There can be no question that the initiation of this work came from Sir John, and his wide knowledge of Scottish authors and literary matters must have constituted the main support of the effort. But Johnston, a poet of European reputation, exercised editorial oversight of the contents and their arrangement. While the book was in preparation Sir John visited Amsterdam and assisted in correcting proof sheets. It was then that he made acquaintance with the printer Blaeu. "Twice", he says, he was "in the Low countries for printing the Scots poets and the Atlas, and he paid to John Blaeu a hundred double pieces for printing the poets."[3]

In writing of this undertaking, Sir William D. Geddes, the eminent classical teacher who edited a collection of Aberdeenshire verse including Johnston's work, says with due appreciation of the value of the production in contemporary Continental estimation: "After Scotus Erigena and Michael Scot there is no one of the name of Scot as famous as was Scotstarvit until the rise of Sir Walter."[4]

Arthur Johnston was the son of an Aberdeenshire laird and on his mother's side a grandson of the seventh Lord Forbes. He graduated as a doctor of medicine at Padua in 1610, and having travelled much abroad returned to England at the time of the

[1] *Edinburgh Bib. Soc. Publications* I (1892-93) No. 12.
[2] Note No. 23, p. 222.
[3] The *Staggering State*, p. 163.
[4] *Musa Latina Aberdonensis* (Spalding Club), I, p. 4.

death of James VI in 1625.[1] We do not know when the two scholars first met but the editor just quoted suggests that they were acquainted at least by 1622, and connects Sir John's election as an Honorary Burgess of Aberdeen in that year with the poet's influence.[2] Sir John must in some way have approved himself to the Aberdeen Council. An item in the accounts of the Burgh, 1629-1630, reads: "For ane barrell of salmond to Sir John Scot for his consultation and freyndlie advyse in the tounis affairs at the late Conventioun of Estates."[3]

In 1625, however, on the occasion of the royal funeral, Scot was in London, and as Johnston also was present they would almost certainly meet. We trace their connection later in several Privy Council reports belonging to the year 1630, when Scot was an arbiter in a dispute in which the poet was a party,[4] and 1631, when the poet was apparently residing in Edinburgh.[5] It is clear from the indications that they would have opportunities for intercourse and would gather increasing knowledge of each other's interests and prepare the way for future collaboration.

Johnston in 1632 published his book of Epigrams, said to be the finest of his verse. His poetical paraphrase of the Songs of Solomon appeared in 1633, and brought him the notice of Laud who met him in Edinburgh in that year. In 1637 he published in Aberdeen his full poetical version of the Psalms of David. They are said to have rivalled (and Laud is said to have hoped they would out-shine) the similar work of Buchanan. In the year which marked his greatest literary activity (1637) he was appointed Rector of King's College, Aberdeen. He died at Oxford in 1641.[6]

With his rapid succession of achievement between 1632 and 1637 this scholarly poet established an extensive and well-sustained reputation.[7]

The *Delitiae Poetarum Scotorum* was produced in two parts, each a neat diminutive volume, flexibly bound, and with a small but very clear type. The inside of the title page contains the

[1] *Dict. Nat. Biog.*, X, p. 946.
[2] Johnston was admitted a free burgess of the Guild of Aberdeen on 5th August 1622, and Scot similarly admitted on 31st August. *Burgh Records*, Spalding Club, p. 377.
[3] *Spalding Club Miscellany*, V, p. 148.
[4] Reg. P.C. 1629-1630, p. 473.
[5] *Ibid.*, 1630-1632, p. 107.
[6] *Dict. Nat. Biog.*, X, p. 947.
[7] Note No. 24, p. 222.

licence of the Archbishop of St Andrews warranting "That there is nothing contrary to Christian doctrine, injurious to customs, or which would give offence publicly or privately. We testify them to be worthy of the title which they profess." Scot, to whom it is dedicated, is called a "Noble Maecenas". In all there were thirty-six contributors.[1] It was said of the Baron of Bradwardine in *Waverley* that "for literature he read the classic poets, and Arthur Johnston's Psalms of a Sunday, and the *Delitiae Poetarum Scotorum*".[2] Dr Johnson also commended it: "This work would have done honour to any nation".[3]

After Johnston's death Scot immediately set about collecting the works of his friend and published them at Middelburg in 1642. Here again we find a narrow diminutive volume, but carefully arranged and clearly printed. It is claimed that the contents had all already been diligently revised by the author in separate issues and are now for the first time appearing in complete form. Scotstarvit's extensive knowledge directed the venture, but the Reverend William Spang, minister of the Scots Church at Campvere, was agent and assistant on the spot. There can be little doubt that in the wide circle of European scholarship and culture this production would be reckoned as a notable event, and the work must have delighted the classical taste of numerous readers in that day.

Another proof of the scholarly activity of Scotstarvit was his translation from Latin of the *Jus Feudale* of Sir Thomas Craig (1538-1608).[4] This work, which helped to build up the law of Scotland concerning land tenure into a separate system, was produced in 1603 and Scot translated it in 1644. Although this was the first English version of a legal work of historic importance its existence appears to have escaped notice, and P. F. Tytler in his *Life of Craig* prefaced to J. Baillie's edition of the treatise in 1823, makes no mention of it.

The facts are however beyond dispute as reported in Scot's *Trew Relation* of date 1660. Writing about himself in the third person he says: "He was an instrument in causing Craig's book *De Feudis* to be printed, which, *anno* 1644, at the desire of the Earl of Crawford he translated into English, which is ready for

---

[1] Nat. Lib. Ry. III g. 36.
[2] *Waverley* (1846) XIII, p. 129.
[3] *Musa Latina Aberdonensis* III, Introd. XXIX.
[4] Note No. 25, p. 223.

the press, containing 7 quires of paper". In the somewhat in-
definite nature of the statement we assume that he made the
English version as related and that the work was ready to be printed
but not, up to 1660, published.[1]

The Earl of Crawford[2] was appointed Treasurer in 1644, and
his interest in Craig's work may have been provoked by the problems of his office. Scot reports of him in *The Staggering State:*
"He had a liberty, by patent under the Great Seal ratified in
Parliament, for changing the whole ward-lands into feu, which
might have been of great benefit to the King, and to himself also,
if he had put the same into practise. But albeit many urged to have
got their lands changed yet did he never suffer any at all to pass,
but one Charter of his own."[3]

Another work is brought to our notice by Bishop Sage, the
first biographer of William Drummond, who reports that Scot
produced a collection, the first, of the poet's works in 1656, which
was about seven years after Drummond's death.

He thus sealed the long and friendly relationship which he had
always maintained with his brother-in-law. Sage says "Many
of his poems in his lifetime had been printed in loose sheets; some
were lost, and all out of print. Sir John Scot after his death caused
collect them and print them all in one volume, *anno* 1656."[4]

Actually at this date two volumes were issued, the first containing the Prose Writings, namely *The History of the Jameses* and a
selection of pamphlets chiefly of a political kind. The ostensible
editor was Drummond's son who dedicated the work to Scotstarvit,
and it is likely that the latter contributed his aid to the production.
The date was January 1655.

The volume of verse however was entirely due to the initiative
and efforts of Sir John. The state and dispersion of the materials
makes it probable that he required a fair extent of time ere the
poems could be secured and arranged. It is significant that he
chose a London publisher. The publication notice reads:

London: Printed for Richard Tomlins at the "Sun and Bible"
near Pye-Corner. 1656.

The title page sets forth in impressive style—"The Most Elegant
and Elaborate Poems of that Great Court Wit, Mr William
Drummond". The local editing and superintendence through

[1] *Scot. Hist. Review*, XI, p. 190.
[2] *The Staggering State*, p. 46.
[3] Note No. 26, p. 223.
[4] *Works of Drummond* (1711) The Life, p. v.

47

the press was placed by Scot in the hands of Edward Phillips, Milton's nephew, and to him we may attribute the somewhat soaring title. There was a second edition in 1659, "Printed for William Rands, Bookseller, at his House over against the Bear Tavern in Fleet Street".

This book (1656) is a small octavo of 208 pages, tastefully printed and bound, and worthy of the distinguished poet whose greatness Scot obviously held in high admiration. The Introduction by Phillips cannot be said to be too happy, but it is brief. He speaks of "These poems, the most polite and verdant that ever the Scottish nation produced", and proceeds to say (with somewhat rueful truth from a Scottish point of view) that, "not even the choicest poets of England can challenge any advantage above him".[1]

From the literary angle readers will find interest in the fact that the work was issued under the care of Milton's nephew. There may however be a more curious interest in the reflection that its publication was made not long prior to General Monk's appeal to have Sir John restored to his office of Director of Chancery, and that the production must have been advanced concurrently with the earlier efforts made to the same end. Scot was in London in 1654 and 1655.

Was there, we wonder, any significance in the choice of Phillips, who did not share his uncle's political views but lived in friendly intimacy with him? Did it mean anything to Sir John's hopes that his chosen editor was the nephew of the Latin Secretary to the Council of State? It is also a curious reflection of Scotstarvit's interests and acquaintanceships that Phillips was the son of Edward Phillips late head of the English Crown Office of Chancery, and that his step-father, Thomas Agar, had succeeded to that position and was the present occupant.

Moreover, would he at this juncture possibly interview Milton who was then living in his "pretty garden house" at Petty France? Would his personal advantage, coupled with zeal for learning and partiality for scholars, not likely lead him to the house of this genius of learning whose reputation was sufficient to attract scholarly foreigners to come to England for the sole purpose of seeing him?[2] We can only speculate on these possibilities, but we

---

[1] *Poems* 1656. To the Reader, A.3. For a note on Phillips see *Milton* by Mark Pattison. English Men of Letters (1909), pp. 44-45.

[2] Milton lived in his house in Petty France from 1651 to 1660. It is intriguing to think of Sir John's movements when in London, which, he tells us, he visited 24 times in an official capacity.

are sure that Sir John would spare no effort either to regain his office or to add to the sum of his knowledge.

We may here introduce a further proof of Scot's unusual industry by calling attention to an observation made by Nisbet concerning the elder Robert Scot. It is to the effect that he excelled all who had gone before him in his conduct of the office of Director of Chancery: in particular that he personally read over every documentary item before he attested it.[1] It can now be made clear that his grandson not only followed his example but went on to undertake duties of office which Robert Scot probably never attempted.

We are referring to an Inventory of Charters which is lodged in the Scottish National Library. On the fore-leaf there is the following note:

"In the handwriting of Sir John Scot of Scotstarvit. Two other volumes of this register in the British Museum. Wholly taken from the Great Seal."[2]

The record thus referred to is written carefully and compactly in a small neat hand and is arranged in Books which are each witnessed at the close. It covers transactions falling within the long period of 1481 up to May 1630, and as it contains approximately 250,000 words of precisely expressed entries, it gives witness to a remarkable amount of patient and skilful industry. To it must be added the other volumes which are said to rest in the British Museum. Together they may be regarded as forming a remarkable monument to the sheer personal labour assumed by this diversely active but indefatigable worker. From this angle we can see the point of his objection to Jaffray's inexperience, and why at the Restoration he referred to "one altogether unskilled placed to be Director", namely Sir William Kerr.[3]

But his greatest service in the interest of the nation lies in his undertaking to publish the maps of Timothy Pont, a labour of extreme difficulty extending over many years.

There has been some confused writing on this subject, the statement even being made that Sir John Scot set Pont to his task of survey and financed it. The fact is that Pont, a solitary and independent worker of great courage and initiative, probably completed his work before Sir John ever heard of it.

The last authentic date on which Pont appears in history is

---

[1] Nisbet's *Heraldry*, II, p. 292.
[2] ADV. MS. 34.2.4.
[3] *The Staggering State*, p. 163.

December 1610: at that time he was the parson of Dunnet in Caithness. A new incumbent appears in 1614, and it may be assumed that the surveyor and map-maker lived until this year. We have scant information about him and nothing as to his end, but we are not altogether uninformed, thanks to an important letter written to Scot by Robert Gordon of Straloch in January 1648, and to the editorial labours of C. G. Cash and Dr David Laing.

It seems probable that Pont did his work between 1595 and 1610.[1] Gordon writing on the above date (1648) and vouching for his statement by the remark "as I have heard him relate", says that "not being supported by the favour and assistance of any persons of high rank, he himself, unaided, undertook this work more than forty years ago". He indicates that Pont returned home "to bring to perfection the descriptions he had made, but he could not accomplish his intention by reason of the avarice of printers and booksellers, and while he waited for some more favourable occasion to present itself, death took him from us before his time in the flower of his age".[2]

Gordon adds that since the papers were in danger of being destroyed James VI gave instructions that they should be purchased and preserved. This having been done they were again likely to be wasted and lost when Sir John Scot—with conduct in sharp contrast to the indifference and avariciousness alluded to above— took the matter in hand. From a note already reported it seems that his interest was awakened about the year 1631-32.[3]

Timothy Pont, born 1565, and graduating at St Andrews in 1583, was one of two sons of Robert Pont, the Scottish reformer who held charges at Dunblane and Dunkeld and was called to St Cuthbert's, Edinburgh, in 1573, where he remained until transferred to St Andrews in 1581. This distinguished Church leader and frequent Moderator of the General Assembly was so learned in the law that he was appointed a Lord of Session in 1572, being the last to conjoin that office with the office of the ministry.[4] He had marked scientific interests which were inherited by his son, who as a mathematician and surveyor was led to undertake the mapping of the entire territory of Scotland: the first to

[1] Note No. 27, p. 223.
[2] Quoted by C. G. Cash. *Scot. Geog. Mag.* (1901), XVII, pp. 408-410.
[3] Note No. 28, p. 223.
[4] Note No. 29, p. 223.

attempt and complete the task.[1] Pont is entered as one of those who undertook in the Settlement of Ulster, but it is doubtful if he took possession of the land allotted to him.[2]

There is a contemporary note of much interest from the hand of Sir Robert Sibbald in the Foreword of his work on Fife and Kinross. He says,

"I find myself obliged in gratitude to acknowledge from whom I had the best assistance in carrying on this work. And, in the first place, thanks are due to the unwearied diligence of Mr Timothy Pont, who after he had travelled over all the parts of North Britain and the Isles belonging to it, made maps of them, and particularly of these shires (Fife and Kinross), some of which I have. And next to him the nation is obliged to Sir John Scot of Scots-Tarvat, who not only recovered Mr Pont's papers but also supplied them where they were defective; and it was by his procurement that the learned Robert Gordon of Straloch, and his son the parson of Rothiemay, did prepare most of them for the press, and furnished some nicely done. I have the autograph Mr James Gordon did of these shires, and of the towns of Cupar and St Andrews. His father Straloch made two excellent descriptions of Fife in Latin."[3, 4]

In Walter MacFarlane's *Geographical Collections relating to Scotland*, the editor, Sir Arthur Mitchell, K.C.B., quotes the following note by Gordon which was affixed to the Latin descriptions just mentioned:

"But I may have to expiate the wrong if I do not here mention Sir John Scot of Scotstarvit who claims his title from this shire, for to him is due all this work of mine. He has been my sole exhorter to this, and I can truly say that had he not roused me when slumbering, and urged me when hesitating, I should never have applied myself to these tasks."[5]

Who it was who brought the question of Pont's maps originally before the notice of James VI is not made clear. It is not likely

[1] His actual MSS. are preserved in the National Library, the frail sheets having been carefully handled by C. G. Cash. *Scot. Geog. Mag.*, September 1907.

[2] In the official Roll of the Plantation of Ulster occurs the entry: "Mr Timothy Pont, minister; surety Alexander Borthwick of Nether Laich: 2000 acres." Reg. P.C. 1607-1610, p. 330.

[3] *History of the Sheriffdoms of Fife and Kinross* (Edit. 1803) p. xii.

[4] Note No. 30, p. 223.

[5] *Geographical Collections*, II, p. 411.

to have been Scotstarvit, for with his wonted energy he would certainly have pursued it, and, besides, Gordon notes that a stage was reached in the unfortunate history of the maps when Sir John stepped in and took control: this was after the failure of the initial interest and action. We can only regret that the gallant Pont himself did not survive to enjoy the encouragement of such a patron.

The evidence of Scot's efforts appears in various directions all related to the same end; namely, in the resolutions of Parliament and of the General Assembly to advance the project; in the invitation of Charles I to Gordon of Straloch to undertake the work of editing; and in the intercourse and correspondence which Scot had with Samuel Wallace, his agent at Campvere in Zeeland, and with the publisher Blaeu.[1]

The first we hear of it is in Principal Baillie's Letters where he makes the following note on the sitting of the Assembly on 2nd August 1641: "Sir John Scot's petition to have a description of our Shyredoms by some in every Presbytery, to be set before the maps you have in hand, is granted".[2] Baillie was writing to his cousin the Rev. William Spang, M.A., at Campvere. There was a regular correspondence, and the note "maps you have in hand" shows that Spang was collaborating and that before 1641 sheets had been transmitted to him.[3]

The royal letter to the Laird of Straloch asking him to undertake a revision of Pont's maps is also of this year and of the same month as the General Assembly's action. It discloses that the initiative comes from Sir John Scot. The date is August 1641. Charles asks that the cairtts (maps) be revised so that they may be sent "by the director of our chancellarie to Holland".[4]

The patriotic promoter was however not always fortunate in his plans. His proposal for descriptions of shires through action in the various Presbyteries was ineffective, and in 1642 he brought forward a bill in the Assembly which was intended to enforce compliance.

Minute of Synod of Fife, 5th April 1642:

[1] Note No. 31, p. 223.

[2] Sir John had conceived the plan of supplying descriptions on a presbyterial basis, thus practically anticipating Sir John Sinclair's scheme in the first *Statistical Account*. Baillie's *Journal*, I, p. 368.

[3] Note No. 32, p. 223.

[4] Charles's letter to Straloch (Aug. 1641) quoted by Rogers, *The Staggering State* (1872), p. 12.

"Anent the bill given in by my Lord Scotstarvett to the Assemblie, complaining that notwithstanding of an Act of the last Generall Assemblie holden at Edinburgh appointing all severall Presbyteries of this kingdome to set doun the descriptions of thair severall paroches, and to report the same to the Chancellarie betwix then and the first day of January bypast, yet none of the ministry of this province, except nyne of the Presbyterie of Kirkcaldie, has obeyed the same. Therefore the Assemblie, considering the worthiness of the work, tending to the honour of the natioun, appointed the Moderators of the severall Presbyteries to urge the fulfilling of the foresaid Act betwix this and the first of May precisely."[1]

But Baillie sounds a disappointing Assembly note under date 5th September 1643. He says: "Sir John Scot's bill for pressing Presbyteries to describe their own bounds was not so much regarded".[2]

It seems from what happened later that the Presbyteries found it difficult to meet the request of the Assembly's Act and could not be forced to perform a task which was not of an obligatory nature. In the end the zealous promoter of the scheme had himself to dictate in Blaeu's house and from his extensive memory an astonishing amount of information on Scottish topography and possibly genealogy, as is reported by John Blaeu. But various references show that the Gordons also supplied topographical notes, and it would appear both from Gordon's and Sibbald's remarks, that Pont himself not only mapped the country but made descriptive notes. He certainly did so with respect to the district of Cunningham in Ayr.[3]

In the month of September 1645 (the month of Montrose's defeat at Philiphaugh) Sir John Scot arrived at Campvere, and there is some doubt as to the motive of his journey thither. Thomas Cunningham was at that time the Conservator of the interests of Scottish merchants in the Netherlands, and in his Journal he asserts that Sir John's visit was due to the troubles at home.[4]

[1] *Records of the Synod of Fife* (Abbotsford Club), p. 131.
[2] Baillie's *Journal*, II, p. 88.
[3] Note No. 33, p. 223.
[4] *The Journal of Thomas Cunningham of Campvere*, 1640-1654. Scot. Hist. Society, p. 130. Cunningham was an elder in the Church at Campvere and was knighted by Charles II in 1650.

Another and weightier consideration rests in the fact that his visit was regarded as an affair of State. The government of Zeeland commissioned a vessel for his safe conduct home, and in Balfour's *Annals* there is the following minute of 6th January 1646:

"The parliament wreatts a letter to the Estaits and Admirall of Zeeland of thankes for ther kindness shown to Sir John Scot in sending a waighter (ship of convoy) to wafte him owre to Scotland from the danger of pyratts. Which letter the Estaits ordanes in ther name the President of the Parliament to subscrive."[1]

It may be assumed that this reveals the real reason of his going, which was to advance the business of the Scottish Atlas as a project approved by Parliament. When in the Netherlands he wrote to the Laird of Straloch on this matter almost at once and reported the loss of the "cairt of Fyffe" when a Leith ship had been taken by a Dunkirk privateer. Pont's map of Fife having been wasted or gone astray, Gordon junior prepared that which we possess. Scot adds, "You did wysely that caused him keep a doubill of it, or otherways all had been gone".[2]

We next hear of the progress of the scheme in a letter of Samuel Wallace (Cunningham's depute) who wrote to Gordon from Campvere in March 1647. He reported that "The cairte of Fyfe is for the maist pairt performit", and requested that Gordon "and my Lord Scottisstarvit, would endeavoire with all possible diligence to assist his porposs by sending unto him all quhatsomever kan be gotten, aither for supplie, ornament, decore, or illustratione thairof".

Of Scot he says, "I am sure nothing in this world would be of greater pleasure and contentment unto him but that this work before his death might be effectuate, he having taken so many paines in it. And, as you writes unto me, unless he holds the matter in hand I fear it would be opprest again, chiefly in these troublesome seasons."[3]

It is on record that Robert Gordon wrote in January 1648 an important letter to Scot which marked the completion of his work, and also gave us the few biographical details about Pont which are all we have in that connection. The letter is worth transcribing in part, particularly for the tribute it pays to Pont.[4]

---

[1] The *Annals*, III, p. 351.
[2] *Scot. Geog. Mag.*, XVII, p. 405.
[3] *Old Spalding Club Miscellany*, I, p. 54.
[4] Note No. 34, p. 223.

"Sir,

"At length our Scotland presents itself to the world after the great labour which we have sustained and the long time devoted to prepare and render it worthy of being regarded. It will now hold an honourable place among the other countries of the earth in this grand and celebrated Atlas of Monsieur John Blaeu, to which the world has seen nothing comparable, and for which all lovers of geography are under a perpetual obligation to him.

"Scotland will no longer be represented upon simple reports, disfigured by unmeaning fables and contained in a few sheets of paper, quite otherwise than it is in truth. But on the contrary according as Timothy Pont has recorded it in his papers, the memory of which cannot be effaced without extreme ingratitude to his merits.

"For, having but few advantages and not being supported by the favour and assistance of any person of high rank, he himself, unaided, undertook this work more than forty years ago.

"He travelled afoot over the whole Kingdom, which no other person before him had done. He visited all the islands, inhabited for the most part by barbarous and uncivilised people of whose language he was ignorant and where he was often despoiled by cruel robbers—as I have heard him relate—and suffered all the hardships of a difficult and dangerous voyage without growing weary or ever losing his courage.[1]

"Being returned to his home after so much wandering, and to prepare for bringing to perfection the descriptions he had made, he could not accomplish his intention by reason of the avarice of printers and booksellers who refused the necessary costs for its execution. And while he waited for some more favourable occasion to present itself death took him from us before his time.

"His heirs to whom he had left his papers neglected them, and they were likely to be consumed by vermin and in danger of being wholly destroyed, when James the First, King of Great Britain, gave directions for purchasing them from his executors, that they might be published.

"But, what unhappiness! It was as if these papers had fallen from the smoke into the fire: they came into the hands of persons who had the design to conceal them. Thus having merely changed possessors they remained buried in darkness until the time that you, Sir, who was born for the advancement of good letters, taking

[1] Note No. 35, p. 223.

55

compassion for such a great loss, promised that they should come to light, and have taken of them such special care, and sought with extreme diligence for some one to put his hand to the undertaking until it could be presented to the public."[1]

Along with this letter Gordon included a Dedication addressed to his friend and patron to which the latter refers directly in a reply dated 2nd February. The main portion of Scot's letter is as follows:

"To the right honorable my noble friend, the Laird of Straloch, These: Right Honorable,

"I acknowledge that I am not able to render you thanks for this last favour that it has pleased you to bestow upon me, in writing the epistle dedicatory sent hither to me in your last letter. Yet you shall not find me unthankful if ever it fall in my reach to do you, or any of yours, service in these quarters where I live.

"I am, with the first occasion, to send it to Champvere by means of Samuel Wallace, to be sent to Amsterdam, and refers it to his (Blaeu's) discretion to insert it or not insert it at his pleasure, seeing I suspect it will be unpleasant to the great men to whom the several maps are dedicated that any epistle of that kind should be prefixed to such a work bearing the name of such a mean man as I am."[2]

Sir John disclaims his fitness to have the entire atlas dedicated to himself because each individual map had been inscribed to some leading nobleman; but Blaeu entirely agreed with Gordon's dedication and added his own tribute of praise and indebtedness.

Gordon's work was now completed. He had accomplished a great task—assisted by his son—in piecing into one all the sectional sheets of Timothy Pont. It was the more meritorious in that the original surveys, penned often in the most outlandish and difficult places and with scanty materials, were frequently rough and incomplete. No finer revisionist than Gordon could have been found.

But it was another six years before the Atlas was produced, being the sixth volume in Blaeu's great European series and the first Atlas of Scotland. These volumes were large handsome folios bound in cream vellum, enriched with designs stamped in gold. In his preface the publisher described Pont and Gordon as the parents of the work and Scotstarvit as the nurse. The importance

[1] *Scot. Geog. Mag.*, XVII, pp. 408-410.
[2] *The Staggering State*, Rogers, 1872, p. 15.

of the nurse's services in this case was critical, for he rescued the child when it was abandoned and likely to be lost altogether, and he nourished and reared it for at least fifteen years. He, more than anyone else, was responsible for giving Scotland its earliest atlas. The copyright in Britain was secured to Blaeu under the authority of Cromwell in 1654.[1]

[1] *The Staggering State*, Rogers, p. 14.

CHAPTER V

CHURCHMAN AND BENEFACTOR

As we would understand from his places of residence Sir John Scot must have had church connections both with Ceres and Kilrenny, but when he emerges on our notice as a Churchman it is at Kinghorn in the Presbytery of Kirkcaldy, which is sixteen miles from Scotstarvit. It may be that there was a certain convenience in this connection, for the ferry-port of Pettycur was at Kinghorn, and we may almost with certainty assume that this marked his usual line of route to and from Edinburgh.[1]

He took his local standing in right of his ownership of the lands of Inchkeirie, and it is noticeable that James Melville of Halhill, whose daughter he married in 1639, was also a member of the same Presbytery, both he and his son Sir James being heritors and elders of the parish of Burntisland.

Scot had established his interest in Kinghorn by 1638, for in April of that year he is reported as competing with the laird of Balmuto (a Boswell) for a seat in the kirk which had pertained to the late laird of Piteadie. In a Presbytery minute of 20th February 1640, the names of the elders of Kinghorn are given and "My Lord Scott-tarvett" heads the list. The same minute reports him as presenting a supplication craving the brethren to sever his "rowne of land", which was Inchkeirie, from Aberdour, and to annex it to Kinghorn to which it was "ewest", or nearest.[2] We seem to hear the Lord of Session and Director of Chancery speaking in these ancient terms of territory. Rowne (room) indicated a holding of land.

This matter was remitted to the Synod but was not easy of adjustment or readily disposed of, as he was still supplicating in the year 1647. On the 2nd June of that year the Presbytery decided to recommend to the Commissioners for the Plantation of Kirks that the lands in question be annexed to the Kirk and Parish of Kinghorn.[3]

[1] Note No. 36, p. 224.
[2] *The Presbytrie Booke of Kirkcaldie* (Stevenson), p. 163.
[3] *Ibid.*, p. 311.

We have a reference to the small estate in question in a charter of 1611, where there is mention of "One half carucate of land at the church of Sanct Maling, now called Inchkeirie, with the chapel of Buchadlach now called Eglismaly".[1]

A carucate was originally a measure of land equal to what a yoke of oxen could plough in a season, and said to contain 104 acres: the terms would appear to signify a not very large possession. Inch indicates the flat land beside a small stream where the chapel also stood. It lies between Grange Castle and Piteadie, not far from Invertiel in the neighbourhood of Kirkcaldy. The Gordons of Straloch were aware of Sir John's property and give the name Inchskirrey in Blaeu's map. A peculiarity of the site was that it lay within a detached portion of the parish of Aberdour, which accounts for its owner's application to the Presbytery.[2]

In July 1640, Sir John is seen moving into the uncertain waters of presbyterial procedure as it relates to ministerial appointments. Then, as now, the floor of the Church courts was a floor of equality and the principle of decision popular. Here in keen debate the ministers of the Kirk have been accustomed to expound and apply a body of law which is perhaps more intricate than majestic. Into this arena we see Scotstarvit enter with zeal and depart with caution, mingled, it seems, with relief.

On the date mentioned, with the Presbytery meeting at Dysart, he "craved judgment anent his proceeding with the Presbytrie of Dunbarr in presenting Mr William Forbes to the kirk of - -".[3]

The Presbytery approved of his presentation and recommended it to the Commissioners, but as we hear nothing further of a minister of that name it is presumed that the Commissioners disagreed; nor do we know in this instance of what church it was that Sir John controlled the right of presentation.

Nine months later he took action in a similar way but with results which became rather complicated and not a little amusing. The record tells us that in April 1641, "My Lord Scottistarvet and John Betone of Balfour" appeared before the Presbytery of

---

[1] Reg. Gt. Seal, VII, 442. Of these names the only one now known is the last locally called "Eggsmalee". Professor Watson gives Maillidh, name of a Celtic saint: Eaglais Maillidh, the Church of Maillidh. *Celtic Place Names of Scotland*, p. 290.

[2] Note No. 37, p. 224.

[3] The Presbytery minute does not name the parish. *The Presbytrie Booke of Kirkcaldie*, Stevenson, p. 183.

Kirkcaldy craving on behalf of the parishioners of Kilrenny that Mr Mungo Law, minister of Dysart, be transplanted to the former charge.[1] The crave was persuasively and somewhat ingeniously presented, but was not granted, and subsequent proceedings show that "My Lord Scottistarvet", in the manner which was later to become a classic tradition, carried the question to the Synod, and, being there frustrated, took the perilous road that leads to the General Assembly. But this pilgrim was stout-hearted, sagacious, and also, as the sequel proved, astute.

In supporting their appeal before the Presbytery Sir John and Beaton of Balfour had presented several appropriate papers. The first was a petition subscribed by the heritors and parishioners of Kilrenny. Next, an Act of Presbytery of St Andrews allowing the same. And thirdly a gift of presentation from the King to the kirk of Kilrenny in favour of Mr Mungo Law. This last the local commissioners evidently thought to be irresistible: "Whilk we, the commissioners aforesaid, think by itself is sufficient for enjoying the said place, and seeing the same has not been done befoir by his Majestie, they expect it sall not be refused".[2] The petitioners must have been at no small pains to effect the King's assistance. Nevertheless the rejoinder of the Presbytery was in the most approved tone of a Court which sees law being broken, presumption aired, and a neighbouring Presbytery acting irregularly:

"We find that the supplicatioun has not come orderly to us from the Presbytrie of St Androis, and that we have heard yet no reason valid to move us to yeild to the desyred transportatioun." They then proceeded to administer their unkindest cut, saying,

"And that whilk they (the commissioners) account thair strongest reason, taken from the King's Majesteis presentatioun, maks most aganest themselffes, because it is aganest ane act of the Generall Assemblie."[3, 4]

The case, as said, went to the Synod where the parties at the bar were the Presbytery and the Kilrenny Commissioners. The Synod ruled stoutly against the crave, but it committed a grave error of procedure in allowing "the whole Presbytery of Kirkcaldy" to share in the discussion, upon which Sir John promptly appealed

[1] *The Presbytrie Booke of Kirkcaldie*, p. 200.
[2] *Ibid.*, p. 200.
[3] *Ibid.*, p. 201.
[4] Note No. 38, p. 224.

to the Assembly which was to begin a sitting in July at St Andrews. Principal Baillie writing to his relative William Spang presents a diverting account of what happened. He says,

"Tuesday 3rd August (1641) was taken up by a very factious question of your good friend, Sir John Scot. He had promised to Mr Mungo Law, second minister at Dysart in the presbytery of Kirkcaldy, a presentation to the kirk of Kilrennie in the presbytery of St Andrews. The presbytery of St Andrews not very curious to crave his transportation, Sir John in the Provincial (Synod) of Fife urges it. In the voicing not only the whole presbytery of Kirkcaldy gets voice but some burgh's two ruling elders. Upon this and some other informalities Sir John did appeal to the General Assembly. By strong solicitation, and a world of merry tales in the face of the Assembly, he gets a sentence for his appellation, to the great indignation of the Synod of Fife and the Moderator's malcontentment." Sir John held himself satisfied with this advantage, and abandoned his plan for the minister's transportation, "which", says Baillie, "made many take him but for a wrangler who did seek more the Synod's disgrace than any other contentment."[1]

It is obvious that the annalist relishes the contrasts in the situation. The Sir John he presents is indeed a different Sir John from "the crusty knight" pictured elsewhere by Professor Masson. He might it seems have pleaded the merits of the case for translation but contented himself with worsting the Synod to the indignation of its members and the confusion of the Moderator.

In approving and pursuing Mungo Law he had his eye on a much sought-after minister: Kirkcaldy also endeavoured to secure him. This individual had a high reputation in his day both as a preacher and a man of talent, and had calls from a variety of parishes during his incumbency of the second charge at Dysart. In 1638, after a keen contest in Presbytery he was chosen as one of three assessors to the famous Glasgow Assembly, George Gillespie going also.[2] In January 1644 he was ordered by the General Assembly to transport himself to the charge of Greyfriars, Edinburgh, which he accordingly did.[3] There is a note in the New Statistical Account which says that he was with the force of occupation in Edinburgh Castle when the fortress yielded to

[1] Baillie's *Journal*, I, p. 369.
[2] *The Presbytrie Booke of Kirkcaldie*, p. 134.
[3] Fasti, II, 537.

Cromwell in 1650 and was one of six ministers who protested against the surrender.[1, 2]

Almost the last note we have of Sir John's presbyterial activities exhibits him protesting in January 1645 against the action of Robert Kirkcaldy, the laird of Grange, for removing and enlarging his seat in Kinghorn church whereby he impeded Sir George Erskine of Invertiel from seeing and hearing the minister. Sir George was a fellow Lord of Session and worthy of sympathy.

In the above case the laird of Grange in enlarging and shifting his family pew had transgressed a ruling of the Session, and as the offender was obstinate the Presbytery made a "visitation". Patrick Gillespie, future Principal of Glasgow University, was the preacher, and he chose as his text, Ezekiel III, 17: "Son of man, I have made thee a watchman over the house of Israel; therefore hear the word of my mouth and give them warning from me."[3]

The figure of a watchman on a tower was no bad simile for the lynx-eyed care of Presbytery in supervising the doings of the community in those times, and in this case the sermon and visitation had a salutary effect. Kirkcaldy acknowledged his error, "for whilk", he said, "he deserved that the seatt might be cast to the kirk door". This hearty and extreme proof of his mood of repentance appeased the Presbytery and gained the approval of all parties.

There came a day when Scotstarvit asked to be relieved from office in the Kirk Session for the space of a year. As he made this supplication in June 1647 it obviously synchronised with a national period of great stringency and difficulty in which the pressure and burden of his various offices of State must have been severe. In the Presbytery record which continues to September 1653 there is no further mention of him. At this latter date he was neither a Lord of Session nor Director of Chancery, and as the minutes are wanting until the year 1693 this field of information is thereby closed.

But curiously enough he returned to the same ecclesiastical sphere in 1659 and came in a whirl of contention for which he was by no means initially responsible. It will be remembered that his kinsman the Earl of Buccleuch had by his will appointed him a Tutor Testamentar, *sine quo non*, with respect to his family and

[1] Nicoll's *Diary*, p. 56.
[2] Note No. 39, p. 224.
[3] *The Presbytrie Booke of Kirkcaldie*, pp. 280-281.

affairs. He was named first among the guardians who, as noted, could not convene without his presence, and necessarily he led in any required action.

On the death of Buccleuch the dowager Countess had married the Earl of Wemyss, and these parties now planned a marriage between the youthful Countess and the Right Honourable Walter Scott, son of Scott of Highchester. The prospective bridegroom was aged fourteen and the prospective bride had completed her eleventh year. This union, premature in character and hurried in its arrangements, and intended it is said to defeat the intrigues of the Earl of Tweeddale, was effected in February 1659, apparently to Scotstarvit's surprise and indignation.[1] Knowing that the girl was still minor he endeavoured to have the contract reduced, and brought a complaint against the Presbytery of Kirkcaldy before the Synod of Fife for their action in dispensing with the proclamation of banns.

He was there present and moved the Synod to censure the Presbytery. But after discussion the Synod declared that the Presbytery had done nothing contrary to any known Act of the Church.[2] The proceedings threatened at one stage to take an alarming form, "for this business was vigorously pressed in the Synod by the Lord Scotstarvit and defended by the Earl of Wemyss, who in the face of the assemblie as much as challenged Scotstarvit to a combat. The reason being that the latter, speaking of the house of Harden, said if the lady had married Harden's son or grandson there had been no stain upon her. Wemyss took this so highly that he said that if he had not a respect for grey hairs he should cause him make that good before he sleeped. But the Moderator commanded them both to silence."[3] Wemyss certainly had good reason to be incensed.

It seems that in spite of the Synod's decision the balance of right lay with the petitioner. An Act of General Assembly of 1600 forbade "untymous marriage of young persons before they had come to age meet for marriage." The gist of the Act on which the Presbytery rested its conduct did in fact deplore the dangerous

[1] *The Scotts of Buccleuch*, I, p. 351.
[2] *Ibid.*, I, p. 358-9.
[3] *Diary of John Lamont of Newton*, pp. 112-114. Sir John was now 74 years old. The Moderator was Robert Blair, ancestor of Robert Blair of *The Grave*, Lord President Blair, and the Rev. Dr. Hugh Blair. His burial place is in St Columba's churchyard at Aberdour.

effects produced by marriage without banns and enjoined proclamation, but gave Presbyteries power to dispense with it "in some necessary exigents". The only visible exigent in this case was the haste of the interested parties to have the marriage compacted before the tutors could know anything of it.

The former Senator now had recourse to civil law, and his plea for a dissolution of marriage on the ground that the Countess was a minor was granted by the Commissary, the famous Sir John Nisbet of Dirleton, later the Lord Advocate, and a severe judge during the Covenanting persecutions.[1] It is a peculiar revelation of Sir John's many alliances by family and marriage that the Commissary was married to one of the Monypennys of Pitmilly, presumably a sister to Sir John's third wife. By order of the Court the person of the young bride was sequestrated, the Countess of Mar and General Monk both being concerned in her care until her minority was completed, when the marriage was immediately ratified. This unfortunate and ailing girl, the greatest heiress then in Scotland, died early and untimely in 1661, aged fifteen.[2]

The Countess of Wemyss, "a wittie active woman" says Baillie, on hearing of the decision of Sir John Nisbet declared that the distinguished lawyer was "a malicious knave". However in subsequent history there was an amicable arrangement of terms, and for their aliment to the young Countess the Earl and Countess of Wemyss received 10,000 merks Scots from the tutors.[3]

*　　*　　*　　*　　*　　*

When we consider Sir John Scot in the character of benefactor, a role which has some affinity with his interest as a churchman, it is not surprising to find that he linked his benevolence with a zeal for learning and applied it to schemes of progressive education. It is gratifying, particularly with respect to the disappointing age in which he lived, to perceive him so early and assiduously at work. In 1620 he made a donation of books to the library of St Leonard's College, St Andrews, thus anticipating by seven years the action of his brother-in-law, William Drummond, in making his munificent donation to Edinburgh University.

[1] *Scotts of Buccleuch*, I, p. 354.
[2] *Ibid.*, I, p. 371 and p. 379. Her husband was created Earl of Tarras in 1660. Note No. 100, p. 229.
[3] *Ibid.*, I, pp. 362 and 374.

Sir John's gift consisted of nine works given by himself and more than fifty others which he persuaded his friends to give, among these donors being Drummond, who may then have had his attention directed to an important existing need. The University's Guide to the Library shows that Scot's action was a notable one in point of time, and had the distinction of being a selective contribution intended to support the study of Humanity, for a Chair in which he at the same time made an endowment of lands and rents.[1]

In the above connection we are told that between the years 1607 and 1611 James VI agreed to found and build a University Library. The instigation had a St Andrews origin associated with the name of Archbishop Gledstanes, who was supported by Abbot, the Archbishop of Canterbury. The latter made the first gift of books and the King himself with other members of the Royal family made gifts in 1612.[2] It will be seen that Scotstarvit was alert in his interest in a matter of high academic value.

In 1620 he was thirty-four years old, and his warm and generous temper may be gathered from his statement that he made these donations "out of my love and affection for the advancement of learning".[3] Again and more particularly he declares that he acted, "being moved in the year of God, 1620, for the love and favour I did carry to St Leonard's College in St Andrews, where I and my umquhile father were educate in Philosophie".[4] The benefaction of a Chair in Humanity was an outstanding proof of his perception of an existing need, as well as of his scholarly zeal and generous desire for the weal of his fellow-countrymen and the prestige of his native land. It so happens that the reasons for the foundation, with the conditions attaching to it, were fully exposed at a later date, due to a difference which arose between the two Colleges, which is worth reporting.

The first person appointed to the new Chair was Alexander Scot, who may have been related to the founder, but in 1642 the Professor was Robert Norie, who appears to have achieved too much popularity in his office, for it was now that the Regents or

[1] St Andrews University. Illustrated Guide p. 46.
[2] *Ibid.*
[3] Report of Univ. Commissioners. *The Staggering State*, Rogers (1872), p. 7.
[4] *The Staggering State*, Rogers, p. 9.

Professors of St Salvator's College complained that the classical lectures at St Leonard's were attracting the students to that College and causing a diminishment in the number at theirs.

With a view to adjusting the difficulty the Estates of Parliament and the General Assembly nominated a Joint Commission to go to St Andrews and hear the case. The Chancellor of the University, the powerful and ill-fated Marquis of Argyll, who had himself been a student at St Andrews, was President, and among the Commissioners was the celebrated churchman, Alexander Henderson, "incomparablie the ablest man of us all for all things".[1] The hearing occupied the attention of the Commissioners on 10th August 1642, and involved a review of the terms of the foundation. The judgment was as follows.

"The Commissioners, considering the Desires and Papers given by Sir John Scot of Scotstarvit concerning a School of Humanity in St Leonard's College, and being desirous to cherish every motion that may conduce for the advancement of learning and the good of the University, but being unwilling to settle an inequality in the number of students betwixt the two Colleges of Philosophie, lest the increase of the one should be a diminution, and tend to the ruine, of the other, desire the Marquis of Argyle to represent to my Lord Scotstarvit their council and resolution, beyond which they could not go, to this sense:

"That they think fit that there be a public Professor of Humanity in St Leonard's College, or within any other public place where it should be found expedient. That the Professors of the old College (St Salvator's) shall have their leassouns. That the Professor of Humanity shall have for his maintenance an equal portion with the Regents of Philosophie in the new augmentation. That he be called Professor of Humanity. That he teach no scholars in private neither in school nor chamber, because it is intendit that the number of the classes in the two Colleges be equal. That by reason of his profession, which is posterior to Philosophie, the four Regents of Philosophie have precedencie before him."[2]

This arrangement, it appears, while granting the plea that there should be a Humanity Professor at St Leonard's, seeks to establish an equality of opportunity between the Colleges by making his lectures public there or at any other expedient place. This it

[1] Baillie's *Journal*, II, p. 59.
[2] *The Staggering State*, Rogers (1872), p. 7.

may be judged was not a very happy compromise. The new Professor, having his status in St Leonard's, was yet not exclusively attached to it. He would share equally in its revenues while serving the gownsmen of both Colleges, and as an additional member of the Staff his appointment would presumably lessen the individual emoluments of his colleagues. It is not surprising that the Principal and Regents of St Leonard's College intimated a renunciation of the Scotstarvit endowment. As this development threatened to defeat Sir John Scot's laudable intention he therefore complained and craved the aid of the Commission.

In the minute which follows he reveals his reluctance to drop the scheme, and says, perhaps significantly, that inequality of the classes is "pretended" to be the reason. He may here hint at the more personal objection relating to finance, a reason which is explicitly alleged in a further appeal of his, and is in fact answered on this occasion by the proposal of the Commission when it sought to improve the Regent's prospects by permitting him to take up a school and teach scholars in St Andrews. Sir John's reference is as follows.

"21st March 1643. The whilk day the Commissioners sitting in full number: the Supplication underwritten was presented, whereof the tenor follows.

"To my Lords Commissioners appointed by the late Parliament and Generall Assemblie to visit the University, unto your Lordships, humbly shews Sir John Scot of Scotstarvet and one of the Senators of the College of Justice—That whereas out of my love and affection to the advancement of learning I have mortifiet to the College of St Leonard certain lands, rents and books, to the avail of 8000 merks, for the use of a Regent of Humanity in the said College, upon special conditions contained in a contract betwixt them and me, and in case of failyie of performance of the said contract, that the hale sums, lands and books return to me.

"And now they, finding themselves not able to perform the same, have subscribed ane renunciation, whereof I am yet unwilling to make use, if your Lordships shall be pleased to find out any means how I may have satisfaction; and since inequalitie of the classes in the Philosophie Colleges is pretended to be the main hindrance, that your Lordships will think upon some way how that will be remedied.

"Therefore I entreat your Lordships to take this into your

consideration, and (in order) not to suffer so good and charitable a work to perish this way, to let it at the least be transferred to another University."[1]

The Commissioners' answer was:

"Whilk Supplication being read and considered, and the said Commissioners being therewith well advised, they have ordained in addition to their former act that this offer be made: That the Master of Humanity in St Leonard's shall have libertie to take up ane school and teach scholars in such an indifferent place within the citie of St Andrews as the Senatus Academicus shall think fit and expedient, providing always that he shall teach no Grammar to his scholars. And ordained an act to be made hereupon."[2]

This offer failed to satisfy the founder of the Chair: he recalled his benefaction and repossessed himself of the endowment, and there must have been a short period when the Professor discontinued his office. But Sir John with scholarly and patriotic zeal pursued the matter further, and a year later laid it before the General Assembly.

In his statement he recounts the reasons for which he originally acted and underlines the conditions on which the professorship was established: "the Regent of Humanitie should enjoy and be capable of all liberties and dignities of the Universitie in an equal degree with the Principall and existing Regents". He charges the latter with breaking the compact by denying to the newly-appointed Professor his due share in the College endowments, and explains how this had led him to withdraw his mortification and to the annulment of the office.

Since then, having been informed of the ill effect which this had on St Leonard's, he was desirous of remedying the situation. To this end, and "for the advancement of learning and for the weal of the College, to be a seminarie of youth to the church and state within this kingdome", he appealed to the Assembly to intercede with the ensuing Parliament, so that an Act might be obtained for establishing the Regent within the College in his just integrity and that he might be made along with the others equally participant in the rents and endowments.[3]

On 13th June 1644, the Assembly complied, and an Act was passed by the Estates ratifying the deliverance of the church,

[1] *The Staggering State*, Rogers, p. 8.
[2] *Ibid.*, p. 8.
[3] *Ibid.*, p. 9.

68

and constituting a Regent and Professor of Humanity to St Leonard's College on the original terms.[1]

It cannot escape notice that Sir John in this important matter was actuated by highly enlightened motives in every respect. His zeal for learning is abundantly evident. His intention—or indeed his express condition—that the new professor should have a status of equality with his teaching brethren and an equal share in the College endowments, was generous and honourable. His attitude also to the already instituted Staff was forbearing and reasonable, and he was patient in endeavouring to apply for their welfare and the success of the College the beneficence which his interest and affection had moved him to bestow. The new Chair was therefore secured to St Leonard's, and St Salvator's was not long left at a disadvantage, for a Professorship in Humanity was founded there in 1645.

Subsequently the two Colleges of St Leonard and St Salvator were united by Act of Parliament (1747). In the University the present Chair of Humanity—although the title makes no reference to it—is the authentic continuation of Sir John Scot's foundation of 1620, and until private patronage was abolished in 1891 his descendants held the right of presentation. The endowment also must still operate but is probably a small part of the modern emoluments of office.

Sir John's deprivation of office at the Chancery in 1651 formed a serious and regrettable anti-climax to the double decade of special "busyness" when we see him moving as an honoured and powerful figure in the public affairs of the nation. But his misfortune under Cromwell failed to diminish his enthusiasm or generosity where he could at once assist the needy and advance the enlightenment of which he was a life-long apostle and practitioner.

It so happened that on the 17th of June 1652, or as soon thereafter as the word could carry, Scotland was startled by news of a destructive fire which had occurred in Glasgow, then the second largest of Scottish cities. About eighty streets or alleys—a third of the burgh—were burned down in the residential centre, and the Corporation apprehended that unless help came from outside the city would be ruined.

In answer to this appeal Scotstarvit made a bequest which betrayed not only his generosity but his practical bent and liberal

[1] Balfour's *Annals*, III, p. 185.

ideas on how a bounty might operate. He accordingly negotiated a contract with the Magistrates and Council of the Burgh, dated 13th June 1653, the object of which was to train a number of lads in a useful trade and to see them established as burgesses upon reaching journeymanship. This first contract revealed in its terms his wonted concern for places involving his own family relationships. Thus he speaks of his love for Glasgow—"the prime city of the west"—of which country he claimed descent, apparently on the maternal side.

In consideration of the city's calamity he mortified and disponed to it, "the lands of Pickie and Pickiemiln lying in the parish of St Leonard's and sheriffdom of Fife: worth three score boll victual yearly in bear and meal". This was for the behoof of six prentice boys: five to be presented by Sir John or his successors and one by the magistrates. Their prentice fee was to be ten bolls each to their masters at the St Andrews market rate. The contract expressed a preference for "Scots bairns within the toun rather than others."[1]

We find the parties to this contract revising it in April 1658, and improving it by reducing the number by one, confining it to "poor" boys only, and laying aside part of the annual rent to provide a small stock of capital for them when they became burgesses.[2]

Eleven years after Sir John's death his successor made arrangements to increase the number to six, and when the instruction of apprentices for payment made to masters was no longer in force, twelve boys were educated yearly under the Trust in local seminaries. They were known as "Scotstarvit Boys", and one can imagine how rich a contribution this must have meant in those times to the individuals concerned, and to the community.[3]

It is a note-worthy fact that the Benefaction made in 1653 and 1658 is still in existence. It was incorporated with other charities of a similar nature in 1885, and the funds were held and managed by the Glasgow Educational Endowments Trust, and afterwards by the Glasgow Educational Trust set up in 1936. The ancient bequest still adds its quota to the massive funds which are required to meet the educational needs of the great city which Scot called "the prime city of the West".[4]

[1] Dr Strang's Bursaries, etc. of Glasgow, pp. 71-74.
[2] A note-worthy benefaction. *The Staggering State*, Rogers, p. 17.
[3] Charters and Documents Relating to the City of Glasgow, Vol. II.
[4] Reported by the City Chamberlain of Glasgow.

It might seem odd to suggest that other influences besides the appeal of humanity actuated Scotstarvit in what he here did, but it sometimes happens that a benefactor's action is quickened where the situation specially attracts his interest and sympathy.

We are referring to the fervour of the Covenanting spirit among the Glasgow people who were deeply and obstinately anti-prelatical. Montrose mulcted them heavily after the battle of Kilsyth in 1645, and three years later the Provost and Magistrates were deposed for contumacy to their Sovereign.

Such being the temper of the city, it may be taken as granted that it was because of his pronounced Covenanting principles, as well as his ability, that Patrick Gillespie was called in May 1648 to the charge of the Outer High Kirk, going thither from the Presbytery of Kirkcaldy where Sir John Scot had been an elder for ten years. As has been related Gillespie made alliance with Cromwell in the Occupation and was appointed Principal of Glasgow University in April 1653, two months before Sir John arranged his laudable contract with the civic rulers.[1]

It is clear that the minister and judge must have been well-known to each other, and it is possible that Scotstarvit during these transactions may have strengthened the bond which constrained him in 1654 to present to Cromwell and the English Council the certification of his good standing attested by this same Patrick Gillespie and his colleague Livingston. Nevertheless his Glasgow beneficence was a generous-hearted and enlightened act of social and public service.

[1] It is a point of interest that George Scot, the son of Sir John and Dame Elizabeth Melville, was baptised by Patrick Gillespie at Kinghorn in April, 1643. *Baptismal Records*, Ref. No. 439, vol. I.

Chapter VI

THE TREW RELATION

Apart from his authorship as a composer of Latin verse Sir John's name is associated with two pieces of prose writing which were left in manuscript and were afterwards printed. The better known is that containing his brief notices about Scottish noblemen and statesmen: *The Staggering State of Scots Statesmen.* The other is a little known piece of writing called the *Trew Relation.*[1] This is found in a collection of manuscripts belonging to the Mitchell Library, Glasgow. Bound up with it are two works by different authors, namely *Hope's Practicks*[2] and *Ane Table of Summons.* They are all three thought to have been transcribed by John Thomson about the years 1660-1663, which would be shortly after the composition of Scot's narrative. The full title of this curious and valuable tract is as follows:

"Trew relation of the principall affairs concerning the State, acted by Sir John Scot of Scotstarvit in the raigne of King Charles ye first, vindicating him from ye aspersions laid upon him by Mr Sandersone in the history of the life of the said King Charles, 1658. Written at Edinburgh ye 9 August, 1660."[3]

A full version edited and annotated by Dr George Neilson was published in *The Scottish Historical Review* within the years 1913-1916. The work is a narrative on the lines indicated in the title, consisting of about thirty thousand words. It deals with various matters of government and law in the seventeenth century, but principally with the accusation that Scot had wronged the Earl of Menteith. Dr Neilson calls it "The Thrilling Story of the downfall of the Earl of Strathearn."[4] Sir John as an apologist makes his motive clear, and in the first page of the manuscript he writes thus of the attack made by Sanderson.

"His clause concerning me is that the Covenanters persuaded

---

[1] *Scot. Hist. Review*, XI, p. 164.
[2] Note No. 40, p. 224.
[3] *Scot Hist. Review*, XI, p. 167.
[4] *Ibid.*, p. 165.

me to accuse an eminent worthie persone, the Erle of Menteith, to his majesty, who (Menteith) had done him notable services; and subjoynes the epithet that I was ane bussie persone, and sayis that Airth was extremely and speciallie aymed at by the contrivers of his ruine, viz the Covenanters."[1]

The serious charge made by Charles's biographer was expressed as follows: "Some upright and honest Scots were in policy taken off either by subtilty or force. And because the Earl of Strathern, a bold man, had the King's ear, and deservedly too, being faithful and true, these men set on Sir John Scot (Directour of the Chancery) a busie Person, to inform against his descent as Heir to David Earl of Strathern, pretending to the Crown."[2]

The situation lying behind these matters arose from a transaction carried out at the instance of Sir Thomas Hope between the King and Menteith, in which the latter was acknowledged to be Earl of Strathearn and the true heir to David, Earl of Strathearn, son of Robert II.

Involved in this admission lurked a serious problem as to the true line of royal succession. This hinged upon the fact of the two marriages of Robert II which in the past had caused doubt and confusion; and it now appeared, in a certain view of the matter, that Menteith, established as the Earl of Strathearn, could have challenged the prior right of Charles as King.

It so happened that Sir John Scot was made aware of this dangerous possibility and thereupon prepared a paper called "A Relation of William, Earl of Menteith's Affair", in which he reviewed the above transaction and exposed its questionable implications.

A printed copy of the statement, which in its original form may have been privately used or circulated, is to be found in the National Library at Edinburgh.[3]

It was to Sir John's consequent actions and the serious results which followed for Menteith that Sanderson referred in his history, and in respect of which he made his charge of complicity between him and the Scottish Covenanters, with the lawyer allegedly acting as a tool for the leaders. To this the *Trew Relation* is Scotstarvit's defence.

---

[1] *Scot. Hist. Review*, XI, p. 167. The Earl of Menteith was later made Earl of Strathearn and finally took the title of Airth.

[2] *Compleat Hist. of Life and Raigne of King Charles*, Sanderson (1658), p. 230.

[3] Nat. Lib. 6.234(10).

"The historical and literary eminence of its author", says Dr Neilson, "offers the best guarantee of the claim that his narrative makes on the attention of the student of the period between the death of James VI and the Restoration."[1]

It is possible that in preparing this paper Scot may have been actuated in part by sympathy with his brother-in-law, Drummond, whose personal pride of race was directly linked with the status of Robert III, inasmuch as the King's wife, Annabella Drummond, belonged to the ancestral line of the poet's family. Drummond himself took part in the future course of events.

It is also not at all improbable that inasmuch as Charles II returned to England in May 1660, and Scot brought his apologia to completion in August of that year, he intended it as a means of justifying his conduct, or at any rate of proving his loyalty to the Stewart House.

With reference to Sanderson's phrase that he was "ane bussie person", it is significant that Sir James Balfour, the annalist, a man conversant with the personalities and movements of that day, used against him the same expression, which as then understood seems to have implied a "busybody". He calls Sir John "a bussie man in foule weather", and appears to blame him for reporting to the King certain evasions in the payment of dues or taxes connected with transactions of estate, which was depriving the King of just revenue.[2] There is a degree of correspondence between Sanderson's and Balfour's references, and it may be said that these are not the only evidences which suggest that Sir John Scot applied to the conduct of his contemporaries standards of rectitude which were both severe and troublesome.

The *Trew Relation*, in which the term "Trew" echoes a note of correction and defence, was completed and published in Edinburgh in August 1660. The author was then seventy-four years old. Sanderson wrote two years earlier and the intervening time would be required to frame a reply. The narrative depicts Scotstarvit operating as a trusted and intimate counsellor of Charles I in the three important fields of affairs which are treated.

Although the title refers in a strict sense to the treatment of the Earl of Menteith's affair, yet on examination it is seen that Sir John was justified in bringing in two other matters, for they form a sequence, and have a personal justification in respect of the

[1] *Scot. Hist. Review*, XI, p. 164.
[2] The *Annals*, II, p. 147.

74

author's interests, and also a logical justification in respect of their content.

The composition is arranged in three chapters, with an addition consisting of an oration made in 1648 before the Lords of Session by James Dalrymple, afterwards the distinguished Lord Stair.[1] It was then that Sir John was pleading before Parliament the wrongs which were being enforced on the smaller Barons, or Gentry, by the Lords of Erections, and Stair's oration is included because on the involved question of feus, superiorities, and vassalage, it supports Sir John's contention, if not in precise argument at least in its liberal spirit.

In his address to the Reader the author makes an intimate approach and gains immediate sympathy. He wishes to dispel the aspersions laid upon him and to publish to the world the truth of matters of State in which he was "a special actor" during the time that he was a Lord of Secret Council, of Session, and of Exchequer, being at this time also Director of Chancery. He here strikes at Sanderson not only for his ignorance of facts, but "because in his whole history he has not one good word to say of the Scottish nation".[2]

It is well to remember that we are dealing with a passage of affairs in which there were various and indeed many actors. But although there are contemporary letters of some of the people involved, with a variety of annals and well-known diaries, yet there does not seem to be any record similar to that of our author and dealing with the same events. We are therefore left somewhat at the mercy of a solitary apologist, and must weigh the value of his account by the criterion of his personal dependableness in general, and the bearing of the evidence of accepted history on the story he tells.[3]

The singular merit of this work is that it gives us an intimate account of how serious matters of State were discussed in early stages by the King and his councillors. The legal ability, the human passion, the frank and often rude style of address between monarch and subject, the tugging conflict of interests, the imperious temper of Charles, and the scarcely veiled resistance of the privileged nobility—all this is exposed in these pages as probably in few other printed records. These things make up

[1] *Scot. Hist. Review*, XIII, pp. 380-391.
[2] *Ibid.*, XI, p. 167.
[3] Note No. 41, p. 224.

the value of Scot's memoir of events in the opening years of the reign of Charles I.

In a preface the contents of the chapters are recounted thus:

First, concerning the business of changing the Lords of Session proposed by Charles I on his ascent to the throne.

Second, the affair of the Earl of Menteith.

Third, concerning the temporal erections of former Church lands by the Nobility, to whom the King had given the superiorities contrary to the laws of the nation.

It is reported in the narrative, and is a historical fact, that, from whatever prompting, the King late in 1625 had decided to make alterations in the composition of the Court of Session.[1] When the Earl of Nithsdale came to Edinburgh at the time of the Convention of the Three Estates in November of the above year, one of the royal instructions which he carried was that he should acquaint the Gentry of the King's intention to choose some of their number for the Session and remove those of the Nobility who had been brought in at the end of the preceding reign, so that the Court might conform to the first institution of the College of Justice.[2]

This intention to apportion representation more justly was, however, but little regarded by those whom it was designed to benefit, inasmuch as the Commissioners of the Gentry, or "small Barons" as Scot calls them, actually professed in the Convention that they had no desire for innovation. There is a hint that this rejection was in some way influenced by the Nobility and it had the effect of retarding the proposed reformation, at least temporarily.

The account gives us an insight into the reasons for the King's action. Sir John reports that it was founded upon information received, disclosing that the two judicatories of Privy Council and Court of Session were being conducted in some confusion, being controlled by the same set of leaders who were assuming the whole management of State and thereby unduly enlarging themselves in credit and in means. His Majesty thought to correct

[1] Reg. P.C. I 1625-1627, pp. 173. At the accession of Charles in 1625 the Court was composed of the Lord Chancellor, the Lord President, fourteen Ordinary Lords and four Extraordinary Lords.

[2] *Scot. Hist. Review*, XI, pp. 168-169. The College of Justice was instituted by James V in 1532. Robert Maxwell was created Earl of Nithsdale in 1620 (d. 1646).

this by giving its distinctive duties to each judicatory, and by reforming the Session in the way indicated.

Having failed to advance this through the Convention of Estates he now began to deal from his Court, and apparently through Nithsdale, with individuals, and asked the following parties to take notice of his intention, and to give over their places of Session:—the Earls of Melrose and of Lauderdale, Lord Carnegie, Sir William Oliphant the King's Advocate, Sir Richard Cockburn the Lord Privy Seal, and Sir John Hamilton the Register Clerk.

The only one who consented and demitted office was Thomas Hamilton, Earl of Melrose. Lauderdale and Carnegie answered that they had as much right to their places as to their lands, and asked to be heard. The others took the same stand, and "the Earl of Nithsdale being crossed in many of his Majesty's instructions by the discontent of the great ones returned to Court to give an account of what he had done".[1]

This is the stage at which Sir John Scot, then a member of Privy Council but not of Session, enters on the scene and manifests that boldness which he brought to the service of many a cause. That he should thus early have been called into intimate council with the King and should have been invited to pronounce upon weighty matters of State, suggests that, apart from any share he may have had in instigating the change, his qualities as a clear-sighted debater on questions of law had been recognised.

We find that early in 1626 he was in London,[2] and when the Earl of Nithsdale returned with the discouraging account of his Scottish visit, Sir John was invited to Hampton Court to advise the King and if possible clear up the difficulties of the situation. The report tells us that the King, Nithsdale, and he, conferred together, and the lawyer undertook "to prove by the law and ancient practice of the Kingdom that his Majesty might at pleasure input or output any he pleased either from the Council or Session; and promised within few days to instruct by writ and evidences what he said".[3] The undertaking he gave illustrates his ready command of resources, unless it is assumed that his promise to supply "writ and evidences" within a few days indicates a too definite preparation of his brief before coming south.

[1] *Scot. Hist. Review*, XI, pp. 168-169.
[2] *Ibid.*, p. 169.
[3] *Ibid.*, p. 170.

It would, even for Charles, have been unthinkable that such a serious matter of State should be settled by his own authority without consultation with the nation's leaders. Accordingly the Earls of Mar, Morton, Roxburgh, and Melrose, with Sir George Hay, the Chancellor, and Spottiswoode, the Archbishop of St Andrews, were commanded to come to London with all diligence.[1]

The King, in the meantime, having received Sir John's Reasons submitted them to Sir James Skene, who was significantly at hand, and desired to know if in his opinion "they would hold". Sir James who was a Lord of Session answered that they would, and "in testification thereof resigned his place". His instant yielding presumably raised him into royal favour, for Charles a little later appointed him President of the Session.

The Scottish Earls having arrived were forthwith given audience "in the withdrawing chalmer at Whitehall", and received a shrewish welcome from the King, who was deeply displeased because his Commissioner Nithsdale had been so coldly treated and frustrated. Angry charges were thrown at each and all of the offending Councillors, but, as the matter is reported, they made fair and reasonable answers. There was however one explosive moment. The King had offered Melrose the Presidency of the Council, which he had refused, and he now excused himself by saying that, being but lately raised from the degree of a gentleman it would be presumption on his part should he thus precede the rest of the Nobility. Nevertheless he added that if it pleased his Majesty to command him he would obey.[2]

At this point Morton interjected that if his Majesty could do that he might make such a number of officers of State as would sway all their votes in Parliament and so carry whatever he pleased.

Charles in an outburst of anger told him that his speech was seditious, and asked who had exalted him and his predecessors, and if it was not in his power to create such offices as he would?

"Whereupon Morton craved pardon on his knees; and that matter there ended."[3] In this incident these statesmen were having a glimpse of the royal despot whose views of kingship were to be so disturbing to the kingdoms and so disastrous to himself. Morton's rugged protest contained an echo of the principle of

[1] *Scot. Hist. Review*, XI, p. 170 (Feb. 1626).
[2] Note No. 42, p. 224.
[3] *Scot. Hist. Review* XI, p. 171.

collective responsibility in the Council which had been only too successfully undermined by James, whose example had not been lost on his wayward and unwise son.

After the Chancellor, Sir George Hay, had explained and excused the proceedings of the Convention of Estates which had resisted the King's plans, "His Majesty pulled out of his pocket the Reasons proving that the Sessioners had not their places *ad vitam*". These he called on the leaders to answer at an early meeting of the Council. Before they left the Earl of Mar had the curiosity to enquire "By whom these reasons were authenticat!", and the King bade Sir John to avow them. A meeting was then arranged under the presidency of the Duke of Buckingham, and Melrose—an astute and experienced advocate—was directed to answer the Reasons in writing, and to communicate his defence to Sir John Scot.[1]

Three days later the parties met at the "Counsell Table" at Whitehall. This was, as the expression just quoted indicates, and as Sir John pointed out later, a meeting of Privy Council. Sir John says, "By the King's orders a Scots counsell was appointed to sit at Whytehall, where never any had sittand before, nor was liklie to sit after".[2] It is stated that there were eighteen Scottish and English Councillors present, along with Buckingham, who was appointed to hear the reasoning.

The purpose of the meeting was then debated; namely, whether the King might remove at his entry to be King those occupying places in the Court of Session.

Sir John in his Reasons concentrated on the principle that the appointment was made not for life, *ad vitam*, but at the King's pleasure, *ad bene placitum regis*.[3] He argued thus:

In the institution of the College of Justice in 1532 there was no stated condition of *ad vitam*.[4] (He admits two express exceptions which strengthen his plea). In custom the Sessioners were for various reasons removed. Being removed others were appointed during their lifetime. He quoted Thomas Craig the jurist, who likened all offices and places granted by the King to a kind of feu,

[1] *Scot. Hist. Review*, XI, p. 172.
[2] *Ibid.*, p. 177.
[3] *Ad vitam aut culpam:* for life or until fault, i.e. until some misconduct is proved.
   Ad bene placitum regis: at the King's pleasure.
[4] Note No. 43, p. 224.

and pointed out that all who had public charges in the common-wealth took new gift of their places at the inauguration of James VI. Craig, having enquired at the learned Bellenden the reason for this, received answer, "That all those diginities, procurations, and offices of the Crown, did end as well with the death of the giver as of the receiver".[1]

Moreover, argued Sir John, the senators had no gift under any seal but simply a letter from the King desiring the Lords to receive such a man, and willing them to give the new entrant all honour and privileges belonging to an ordinary Lord.

Thomas Hamilton, Earl of Melrose, made the answer. This old and shrewd statesman (he was Sir John's senior by twenty-two years) began by taking a side-stroke at his opponent. Others to whom it better belonged, he said, should have undertaken this task. Such reasons as he offered were but "undigested lines to oppose to the articles so advisedly prepared after diligent search of the register, open so many years to the said Sir John, at his pleasure". This presumably was a reference to Scot's oppor-tunities of access to records as Director of Chancery, with the insinuation that Scotstarvit had come with his case well in hand.

He met the latter's argument of omission by saying that neither was the appointment said to be *ad bene placitum regis*; nor was it stated that, being once lawfully appointed, a judge might during his lifetime be removed. The obscurity of the original foundation was clarified by custom where the rule held that the office was for life, and none removed at pleasure but only for inability or crime, etc. It was not proved therefore that the office was not *ad vitam* because some had been removed. Appointment did not give immunity against deprivation for infirmity, crime, rebellion, absenteeism. The latter cases were expressed by Parliament to be just.[2]

He proceeded to contradict the facts and deny the conclusions of Sir John in some of the cases cited, and was satirical over the fifth reason, saying that "although Mr Thomas Craig and Mr John Ballantyne (Bellenden) were learned men of good fame yet their private opinions were of no greater force nor authority than Sir John Scot's is". He thought it strange that an office should be

[1] John Bellenden (d. 1577) distinguished lawyer and Clerk of Justiciary. He was succeeded as Justice Clerk by his son, Sir Lewis Bellenden, Lord Achinoul. (*Jus Feudale*, Bk. I, Digests 10, 11).
[2] *Scot. Hist. Review*, XI, p. 174.

Thomas Hamilton, 1st Earl of Haddington
1563-1637
Reproduced by permission of the Earl of Haddington

William Graham, 1st Earl of Airth
1591-1661
Reproduced by permission of the Scottish National Portrait Gallery

likened to a feu, but pointed out that a feu was granted for the lifetime of the receiver.

Melrose roundly asserted that it could not be found in the Register where any man, once lawfully provided to a place in the Session, was removed without a cause expressed for which he might have been deprived by warrant of law, except in the instances of infirmity and inability. All the others were declared vacant either by demission or decease.

Finally he made the bold declaration that the appointments did not require the warrant of the King's seal because they were lawfully possessed according to the consuetude of the realm, which is in place and force of law where no law is made to the contrary. The King's letter was not the only warrant of their places, but also the Lords' admission and act made thereupon after trial of their qualification. He quoted an Act of James VI which allowed the Lords to refuse any man presented if they found him unqualified.[1]

The debate was a characteristic example of the ingenuity and resource of two able lawyers when pleading a controversial point of law.

There was now an interlude which must have pleased the nobles and was calculated to be embarrassing to Scotstarvit. By agreement Sir John's Reasons had been placed in Melrose's hands and according to arrangement the latter's answers should have been previously committed to Sir John, so as to establish a parity in both cases. It was now disclosed that this had not been done.

When, therefore, the Duke of Buckingham called on Sir John to reply, the latter manifested distinct surprise, calling attention to the omission and making a protest and a reservation. He hoped the Council would not think less of "the King's cause" if his present replies to answers he had never seen did not fully meet their expectations. This was a Scots Council and he would not wish to have it charged with fatuity by failing to controvert the defence. But he claimed to be "heard by writ" afterwards.

Having made all he could out of the omission, and adjusted the psychological balance, he then undertook *ex improviso* to answer severally every one of his opponent's reasons. In doing this he exhibits a remarkable knowledge of facts and instances.

From what he tells us it appears that his main thrusts were of

[1] Acts Parl. Scot., James VI, p. 6, p. 93.

a personal character which greatly discomposed and displeased Melrose. The first, bearing on the alleged abuse and confusion of office as between Council and Session, which was the basis of the original charge, was to the effect that Melrose as President of the Court of Session and State Secretary had encroached on the office of the King's Advocate.

The second constituted a fatal hit to which the Earl by a rash statement and a lapse of memory had left himself exposed. In his answer he had advanced a challenge that the Register contained no case of a Sessioner whose appointment to office was made specifically on any other ground than for his lifetime. He had first maintained the force of custom in fixing life tenure as the rule, and had then ventured to assert the entire absence of any case of provision to office on any other exclusively stated ground.

Scotstarvit, with disconcerting resource, immediately seized on this, and answered that he (Melrose) could not be ignorant of his own case, where it would be instantly proven and verified that he himself had his place not *ad vitam* but *ad bene placitum regis*. The narrative proceeds thus: "Which Melrose knowing to be the truth, and that it would be instantly verified, answered that it was no marvel if he had forgotten, seeing that it was thirty-five years since he had received that gift. . . . Which gave the Duke of Buckingham such contentment that instantly he dissolved the meeting and went in to the King."[1]

The *Relation* gives an account of two other meetings in which Charles was personally present and exhibited both his ability and his wit. In the first the Chancellor pleaded for the retention of the Earl of Lauderdale and Lord Carnegie on the Session, saying "They were such men as he had not the like in his kingdom". To this the King satirically replied that he was sorry the kingdom was so ill provided with able men. The Bishop of St Andrews also supported the cause of the two Lords, entreating that they might at least be placed as Lords Extraordinary, which it appeared the King might be willing to concede. In the final meeting an incident arose which provoked Scotstarvit to defend himself, and two interesting matters were proposed for judgment by the King. The incident centred on a remark made by the Earl of Mar, an elder statesman, who when the reasoning about a reformed Session was ended took occasion to complain that his Majesty

[1] *Scot. Hist. Review*, XI, p. 177. Melrose was appointed and November 1592. Brunton and Haig do not state the condition of appointment.

should give more trust to Sir John Scot than to those of his closest Council. To this Sir John made a spirited reply:

He answered that he had the honour to serve his Majesty's father of worthy memory as one of his Council; that he should say nothing in his Majesty's presence without good warrant, and albeit he might not compare with noblemen as not being of their degree, yet he might affirm that himself, and five of his lineal predecessors, had served his Majesty and his noble progenitors continually without intermission since the days of King James the Third in places of State as councillors, clerks of register, clerks of the session, or directors of the chancellary. And that amongst their writs there was not a remission for any fault committed against their King or country.

This assertion carried a sting of reproof, inasmuch as Mar who belittled him had been condemned as a traitor for his share in the Raid of Ruthven, and had been guilty of acts of insurrection.[1] The King's response was, that he could not but give Sir John Scot his trust seeing that the grounds of his reasons were fair and sound.

He now presented the question: Who should be the judge of this matter? The nobles alleged that the Session itself was invested with this power; which, the King observed, was like the Church of Rome making a shield for its errors under the doctrine of the Pope's infallibility.

Sir John maintained the contrary, his argument being that the judges were the Privy Councillors, or any other delegates of that number whom his Majesty would appoint, and for proof produced an Act of Parliament of James VI, which declared that the King and his Council were judges of all persons and causes within the kingdom.[2]

Mar said that this act referred only to some turbulent ministers who at that time disclaimed the late King's authority. Sir John made the response that all the acts of Parliament had particulars on which they were grounded, but their conclusions as positive laws became obligatory for the subjects.

The King then proposed a final point: Which was the supreme judicatory, the Privy Council or the Session? The nobles answered

---

[1] John, Earl of Mar (1558-1634), *Acts Parl. Scot.* (1584), III, pp. 295-296.

[2] One of certain Acts known as the Black Acts. Omond discusses this in *Lord Advocates of Scotland*, Vol. I, pp. 98-99.

that they were both equal. Sir John asserted that the Council was "farre above the other", as treating and judging of the highest matters of State concerning the Crown, Government, Finance, Peace and War, whereas the Session treated only of debates of Law between parties. At this point he endeavoured to clarify the matter by referring to a somewhat rare occurrence.

During the reign of James VI a plague broke out in Edinburgh at a time when the Court of Session was meeting. The Council, fearing a spread of the plague throughout the country due to the frequency of people resorting to the city, and presumably to the Law Court, thereupon by their act and decree discharged the Session from sitting until the Council should give them warrant.[1] Since they had this power to prorogue the Session he concluded it to be clear that the Council as a judicatory was above the Session.

The King then said that he would help Sir John with an argument pursued *a majori ad minus*, for, said he, "If I have power to alter these of the Council, *multo magis* have I power to alter these of the Session".

That same night he sent for the Signet from Douglas the Secretary Depute and delivered it to Sir William Alexander (the poet, who became the Earl of Stirling). Sir John Scot was instructed to draw up forms of presentation in the style, not *ad vitam* but *ad bene placitum regis*, blanks being left so that names might be entered.[2]

Charles accepted two proposed lists, one from Nithsdale and those on that side, and one from the Chancellor with the Earls of Melrose, Lauderdale, Mar and Morton. In the new appointments the following were rejected from their places as Lords Ordinary: Sir William Oliphant the Advocate, Sir Richard Cockburn the Lord Privy Seal, Sir John Hamilton the Clerk Register, the Earls of Lauderdale and Melrose, and Lord Carnegie. But (in this account) Lauderdale and Carnegie were appointed Lords Extraordinary. Sir James Skene was made President of the Session, "as the King had promised at Roystoun". The date of Commission was 14th February 1626.

It appears that this report is correct but incomplete; the Register shows that Sir Archibald Napier of Merchiston, then Depute Treasurer, and Patrick Lindsay Bishop of Ross, were also appointed Lords Extraordinary. Eight members of Session

---

[1] Reg. P.C. 1604-1607, p. 263.
[2] *Scot. Hist. Review*, XI, p. 186.

accepted continuance under the changed conditions and seven were added.[1]

In this year Sir Thomas Hope began his long and eminent career as Advocate, the Earl of Melrose was made Lord Privy Seal, and Sir William Alexander took office as Secretary conjointly with Sir Archibald Acheson. Sir John Hamilton remained as Clerk Register.

"Immediately thereafter", says the narrative, "his Majesty despatched the whole number homeward, telling them he would acquaint them further of his royal intentions at his next leisure, and caused a packet to follow them containing a commission for the Council and the Session, of which number he made Sir John Scot one."[2]

For comparative purposes the observations made by Professor Masson on this subject may be noted, and it may also be noted that he makes no reference to Scotstarvit's narrative.

It is true as he says that Charles did not permit the obstructions of the Estates or the bold remonstrance of the Council to hold up his revolutionary plans, but it was after such debate and negotiation as has been recorded that he sent to the Senators concerned the letter which we shall later quote, and from which may be inferred his adoption, on his own authority, of two radical changes in the terms of appointment as hitherto understood and practised. We quote Professor Masson's statement on the character of these changes.

He says: "Whereas till now the presumption, ratified by almost unbroken practice, had been that the Judges of Session when once appointed by the Crown and installed in office were not removeable at the mere pleasure of the Crown, it was now intimated that Charles recognised no such rule: also that the existing judges must regard their appointments by his late father as defunct, and that such of them as were to continue in office must take out fresh appointments formally from him."[3, 4]

Brunton and Haig in the introduction to their *Historical Account of the Senators of the College of Justice*, accuse the young King ("determined on trying the hateful strength of his prerogative in every department of State"), of substituting a new doctrine of

[1] Note No. 44, p. 224.
[2] Note No. 45, p. 224.
[3] Reg. P.C. 1625-1627. Footnote pp. 221-222.
[4] Note No. 46, p. 224.

the tenure of Judgeships for the traditional supposition of an *ad vitam aut culpam* tenure.[1]

The debate raised at Whitehall seems to show how open these matters were to doubt and questioning. Professor Masson speaks of "almost unbroken practice", and Brunton and Haig quote a "traditional supposition". It may be pointed out that Charles's assumption of right in this matter was rejected by Parliament in 1641, when judges were appointed *ad vitam vel culpam*,[2] and a reversion to the practice of appointing *ad bene placitum regis* by James VII was one of the reasons for declaring that he had forfeited the crown of Scotland in 1689.[3]

Sir John Scot in the argument he offered at Whitehall was clearly breaking a lance in a cause which was contrary to the temper and judgment of the nation's leaders.

The other change referred to was involved in the resolution that no noblemen or State Officer should hold a judgeship, and consequently, that such of the existing Ordinary Lords of Session as stood in these categories should at once vacate their judicial post.

At this point Professor Masson proceeds to say that what was intended was that no Privy Councillor should also be an Ordinary Lord of Session, but that the Privy Council as the supreme executive and administrative body of the land, and the Court of Session as the supreme judical body, should henceforth consist of different sets of persons.[4] But it must be said that although this may have been originally contemplated the King did not seek to give effect to it.

From Sir John Scot's account we gather that the King's real purpose—and it was on this that the whole matter was raised—was to break the power of those who, being high officers of State or ruling noblemen in the State, were also both Councillors and Sessioners, and were wielding their influence for other than the national good. The principle of a complete difference in personnel is not actually brought into light, nor does Sir John in his final explanations refer to it. Moreover the practical steps taken by Charles apply exclusively to those in the Session whom the aforementioned conditions would disqualify, and the royal nominations

[1] Brunton and Haig, Introd., p. xxxix.
[2] Acts Parl. Scot., V, p. 355.
[3] *Ibid.*, IX, p. 34.
[4] Reg. P.C. 1625-1627, Introd. xxxiv-xxxv.

referred to in "the packet" when the statesmen were dismissed from Whitehall permitted plurality of office as between Council and Session to continue, as is shown by the composition of the new bodies. Sir John was himself for many years both a Privy Councillor and Lord of Session.

Professor Masson names seven to whom the order for retirement applied; namely, the Earl of Melrose, Secretary of State; the Earl of Lauderdale and Lord Carnegie, Peers; Sir Richard Cockburn, Lord Privy Seal; Sir William Oliphant, King's Advocate; Sir John Hamilton, Clerk of Register; Sir Archibald Napier, Treasurer Depute.[1]

Sir John in his list omits the last named, and says of the other six that Melrose alone consented to the change at once and that the King agreed to appoint Lauderdale and Carnegie Lords Extraordinary, as he had been solicited to do. This left the Privy Seal, Clerk of Register, and Advocate, and it will be seen that this account is supported by the following formidable letter of date 26th January 1626, which was sent to the parties named because at the first notice they had failed to comply with the King's wish. The direction on the back reads:

"To our right trustie and weilbeloved counsellouris, Sir Richard Cokburne of Clarkingtoun, knycht, Keepar of our Privie Seale, Sir Johnne Hamiltoun of Magdalenes, knicht, Clerk Register, and Sir William Oliphant, knicht, our Advocate.

"Trustie and weilbeloved counsellouris, wee greit yow weill. Haveing resolved after goode consideratioun to reduce our Judicatorie of the Sessioun, as near as it can convenientlie be done to that estait wherein it was settled at the first institutioun, we have determined that no Nobleman nor Officer of Estate sal be admitted for a judge thairin—as hathe been heirtofore impairted unto yow.

"In regaird of your offices, whiche, requiring attendance other-wayes, may be more serviceabil unto us and more beneficiall unto yow, we desyre yow to leave your places in the Sessioun, because we do conceave them to be void by the death of our deare late father, so that we may provide other personis for the same. And if yow willinglie do not condiscend unto this do not complain heerafter if, finding by a lawful course bothe your offices in the State and your places in Sessioun at our gift, we dispose of thame otherwayes. For we desyre no way to harme yow further than

1 Reg. P.C. 1625-1627, p. 222, p. 236.

87

the intended reformatioun doeth of necessitie require, seeing (being weill informed of your sufficiencie) we intend to use yow still in the places of gritest trust, hoping that yow will strive to deserve the same. So we bid yow fairweill. Givin at our Court at Whitehall, the 26th January 1626."[1]

It is made clear from what followed that these three gave up their judgeships; Earl Winton reported this, and they also wrote: the date was 14th February 1626. The omission of Sir Archibald Napier from Scotstarvit's list is not explained but it may be that his removal had not been decided at the time of which Sir John is reporting. Actually Napier assisted Winton in carrying through the delicate business and as he was not written to he must already have resigned. He was appointed one of the four Extraordinary Lords whose duty was "to assist and remark the proceedings of the rest", and in the following year was raised to the Peerage.[2]

Our author rounds off this chapter by revealing with characteristic candour, "the reasons why he so willingly contributed his help to change the *great ones* off the Session".

Firstly, he says they had wronged him. The explanation under this head is that he claimed to have a warrant from King James to sit in the Inner House to hear causes reasoned, and the Session refused to acknowledge his right, saying it was against the order to do so. The real reason, alleged Sir John, was a compact made between the Lord President (the Earl of Melrose, later Haddington) and the Earl's brother-in-law, Sir William Scott, who for a time held the office of Director of Chancery. Sir John averred that the Court in excluding him was submitting to the pressure of powerful personal interests. Had he enjoyed the liberty of attendance he might have won the favour of the judges and obtained a sentence restoring him freely to the Directorship.

His second reason was that the Lords had given a decree on behalf of Lauderdale, one of their number, making him Lord of the Erection of the Abbacy of Haddington and superior to Sir John in his lands of Easter Pitcorthie, thus no doubt causing the imposition of fees of superiority, and doing him an injustice.

And thirdly, "he so willingly contributed to change the great ones off the Session . . . because of their exorbitent power, and his Majesty's earnest desire to have it curbed". He thought it

[1] Reg. P.C. 1625-1627, p. 220.
[2] Note No. 47, p. 225.

"his duty to assist in so just a demand, especially as he was earnestly desired to do so".[1]

His motive seems largely personal, but we may admit that to suffer the results of unjust decrees and policies is an experience which sharpens one's perception of wrong principles and stimulates indignation to take the form of action.

[1] *Scot. Hist. Review*, XI, pp. 190-191.

Chapter VII

THE BUSINESS CONCERNING THE EARL OF MENTEITH

William Graham, Seventh Earl of Menteith, was born about the year 1590 and lived until 1661. In his brief public career he reached higher distinction in political office than any other of the house of Graham; whether this was due to outstanding merit or fortunate circumstances must be judged by the facts of his history. In his portrait painted by Jameson we see a bold and handsome face with something of unreflecting audacity in the eyes, and much suggesting a presence which might captivate a prince like Charles who was affectionately inclined and susceptible to pleasing personal gifts. Probably here as in the case of Buckingham sentiment displaced judgment and assigned the role of statesman to one unfitted for it.

Menteith fell heir to the earldom in 1610 and was married in 1612. It is noted that there was litigation between himself and his mother concerning the lands of Kilpont, the difficulty being settled in 1618.[1] There is a possibility that this action quickened in him a natural vein of curiosity as to his ancestry, for he now set himself to inspect his family charter chests, and he prepared inventories of their contents which bear the date of April of the above year.[2] That he had ambitions to enlarge his possessions is proved by his policy, already established, of redeeming lands which had formerly belonged to the earldom. It may be that these transactions which he pursued vigorously brought him to the notice of Scot in his Chancery office. All this is of distinct interest in view of what followed.

The only royal notice taken of him during the reign of James was the King's request to him for terriers—"earth dogges"— for fox hunting—which suggests a keen sporting interest—and a somewhat routine appointment as justiciar for a year over the district of Menteith. He is said however to have conducted

[1] *Red Bk. of Menteith*, Sir W. Fraser, I, p. 332.
[2] *Ibid.*, p. 333.

himself with commendable thoroughness in his judicial office, and this spirit of practical application may be taken as a characteristic quality. It is also a mark to his credit that he was concerned to provide a place of worship and the ordinances of religion for his tenants. The Register in addition makes it clear that on his appointment to the Privy Council he became regular in his attendance, a virtue not exhibited by every Councillor. That he possessed a strong sense of duty and was industrious and diligent in his affairs cannot be doubted.

It must however seem curious that a noblemen living thus inconspicuously should be selected and appointed a member of the Council, as he was in January 1627, and the explanation offered by Sir John Scot that the appointment was made on his recommendation so that a representation of the older nobility might help "to make an equilibrium in the State", may be accepted as probable.

Thereafter from almost countrified obscurity Menteith rose rapidly to be the most influential figure in Scotland, having high honours by royal prerogative conferred upon him in quick succession, and enjoying the friendship and full confidence of the King. In February 1628 he was appointed Lord President of the Council[1] and later in the same year he was created Lord Chief Justice.[2] In 1630 he received the distinction of membership of the Privy Council of England.[3] It was through his medium that all important communications on Scottish affairs went to Court.

But at the very zenith of his career his place was shaken and his power destroyed by actions provoked by his unwisdom in negotiating with the King over the rights of the Earldom of Strathearn to which he laid claim. The unhappy dismissal from office which then occurred left him in a lower situation than that which he originally occupied, and although he lived for long years he did not emerge again upon the Scottish scene.

To proceed to explain what was a very extraordinary event it is important to note that in 1617 James VI passed an Act Anent the prescription of Heritable Rights which necessitated the lapse of a period of thirteen years before claims could be made on heritable lands: the prohibition thus ceased in 1629.[4] Meanwhile it is suggested that Menteith had continued to investigate his

---

[1] Reg. P.C. 1627-1628, p. 233.
[2] Ibid., p. 364.
[3] Red Bk. of Menteith, I, p. 340.
[4] Acts Parl. Scot., IV, pp. 543-544.

family titles, and that he now had aspirations directed to the Earldom of Strathearn, to which he assumed a right as the direct heir-male of David Stewart, son of King Robert II, who held that Earldom. Menteith based his right on the marriage of David's only offspring, the Countess Eupham, with his ancestor Sir Patrick Graham. It appears, therefore, that as soon as the legal bar imposed by the Act of James ceased to operate he took steps to effect his ends and for this purpose communicated with Sir Thomas Hope, the King's Advocate.

Menteith later avowed that he acted throughout under the direction of the latter, but, when we remember the interest which he had earlier displayed in his family charters, it would be unreasonable to believe that this venture originated elsewhere than in his own ambition and will. The early stage of motive and decision must remain unclear, but at all events in the Advocate, who was at this time his supplicant for important favours, he had the assistance of the ablest legal mind in questions of land law that Scotland could at that day provide.

It is plain that in the course of 1629 considerable progress had been made, for in September the King directed the Advocate to draw up a form of Surrender for all lands of royal property contained within the Earldom of Strathearn,[1] and in November he issued a commission to the Clerk Register to give fullest access to Menteith to search the official registers, an action which brought to light two Charters of King Robert II granting to his son, David Stewart, the Earldom in question.[2]

Thereupon ensued that transaction whereby the King, having been approached by two trusted State officials, was persuaded to accept a renunciation of lands by a nobleman who, in the existing state of things did not possess them, and in doing so to grant to the said nobleman a considerable financial award. The business involved on the King's part an admission that these crown lands were not his, with a further admission of Menteith's direct heirship to Earl David, and a clouding of the royal family line. The date of the Renunciation was 22nd January 1630.[3]

This happening sheds some light on the trust which Charles was accustomed to impose in his intimate counsellors,[4] and in

[1] *Red Bk. of Mentieth*, II, p. 21.
[2] *Ibid.*, II, p. 24.
[3] *Ibid.*, I, p. 344.
[4] Note No. 48, p. 225.

view of what transpired it reveals in Menteith, and in the legal agent who encouraged his suit, a strange obtuseness as to the nature of possible reactions, public and private.

These two men offer a considerable contrast in character and gifts, but no two could have been better matched to assist each other in the realisation of his respective ambition. Menteith, a noble of ancient lineage, and an eager if inexpert statesman, wished to be rehabilitated in the high state of the race from which he sprang.

As revealed by his letters he was a plain practical person; "no complimenter", no lover of "idle professions without effects". Homely expression was characteristic of his style which abounded in pithy or proverbial Scottish phrase. He says to the Earl of Morton, "tak me as you find me", and of the despatch of a letter by messenger: "This ould bearer goes faster than I, for I will mak no more haste nor is fitting for ane sair back".[1]

It may be that a love of picturesque native phrase, and a habit of blunt speech infused with a humorous quality, made up part of his attraction, and this feature of his address may account for the expression about "neck-breaking" which he later used as a threat to Sir John Scot, and even for the unfortunate boast which was flaunted by his enemies and did him so much harm, namely, that he had in his veins "the reddest blood in Scotland". Traquair seems to vent what was common knowledge when he speaks of his "rash tongue".[2]

Along with these impressions of unguarded speech we must assume a habit of life which was unaccustomed to clerkship and formal correspondence. Writing to Earl Morton in September 1630, he can say naïvely, "I know you doo not expect that I am a writer of newes: you shall have them from uthers and it will save me a labour". Late in 1632 he refers with an ingenuous air and a trace of humour to the frequent transmission of notes: "Nulla dies sine linea" he says, and adds, "This has learned me to be a writer".[3]

In assessing Menteith's conduct the stresses peculiar to his office should be duly weighed. The evidence of existing documents reveals the flattery directed to him, and on the reverse side

[1] *Earldoms of Strathearn, Menteith, and Airth.* Sir Harris Nicolas (1842). Letters, Appendix, pp. lxxxii-lxxxiii.

[2] *Ibid.*, p. lxxxiii.

[3] *Earldoms of Strathearn*, etc., Appendix, p. lxxxii.

there is proof that he was attacked by envy and the malicious gossip of his enemies. But in all that we read of this man there is no sign of duplicity or diplomatic adroitness.

His legal adviser, Sir Thomas Hope, was a man with a remarkable combination of qualities. An unrivalled lawyer, a subtle and skilled advocate, devoutly religious and passionately devoted to his family. When he retired early in 1644 he had already spent forty years at the bar and for seventeen years had been Lord Advocate. James Melville in his Autobiography tells of Hope's early distinction, when as a novice in 1606 he pleaded in a case of treason alleged against certain ministers, and in his action "missed nothing that the best could have done".[1] Thomas Hamilton, who as Lord Advocate at that time led the prosecution "with gryt sophistrie, craft, and ill-will", declared two years later that Hope was "one of the most learned and best experienced advocates at the bar".[2] After the Revolution he stood in the peculiar position of being the King's ablest minister and yet the friend and adviser of those who had opposed the royal policy in ecclesiastical matters.

His punctilious and steadfast attitude was seen when alone of the Councillors present he refused to sign approval of Traquair's Proclamation made at Stirling in February 1638, on the ground that he had not submitted it to the Council and had exceeded his instructions.[3] He was equally obdurate and astute when the Committee of Estates in 1641 prepared summonses against the Incendiaries and requested his signature. Having no warrant from the King he declined and the Incendiaries were never brought to trial.[4]

His strength lay in the clear distinction he made between civil rights and spiritual rights. He staunchly defended the Royal prerogative as long as it did not encroach on religious liberty, and his superior command of law and principle won for him the respect —somewhat chilly on occasion—if not always the confidence, both of the King and the national leaders.[5]

It is odd to find in a man of such formidable knowledge and adherence to legal principle the fault of an unusual credulity as to

[1] Melville's *Diary* (Wodrow Soc.), p. 621.
[2] *Lord Advocates of Scotland*, Omond, I, p. 101.
[3] *Ibid.*, I, p. 119.
[4] *Ibid.*, I, p. 133.
[5] Note No. 49, p. 225.

the portent of dreams and small untoward happenings, and a zeal for family interest which sometimes led to almost frantic appeals for favour and an undue seeking and striving for place.[1] Of his high character and religious sincerity there could be no question. Scot calls him a Puritan.

At the end of the day it is not surprising that the Earl found his adviser making a politic retreat, unscathed by the critical contest, while assuring his noble client that in what he sought he had been "just in action, and also *in animo et intentatione*", and counselling him "To sanctify God in his hart, and not grieve his Spirit nor the good angel whom He had appointed to keep him in all his ways".[2] Such was the fastidious and gifted lawyer whom Menteith had chosen to present and prove his ambitious claim.

According to the *Trew Relation* the movement involving Menteith began with the desire of Sir William Alexander, made Secretary of State in 1626, to strengthen himself in office by bringing some trusty friends of his into the Privy Council. This desire he confided to Sir John Scot who had recently been prominent in the proposed re-casting of the Court of Session, asking his advice and help. From him he received the opinion that "the fittest way to curb the grandeur of the present rulers was to add to their number some of the old nobility, and so make an equilibrium in the Estate", and he named Menteith as a fit person to be included.[3] The Secretary, armed with the express view of a councillor who was likely to be a good judge in such matters, submitted Sir John's letter to the King, who accepted the advice and wrote to the Council instructing them to assume the Earl as one of their number. Sir William in communicating with Menteith desired him to thank Sir John Scot for the letter on his behalf which had won the King's consent. This being done there followed for some time a situation of intimacy with the Earl acting under the lawyer's guidance.

The latter about this time advised him to go personally and present his thanks at Court, and gave him a letter of recommendation to his friend James Maxwell, a courtier in the King's retinue. Menteith did as advised and gained such credit with the Duke of Buckingham that in a very short time he received, as reported,

---

[1] See his Diary, p. 130, and his Letters to Menteith contained in *The Red Book*, p. 355. To break a shoe-string was a portent of family disaster.
[2] *Red Bk. of Menteith*, I, p. 357.
[3] *Scot. Hist. Review*, XI, p. 284.

considerable honours at the King's hand. It will be seen from this version of affairs that Sir John Scot was practically the architect of the Earl of Menteith's success.

But for whatever reason there was very soon a serious rupture in the relationship. This must have taken place in the year 1628 for on the very day in January 1629[1] on which Scot took office as a Lord Extraordinary, warning was conveyed to him by the Earl of Buccleuch that Menteith had vowed "to break his neck".[2] His loss of place in the Session in November 1630 undoubtedly saw the fulfilment of this threat, for Traquair had reported in a letter to Morton in February 1629 Menteith's assurance that Scot's appointment as a Lord Extraordinary, "was for the interim until he speak with the King".[3]

Some light is shed on what had happened to provoke hostility by the comments of the Advocate in November 1631. At this time Sir John and the Advocate's eldest son were competing for a place as Lord Ordinary,[4] and Hope in writing to Menteith and calling Scot the latter's "professit unfreind", goes on to say "I scarcely think him worthy of addition to the Session who in open Council presumit to injure your Lordship, and in open Exchequer raillet on me for being too busie on his Majesteis service".[5]

Sir John's explanation of the trouble is that when Menteith returned after his flattering reception at Court, the Advocate perceiving him to be deep in the King's regard, persuaded him to be ruled by his counsel and to have no further communication of affairs with Scotstarvit. Menteith's collaboration with Hope had then ensued.

Conjoint with these affairs it so happened that when Sir John was in England in 1630, and after the date of Menteith's Renunciation of the Earldom of Strathearn, he had received from the Earl of Seaforth a paper—he calls it a "brief information"—setting forth the disadvantages to the King of that transaction, and this he had copied for further consideration.[6]

---

[1] Brunton and Haig, p. 280.

[2] *Scot. Hist. Review*, XI, p. 285.

[3] Traquair to Morton, 3 Feb. 1629, in copy of the *Trew Relation*, Nat. Lib. 56, 6.234. (10).

[4] Note No. 50, p. 225.

[5] *Red Bk. Menteith*, II, pp. 128-129, p. 133.

[6] Note No. 51, p. 225.

Sir Thomas Hope, Lord Advocate
circa 1575-1646
Reproduced by permission of the Scottish National Portrait Gallery

George Hay, 1st Earl of Kinnoull
1572-1634
Reproduced by permission of the Lady Auckland of Cromlix

In the now troubled state of his relations, catching at the apprehensions which were there expressed, he set about to examine methodically the original titles in the case, to consider how the terms of the settlement between the King and Menteith reflected upon the King's standing as heir to the Crown, and to study what political dangers might follow from the aspirations of one who (as in an important reservation made by Menteith) laid claim to be the direct descendant of David, son of Robert II.

As a preliminary our author sets forth a brief statement on the marital arrangements of Robert II, and the terms on which he originally granted the Earldom in question to his son.

The facts briefly are that the King in his minority and before his accession to the throne had for his consort Elizabeth Mure of Rowallan by whom he had three sons, John, Robert, and Alexander. The fact of consanguinity between the two had, according to canon law, frustrated regular union, but a papal dispensation in 1349 legitimated the wedding and regularised the position of the offspring. After the death of Elizabeth Mure the King married in legal form Eupham Ross who bore him two sons, David and Walter. These are the bare historical facts.

But as a relevant comment of some importance it may be said that the right of succession established on the family of Elizabeth Mure was not everywhere accepted, and even in the early seventeenth century some confusion seems to have crept into the minds of the genealogists and historians. In an editorial note attached to the brief notice on Sir Thomas Hope in *The Staggering State* there is mention of "the error of our historians that David, Earl of Strathearn, was the eldest son of Robert II's first marriage, namely with Eupham Ross".[1] Certainly David was the eldest son of that union: the error consisted in allowing priority to the marriage contract. The note adds that "this gave occasion to Sir Lewis Stewart[2] to confute that gross error, which he did by producing several authentic deeds of Robert II, particularly one at the time of his coronation (1371) declaring John Stewart to be his true heir and to have the right to succeed after him to the kingdom".

The continuing seriousness of this dispute can be gauged by the publication in 1695 of Viscount Tarbat's "Vindication of King Robert III from the Imputation of Bastardy by the clear proof

---

[1] *The Staggering State* (1754), pp. 140-141.
[2] Sir Lewis Stewart, father-in-law to Johnston of Warriston.

of Elizabeth Mure, she being the First Lawful Wife of Robert II, then Steward of Scotland and Earl of Strathearn".[1]

That Menteith should, in view of the existence of these doubts, claim the Earldom and establish his right of blood as direct heir of David, was not without its grave dangers.

In respect of the other question, that of the grant to David of this Earldom, the crucial point was whether there was a condition that failing any heirs male it should return to the Crown. Sir John admits that he did not find this stated in the charters which he examined, but says it is set down in Scottish history that this was the condition, and that it held of lands in the cases of the brothers Walter and Alexander.[2]

In actual fact David died and left a daughter but no son, and James I finding himself in 1424 in financial difficulties "recognosced" the earldom to the Crown, contending that it was limited to heirs male, and gave instead to Malise Graham, David's grandson through his daughter Eupham, the new Earldom of Menteith, the recall of the Strathearn gift being confirmed by Parliament.[3, 4]

Further study by our author in support of his third premise, namely the political dangers inherent in the situation, leads him to relate how the confusion of families in respect of Robert II's two marriages had already led to conspiracy against the Crown, as witnessed particularly in the case of Walter, Earl of Atholl (of the family of Eupham Ross) who, at the instigation of Sir Robert Graham, assumed that he was rightful heir to the Crown, and formed the plot which led to the assassination of James I at Blackfriars Monastery, Perth, in 1437.[5]

Having made this historical preamble, Scotstarvit then proceeded to draw up a set of Reasons for presentation to his Majesty with a view to persuading him that Menteith had made a dangerous claim, and to effect the annulment of the settlement already arranged. The Reasons are six in number and express the apprehensions of the pleader thus:

That the right of succession to the Crown may again become confused. That colour may be given to the view that James I

---

[1] Sir George MacKenzie, Viscount Tarbat, 1630-1714.
[2] *Scot. Hist. Review*, XI, p. 283, 456.
[3] Acts Parl. Scot., James I, 1424, Vol. II, p. 4.
[4] Note No. 52, p. 225.
[5] *Scot. Hist. Review*, XI, p. 286.

acted wrongfully. That the Act of Parliament annexing the Earldom after James's action would now require to be reduced. That wrong would be done to the tenants, the crown vassals, if there was a transference of superiority. That the King's rent would suffer. That the King's father suffered no one to assume the title of Strathearn, saying it was all he had for the slaughter of James I.

It may be claimed that these are Reasons of expediency, the persuasions of an advocate who is looking at the practical effects which may follow in the State and to the King from the establishment of such a transaction. Certainly, whatever he thought of legal right, he was here concerned chiefly to maintain the royal succession and guard the peace of the realm.[1]

It was the late autumn of 1632 before this movement of protest reached the point of action. In September we find Sir John in communication with Sir James Skene, President of the Court of Session and with the joint Secretaries of State, who are both named, although from that point onward Sir William Alexander drops from notice and Sir Archibald Acheson acts as a chief and responsible agent.

At the critical juncture in question it happened that there were in Edinburgh James Maxwell and Sir Robert Dalzell, who both had places at Court and were about to return thither. The Secretaries, says Sir John, advised that the assistance of these courtiers should be sought in the endeavour to bring the matter to the royal notice. But it was found when the proposal was made that Sir Robert Dalzell would take no part until they had the opinion of the Earl of Haddington.[2]

Here was Scot's former antagonist, the elder statesman whom apparently Sir John regarded with unfriendly respect. Born in 1563 he became an Ordinary Lord of Session in 1592, and in 1596 was one of the eight statesmen appointed by James to manage his finances. In the same year he assumed the office of Lord Advocate. When the King removed to London in 1603 Hamilton was entrusted with a large share of Scottish government, and he attended the Hampton Court Conference on Union in 1606 where, along with the subtle intellect of Francis Bacon, he employed his talent in casting into appropriate legal form the proposed scheme. In 1612 he became Secretary of State, and

[1] Note No. 53, p. 225.
[2] *Scot. Hist. Review*, XI, p. 288.

further enhanced his power four years later when appointed President of the Court of Session. The office of Secretary he retained until 1626 when he took over the post of Privy Seal. It will be seen that few had served in a wider range of high office than he. In 1613 he was raised to the peerage as Lord Binning and afterwards received the honour of an Earldom, being first designated of Melrose and then of Haddington.[1]

Although there is an air of facetiousness about the soubriquet "Tam o' the Cowgate", it cannot be concluded that its bearer was a man given to pleasantry and humour. Sir John who knew him intimately noted as his chief characteristics his learning and irascibility. Educated as a Roman Catholic he was regarded generally with suspicion, and his enemies declared with bitter emphasis that "the dregs of his Roman profession stuck fast to his ribs". Nevertheless he was guided throughout—and not least in the present affair—by that "singular wisdom and dexterity" which James once took occasion to extol.[2] Haddington was definitely of a scholarly bent, with a specialised interest in early historical documents, of which he has left a valuable collection. His existing letters—including six addressed to Menteith—reveal his sensible and statesmanlike mind and convey a serious and reflective tone.

It is of interest to note that this powerful official conducted rather more than a formal correspondence with Menteith on whose curious transaction with Charles he was now invited to adjudicate. Haddington, having no doubt balanced the dangers either way, chose to be seriously concerned over the case as presented by the Director of Chancery, and he assured the hesitating courtiers that they could act without risk and would be doing a good service to the King. Such a recommendation must have carried considerable weight when it was, as it would be, reported at Whitehall.

It is curious to reflect that the Earl himself was not unfamiliar with a charge of treason, inasmuch as little more than a year earlier he, along with the Marquis of Hamilton and the Earls of Roxburgh and Buccleuch, had suffered from "malicious reports" made to the King. The allegation may be judged as to its nature by Charles's characterisation of it as "nearly concerning us". But

[1] Brunton and Haig, pp. 221-224.

[2] *Ibid.*, p. 224. He was cousin to George Heriot, His Majesty's Jeweller, the founder of Heriot's Hospital.

having taken steps to consider and sift the evidence he wrote to the above parties in July 1631 saying that he found them "altogether innocent and cleere thairof".[1, 2]

At this point Scot's *Relation* presents a summarised statement of the objectionable aspects of the Strathearn settlement, with a concluding averment that if the matter be rightly considered, "It will be found that his Majesty has been greatly wronged in many things which, if his Majesty will put to trial, shall be sufficiently cleared".[3]

It appears that to this statement Haddington gave his assent. Accordingly being thus satisfied the messengers repaired to Court and disclosed their momentous news. The result was critical and startling. Sir Robert Dalzell was immediately posted back with the following letter in the King's hand:

"Robin Dalzell, whereas I have been informed by you and James Maxwell that the grant of the Earldom of Strathern which I have given is greatly prejudicial to me both in honour and matter of state, insomuch that he (Menteith) either hath or may serve himself heir to King Robert the Second: Therefore, since this doth seem to lay a heavy aspersion upon a man whom I both do and will esteem until I see evident cause in the contrary, he having done me many good services, I command you to produce your authors, that I may either punish them for this great aspersion, or reward them for this good service in so important a discovery. Otherwise I must take James and you for my authors, judging you as ye shall prove your allegations. Make haste in this for I must not suffer a business of this nature to hang long in suspense. Whitehall, 2nd October 1632."[4]

With the advent of this peremptory missive matters at once took a dramatic turn and the tension of interest heightened. Sir Robert Dalzell had ridden in haste and reached Edinburgh on "the fourth day". Without undue loss of time and evidently under an arranged plan he convoked a meeting of Sir James Skene, Sir Archibald Acheson, and Sir John Scot, whom he confronted with a Commission also consisting of three, namely Sir Thomas Nicolson, later the King's Advocate, Sir Lewis Stewart, and Mr

---

[1] The charge was made by James Stewart, Lord Ochiltrie. Reg. P.C. 1630-1632, p. 263.

[2] Note No. 54, p. 225.

[3] *Scot. Hist. Review*, XI, p. 288.

[4] *Ibid.*, XI, p. 289.

Andrew Aytoun of Logie. These three advocates were assembled to judge of the reasonableness or otherwise of the charges alleged by the others, who are distinguished by the term "authors" or "informers". Papers containing questions and desiring answers were set before the members of the Commission. Sir Thomas Nicolson (a cousin of Sir Thomas Hope) having heard the first article rose in immediate trepidation and asserted that he would listen to no more. Declaring with an oath that all who were accessory to the prosecution of that matter would be hung, he forthwith left the house.

Despite this defection the other two judges waited, and after hearing and considering the questions, gave their answers, which supported the serious nature of the things contended. The document showing that the royal warrant of enquiry had been complied with is quoted. Dalzell signed it before Andrew Aytoun and Lewis Stewart as witnesses, and it was also signed by Sir John Scot and his colleagues. As the date appended is November 1632 this shows that a few weeks had been occupied in completing the business.[1] It was in this bleak month that Robin Dalzell hurriedly returned to Court bearing tidings which must have brought little comfort to the King, who was at last looking forward and preparing to make his Coronation visit to Scotland.

Action meanwhile moved with definite and alarming pace, for on 9th December Menteith received royal notice that Sir Thomas Hope had been instructed to call to him "Maisters Andro Aytoun, Thomas Nicolsoun and Lues Stewart", and consult "whidder the services and retours whairby you are served and retoured heir to David Earl of Stratherne should be deleit furth of our registers": and Menteith himself was "to cause administer ane oathe solemnly to thame all, and cause thame upon thair oathe to delyver thair opinions and judgements, and sett the same doun in writ under thair hands, and return the same to us".[2]

A curious incident, significant of the political intrigue of that day, now happened in the old winter-ridden capital of the north. On 22nd December in the town house of Lord Durie[3] there gathered as guests to dinner Sir James Skene, Sir Archibald Acheson and Sir John Scot, and, no doubt to their astonishment, they found that the only other guest was the Earl of Traquair.

---

[1] *Scot. Hist. Review*, XI, p. 290.
[2] *Red Bk. of Menteith*, II, p. 47.
[3] Note No. 55, p. 225.

Here indeed in John Stewart they had for companion a powerful and astute statesman: "a man of violent temper who could not brook opposition".[1] This bold and able man, whose changeful career had not yet reached its height, acted on this occasion true to his character.[2]

The fact was that the meeting had been arranged by him, and his purpose was disclosed when he indicated his awareness that important designs were being pursued by the other three. He then said that his one interest in meeting them was to learn if they had any quarrel with himself. On this point they gave him definite assurances and the meal proceeded.

Half-way through the sitting a servant entered and called Traquair to an outer room. On returning he enquired if any of them had any business at Court as he had been speaking to one who would carefully convey their letters thither. The Secretary and President of Session regarded this as an innocent invitation, but Sir John, remembering that Sir Thomas Nicolson was cousin to Sir Thomas Hope, instantly suspected that one or the other of these had revealed their business, and that a plot was afoot to secure the documents and counteract the whole serious effort.[3]

Anyone who reads Scotstarvit's final estimate of John Stewart[4] will understand how even at this stage he knew he was dealing with a dangerous opportunist, and the speed and decision of the action which he now took betrays his profound concern. Without delay on leaving Lord Durie's house he went to the Cowgate and consulted the Earl of Haddington. This stateman's advice was significant. He urged Sir John to ride to Court himself and carry with him all the papers pertaining to the Menteith affair. Sir John therefore set out, having first convened his colleagues and obtained under their hands a commission to go and submit these matters to the King, they pledging themselves in life and estate to stand to whatsoever he should say on their behalf. Here it is best to allow the narrative to tell in brief the somewhat dramatic particulars of the journey south:

"That instant night, before ten o'clock, within three days of Christmas, he rode to Dirleton, and the next morning took post

---

[1] Nicoll's *Diary*, p. 228.
[2] Note No. 56, p. 225.
[3] *Scot. Hist Review*, XI, p. 291.
[4] *The Staggering State* (1754), pp. 40-45.

to Cockburnspath, and the fifth day came to Hampton Court where his Majesty resided; who (Scot) being brought in to the bed chamber by Mr Maxwell, had a long conference with his Majesty concerning the said matter, and shewed him the paper which he had caused Mr William Drummond of Hawthornden, his brother-in-law, to write: which the King instantly desired to be read in his presence."[1]

Drummond's pamphlet is taken up with historical examples of the dangers attending upon the disputed succession to the crown, and implies the risks involved in the negotiations already conducted with Menteith. He pretty broadly hints at drastic solutions in two closing paragraphs, where we must assume that the ferocity of his sentiments belongs rather to his poetical style than to his natural temper. He says:

"It is to be considered if Queen Mary of England who cutted off the head of Lady Jane Grey, and Queen Elizabeth who did the same to Mary Queen of Scotland her kinswoman, were living, they would have suffered any to enjoy the opinion of being nearer to their crown than themselves, and whether a prince may justly keep under the race of those whose aspiring thoughts dare soar so nigh a crown, as they have been kept these two hundred years bygone for reasons of State. Unless the prince exalt them in order to give them a more deadly blow, and extirpate them and their whole race."[2]

Drummond was a fervent royalist but to excuse his drastic recommendations is difficult save on the ground that he believed Menteith to be guilty of treasonable aspirations.

Sir Robert Dalzell, who was present in the bed-chamber, now asserted that distinguished witnesses could avow having heard Menteith say that "he had the reddest blood in Scotland". This information moved the King so deeply that he dismissed the company. "It is a sore matter", he said as his visitors moved out, "that I cannot love a man but you must pull him out of my arms".[3]

In the meantime Scotstarvit's hasty flight to Court and the nature of his errand having been divulged, steps were taken to oppose him. The prime movers in opposition were the Chancellor, Viscount of Dupplin, and the Treasurer, the Earl of Morton. In a

---

[1] *Scot. Hist. Review*, XI, p. 292. "Took post": this signifies travelling with a relay of horses in order to make speed.

[2] Note No. 57, p. 225.

[3] *Scot. Hist. Review*, XI, p. 294.

pact between them they had undertaken to free Menteith from hazard if he would use his influence to get Morton made a Knight of the Garter. It is probable that this agreement with Morton is mentioned because Menteith's failure to implement it became a potent cause of his downfall. Having received assurance to the above effect his powerful agents represented to the King that the charges were frivolous and should be contemned.

Charles however called Sir John to a further meeting, and in it the latter undertook to table full proof that his Majesty was abused both by Sir Thomas Hope and the Earl. What he did apparently was to reveal by a strict examination of the documents the peculiar fact that Menteith instead of being disabled by his renunciation of the Earlship was actually confirmed in it. For this purpose the Renunciation is presented in full and is left to be compared with the succeeding Patent of Honour. The Renunciation with two unimportant excisions reads as follows:

"Be it kenned that me William Earl of Menteith, Lord Graham of Kilpunt, President of his Majesty's Council and High Justice of Scotland, forasmeikle as umquhile King Robert the Second by his charter under the great seal gave to his son David and his heirs the Earldom of Strathern, to be holden in free regality with all fees, forfeitures, and other liberties: Likewise also the said King Robert by another charter granted to his said son and heirs the said earldom with addition of the Four points of the Crown, and forasmeikle as I am undoubted heir of blood and successor to the said David Earl of Strathern, being descended lineally from Patrick Graham and Eupham Stewart, daughter to the said David, and having good and undoubted right to claim the said Earldom, yet, nonetheless, considering that the said Earldom has been bruicked by his Majesty and his predecessors as a part of the annexed property continually since the decease of King James the First: and calling to mind the extraordinary favours bestowed upon me by my gracious Sovereign, Charles, King of Great Britain, therefore, wit ye me to have renounced all right and interest which I or my heirs have or pretend to have to the said Earldom, in favour of my sacred and gracious Sovereign, his heirs and successors, to remain with them and with the Crown for ever: providing these presents do not prejudice me nor my forsaids if need be, to obtain ourselves served, retoured, and seized in the said lands as heir to the said umquhile David."[1]

[1] *Scot. Hist. Review*, XII, pp. 396-397.

The renunciation duly witnessed was subscribed at Holyrood House on 22nd January 1630.

Of the Patent of Honour it may be sufficient to quote the following. It states that,

"William Earl of Menteith stands served and retoured undoubted heir of blood of umquhile David, Earl of Strathern, the son lawful of King Robert II. To the which David and his heirs the said Robert by two different charters, one dated at Edinburgh 19th June, the first year of his reign, the other at Perth, 3rd July the same year, disponed the said Earldom with all annexes and pertinancies thereof."

It admits Menteith's "good right to the said Earldom", and quotes his renunciation of all right and title without prejudice to his "right and dignity of blood belonging to him as heir of Line of David Earl of Strathern". Then, in order that Menteith and his heirs, "may enjoy the right and title of the Earldom of Strathern, and succeed to the same title, place, and dignity due to them by the said two charters", the King "ratifies and approves the title, etc. of an Earl to the Earl of Menteith, who shall henceforth be styled and called Earl of Strathern and Menteith, and shall enjoy and possess the title and dignity . . . with the same privileges and degrees which belonged to David Earl of Strathern and his heirs".[1]

It would appear, therefore, that Menteith renounced a title which he did not at the moment and in appearance possess, and then was granted the same title on the ground of his right established in the charters of Robert the Second. The King disclaimed any right of his to the Earldom which he and his ancestors had bruicked for long, and admitted that Menteith stood in the line of Robert II through Earl David and Eupham Stewart.

Charles, after the initial information and the later report of the Commission, took tentative steps towards deleting the service from the Registers, but certain circumstances caused him to hold his hand for a season. We know this both from Sir John Scot's protest at his leavetaking with the King and from a letter of Traquair.[2] The fact was that Menteith, realising the seriousness of his position, had come voluntarily to Court and prostrated himself

[1] *Scot. Hist. Review*, XII, p. 395.
[2] Letter to Earl of Morton, 29th August 1612. *Earldoms of Strathearn,* etc. App. lxxxi.

with acknowledgement of his fault. Charles being additionally influenced by the pleadings of Morton and Hay received him favourably, and bade him quit the title of Strathearn and take that of Airth, which he did.[1] Scot was chidden for having concealed the matter for so long and for having given out the briefs, to which he made a tart reply and thereupon returned to Edinburgh.[2]

But just at the time of stalemate a development took place which set the whole case into renewed agitation.

Morton, it appears, learned that with the approach of the Scottish coronation Menteith was moving to secure for himself the honour of the Garter which he had promised, and "had foully failed him therein". Stung with indignation he sought along with the Chancellor an audience with the Queen, and unfolding the story of Menteith's claims represented the danger to the succession of the young Prince. Upon this the Queen urgently addressed the King and obtained an assurance that the matter would be effectively dealt with.[3]

There is no doubt that after a pause Charles resumed a vigorous process of recall and redress, and Scotstarvit's account of the Queen's perturbation may well supply the reason.

In the *Trew Relation* the description of the closing movements in this drama is somewhat compressed, but the evidence of the official records shows that the main case having been settled, namely the rectification of a huge legal indiscretion, proceedings suddenly took shape as a trial in a charge of treason, and in a judgment on that charge the case ended.

In the matter of the rectification the appointed panel of lawyers had judged it necessary for the King's security that all the steps taken to serve Menteith heir to Prince David with right to the Earldom of Strathearn, should be annulled, with declarator that his Majesty only had right to the Earldom and was nearest of blood to David the late Earl of Strathearn. Among the reasons proffered in support of this was the absence of any proof by writ that Malise Graham was lawful son of Lady Eupham, or that she was the lawful daughter of Earl David, and that the Renunciation had not been accepted by the King, but by his Advocate, without lawful warrant.[4]

To bring the matter before the Court of Session a summons was

---

[1] Reg. P.C. 1630-32, pp. 56-57.
[2] *Scot. Hist. Review*, XII, pp. 397-398.
[3] *Ibid.*, XII, p. 401.
[4] *Red Bk. of Menteith*, I, pp. 360-361.

raised at the instance of Morton, Traquair, and Sir Thomas Hope. The decree of Reduction was obtained on 22nd March 1633.[1]

Lord Durie has given the Court's decision in these terms: "The decree of reduction was obtained from the Lords of Session who found the Reasons relevant to that end, and declared that the defender was not heir to Earl David or Countess Eupham, nor could be, nor was he of blood to them, but on the contrary the King was sole and only heir":[2] a judgment long subject to adverse comment.[3]

The foregoing matters were scarcely settled when further proceedings were instituted on a charge preferred by Sir James Skene, President of the Court of Session, that Airth had made treasonable speeches, saying that "his blood was the reddest in Scotland and that the King was obliged to him for his crown".[4] Charles appointed a Commission of six which included the three most powerful statesmen in the country, namely Kinnoull, Morton, and Haddington. Depositions alleging seditious speech were made before them at Holyrood House by the Earl of Southesk and the Countess of Mar, so says Scot: but in the official record the names of Lord Ramsay, the Earl of Wigtown, and Sir James Maxwell of Calderwood also appear. This took place on 25th May.[5]

Charles reached Edinburgh on 15th June and appointed the trial for the 24th, but it is doubtful if a trial took place before the King, who remained invariably kind and tolerant in his communications with the accused. In the forepart of July Airth wrote to the Commissioners saying he could not plead guilty,[6] and Charles almost at once instructed Traquair to obtain a satisfactory confession. Accordingly on 15th July Airth made a submission which Traquair deemed acceptable for report to the King.[7]

During the remainder of the coronation visit the monarch left the business alone and it was early in October on his return to England that he wrote declaring that he had found sufficient proof of the charge.[8] On 8th November, Kinnoull, the Chancellor,

---

[1] *Red Bk. of Menteith*, I, p. 363.
[2] *Earldoms of Strathearn*, etc., Nicolas, lxxvi.
[3] Note No. 58, p. 225.
[4] *Scot. Hist. Review*, XII, p. 403.
[5] *Red Bk.*, *II*, Postscript pp. 51-52.
[6] *Ibid.*, II, pp. 152-3.
[7] *Ibid.*, II, p. 154.
[8] *Scot. Hist. Review*, XII, p. 402.

convened the Council and intimated the royal decision and sentence. Both Morton and Scot were absent but Traquair, Haddington, and the Advocate were present.[1] The Earl compeared, heard the judgment and acquiesced. His letter of demission, in which some subtle legal skill had been exercised to qualify the terms of confession, reads as follows:

"Be it kenned that me, William Earl of Airth, forasmeikle as it has pleased his sacred Majesty by his letter directed to my Lord Chancellor, to declare that whereas his Majesty upon the commission for trial of some treasonable speeches spoken by me, has found sufficient proof to believe the same, and that I have confessed as much in effect, together with the great fault committed by me in my service to the Earldom of Strathern; in regard thereof his Majesty has found that I am not worthy to enjoy the charge which I have formerly borne in the State, therefore, and for obedience to his Majesty's sacred will, wit ye me to have resigned and surrendered etc., and for more security, sic subscribitur, Airth."[2]

The King also took a bond from the Advocate, who acknowledged his fault and obliged himself never to give his Majesty cause of offence thereafter, promising if he did any fault to suffer what it merited.

In his *Information of the Trew Estait of the Bussines of Stratherne*, which is quoted in Sir Harris Nicolas's work on the Earldom, Hope gives assurance in a closing sentence that "This is a trew and simple statement of the bussines", which "was done with fidelity and cair to see his Majestie fully and perfytlie secured from all actioun quilk the said Erle or his heirs might pretend to the Erldome of Stratherne or any pairt thairof, notwithstanding quhatsomever of malicious informatioun be made to the contrary".[3]

As to the initiation of the matter he says: "In July 1629 the Erle of Stratherne causit search his Chartour kist, together with the Registers, wharin he fand a number of old Chartours grantit to his predecessours. He shewed his haill evidentis to his Majesteis Advocat, and desyrit his advyse."[4]

Of the vital transaction of the renunciation and the service,

[1] Reg. P.C. 1633-1635, pp. 139-141.
[2] Earldoms of Strathearn, etc., App. liii.
[3] *Ibid.*, App. xxiii.
[4] *Ibid.*, App., pp. xix-xx.

he asserts: "There is no Advocat of skill and knowledge of the lawes that will tak upon his conscience to affirme that his Majestie could be securit by the said renunciatioun, except the said Erle had bene (first) servit heir to the said David his predecessour".[1] He thus rebuts malicious reports and justifies his actions.

The truth appears to be that Hope, having been approached by the Earl and having had the evidence submitted to him, advised the other to pursue his claim, and he himself was engaged to conduct the necessary legal steps. This is the point on which Menteith sought to exculpate himself with the King, saying somewhat lamely: "I went not one foot but by your Advocate's advice and direction. When I was in England he wrote me to serve myself heir to Earl David, which I gave way to, and in my absence he did it."[2]

Convinced of Menteith's right, Hope concluded that the King could be secured only in the manner he recounts. He could thus claim that he was protecting the succession, and doing so justly. In assessing personal motives it cannot reasonably be supposed that he undertook a task so fraught with serious possibilities to the State solely for the sake of family or private advantage, which was certainly weighing with him at the time. His character and record, and the terms which he uses in his "Information", make such an idea incredible.

The spur which quickened Sir John Scot may have been retaliation over the ungenerous attitude of his erstwhile protégé— it is difficult to clear him entirely of such a motive—but he was of a constitution too honest to have acted solely on a personal and accidental ground. Accustomed to study with scrupulous care the documents which passed into his office, and being by nature extremely watchful in the detection of error, he appears to have been convinced that a serious wrong had been done to the King, or might be done, which could have dangerous repercussions in the nation. It was not he who originated the doubts or prepared the paper which gave them expression, and when his efforts to awaken Charles to danger failed of adequate result, it was Morton's agency that brought the matter again to notice, and it was Sir James Skene who took up the charge of treason.

We cannot but be sympathetic towards Menteith. Within a period of six years his public career began, expanded, and ceased.

[1] *Earldoms of Strathearn*, etc. App. p. xxiii.
[2] *Red Bk.*, I, pp. 368-369.

At the end of it he was still only in his forty-third year, and had neither had the time nor a fair opportunity to reach political maturity. There is little suggestion either of craft about his character or that he was disloyal to the King. There is no blot on his record. Having been given an unexpected and perhaps too flattering start in royal favour he seems to have become not unnaturally ambitious of title and of precedence among the Scottish Nobility. What we read of him is void of any indication that he was capable of leadership or that he had, or aimed at having, a partisan following among his peers. Hume Brown thinks he was carried off his feet by his unexpected success, and this probably betrayed him into making boastful utterances in intimate company.[1] This, and the claims contained in his Renunciation, gave his rivals for power sufficient reason to counter his aims and undermine his position.

Airth, as he was now entitled, was temporarily banished to his castle on Inchtalla in the Loch (Lake) of Menteith, Perthshire. In 1639 the King showed his confidence in him by re-appointing him to the Privy Council, but the disturbance of the Revolution and the ascendence of the Covenanting party must have negatived any likelihood of renewed activity.[2] His financial position also had suffered in the alteration of his worldly state, and he had the misfortune to lose his son Lord Kilpont, who followed Montrose and was killed tragically a few days after the battle of Tippermuir. The truth is that his influence and fortunes had suffered a disablement which the future history of Scotland did nothing to amend.

Nevertheless when we remember the vexations and jealousies that troubled his five years of royal favour we may believe that privacy and retirement at Loch Menteith offered the compensations of some genuine happiness and simple contentment. Fortune left him where it found him, in rural scenes, engaged with farms, with the sport of the field and the good of his tenants. There his practical bent would have full play, and the flavour of his Scottish tongue would be a delight to his associates. After long years of retirement he died in 1661.[3]

---

[1] Reg. P.C. 1633-1635, Introd., pp. xliv-xlv.
[2] *Ibid.*, 1638-1643, p. 125, p. 473. He refused to sign the Covenants, and in April 1644 Louden urged him to sign for his safety's sake. *Red Bk.* I, p. 384.
[3] For his later history see the *Gartmore Papers*.

Chapter VIII

THE LORDS OF ERECTIONS AND THE REVOCATION

This chapter presents Sir John Scot's narrative of an effort at reform in which he was interested and active, where the aim was to reduce or abolish the evils attending upon the intrusion of new lordships between the vassals and the supreme lordship of the Crown.

"The Lords of Erections were those members of the nobility or others of the laity, to whom the king, *jure coronae*, made grants of the lands or tithes which had formerly belonged to the old ecclesiastical establishment. They were called Lords of Erections and sometimes Titulars of Teinds, because under their grants they had the same rights to the erected benefices, both lands and teinds, which were formerly vested in the monasteries and other religious houses."[1]

For the origin of this oppressive order—as it came to be regarded —it is necessary to go back to the immediate post-Reformation period when there was a general annexation of Kirk lands to the Crown. This act of confiscation rested on the plenary powers over church property which the crown had asserted at the Reformation and exercised since that time.

Scottish history was still at a stage where the royal favour involving large material grants could be bestowed on this or that nobleman as it suited the whim or purpose of the monarch. Accordingly, in the then state of intimacy which existed between the king and the nobles, royal gifts and concessions of land were made with remarkable freedom, no doubt usually on the ground or plea of service rendered or to be rendered. Apart from bestowals directly linked with the general annexation referred to, numerous instances of the above practice could be cited where titles had lapsed or forfeitures had been exacted. From references in the *Trew Relation* to regalities and bailieries it appears that this could

---

[1] Bell's *Dictionary of the Law of Scotland* (1826), I, p. 545.

also apply, and did apply, to lands where the territorial rights originally and anciently belonged to the king in person. But the possibilities of bestowal were vastly increased when the broad possessions of the Church fell to the royal disposal.[1]

These were apparently regarded as a kind of prize to be competed for by those who had much temporal power and less moral principle. The race quickened in James's minority when Melville reports of the Lords assembled during the Conference at Leith, which was followed by a General Assembly at St Andrews in 1571, that "Everie ane was hunting for a fatt kirk living". The diarist in his account proceeds to allege serious subterfuge on the part of the nobles in their effort to secure the largest possible share of feus, tacks, and pensions.[2]

The records make it clear that in their eagerness to win the ancient temporal wealth of the Church the parties concerned sometimes used questionable means and violated the laws of the realm, and we shall find Sir John Scot reporting the institution of unlawful statutes achieved by corrupt management of the Estates.[3] Private interest was so powerful that the Kirk had extreme difficulty in getting possession of a just portion of the existing revenues.

James Melville reports (1596) how he heard Mr Alexander Hay the Clerk Register—"a man the most exercised of any in Scotland in these matters"—and Sir John Lindsay—"a man of the greatest learning joined with solid natural wit"—debate about a standard plan[4] to provide stipends and endow the Kirk. "The first maintained that it was an impossibility as things stood in Scotland to devise such; or if it were devised to effectuate it: and dee'd in that opinion. The other held that both were possible, and set himself to devise the same and put it in writing." But, says Melville, "concerning the effectuating thereof he dee'd in the same faith as the Clerk Register".[5]

In stating the reasons that warranted his proposed scheme Sir John Lindsay said it was because

"The rents and patrimony which pertained of old to the Kirk

---

[1] Note No. 59, p. 225.
[2] Melville's *Diary*, Wodrow Soc. (1842), p. 31.
[3] Note No. 60, p. 226.
[4] The "Constant Plat" of 1596, devised by Sir John Lindsay of Balcarres, Secretary of State.
[5] Melville's *Diary* (1842), pp. 331-332.

had been greatly damnified and exhausted by the annexation of the whole temporality thereof to his Highness's Crown, and by the Erections of a great part of the said temporal lands of the Kirk—with divers kirks and teinds included—into Temporal Lordships, and by the pretended rights of so many persons' life-rents, assignations, and other dispositions."[1]

It is proof of the steady rate of acquisition that in a fairly short period of years the patrimony of the Church could be possessed by so many secular parties and held fast in what proved to be an almost unbreakable network of law and privilege. This left other injustices than those affecting the reformed Kirk, and provoked the protest of the large land-owning class of the Gentry which forms the special theme of this chapter.

The nature of the evil in their connection was that new superiors were established who inflicted grievous charges on the holders or tenants of the land, and relief was sought from these exactions and from a system which violated the important relationship of the King and the actual landholder or heritor. It appears to be the case that apart from any practical injustices the Gentry were also protesting against the superiority being in the hands of their fellow-subjects.

This particular problem formed the subject of James Dalrymple's oration before the Lords of Council and Session on 15th February 1648. In this notable utterance the great lawyer, the future Lord Stair, posed the question in these words:

"The thing, then, to be judged in this cause is whether it be lawful for any man by indulgency of the prince to accept, or the king to give, such gifts whereby one or other superior may be interponed between him and his vassals, they refusing to condescend to the same."[2]

The contemporary situation he describes by referring to a succession of ages, a gold, a silver, and an iron, illustrating a worsening process in history, the last having then arrived. He says,

"This hard and iron age wherein we have fallen has involved and confounded the dominion of one and the same roome,[3] so that there is one direct dominion and another profitable: one lord superior and another inferior . . . and avarice has so far gone on that all men are desirous and ambitious to seek the dominion of

---

[1] Melville's *Diary* (1842), p. 332.
[2] *Scot. Hist. Review*, XIII, p. 382.
[3] "Roome" indicates a possession of land.

all, to the attaining of which, lest they should be prohibited, they devised imaginary ways whereby they all may be styled lords and masters; in the community in the meantime like slaves all become servants, neither have we any thing proper or free but the air wherein we breathe."[1]

This was a matter of intense social importance promoted by impulses which, although defeated in one age, were bound to be renewed until justice was established.

The beginning of the opposition of forces must be traced to the conduct of James when he reached his majority in June 1587. The influence of his personality had already been felt and it was with a consciously planned purpose that he invoked a meeting of Parliament in July of that year. The House sat for fully a fortnight, and amongst a variety of important Acts none was more so than that entitled, "The Act for the Annexation of the Temporalities of Benefices to the Crown", and the following Act of Revocation.[2]

This was a constitutionally correct proceeding. A young sovereign had the right within a short period of years after completing his majority of revoking and annulling any grants made during his minority if they were deemed to be detrimental to the royal interest.[3] It was perhaps also arguable in feudal law that the gift failed with the death of the giver. This may not have extended to benefices in land but it was claimed to affect appointments to office when Charles took the step of changing the Session.[4]

The aim and scope of the Act of 1587 are seen in the preamble which declared that all the Lands and Revenues, "given and disponit of auld to Abbays, Monasteries, and other persons of Clergy", were national or crown property originally, and as their alienation to the Papal Church had been judged neither necessary nor profitable, and had so impoverished the Crown as to lay inordinate taxation on the subjects, therefore it was now deemed fit to recall them. Accordingly all such lands belonging to ecclesiastical foundations, or to the clergy regular or secular, were declared to be re-annexed and entirely at the King's disposal.

---

[1] *Scot. Hist. Review*, XIII, pp. 282-283.
[2] Acts Parl. Scot., III (1567-1592). Annexation of Temporalities, p. 431. The Revocation, p. 439.
[3] Reg. P.C. 1625-1627, Masson, p. XIX.
[4] Bellenden is quoted by Sir Thomas Craig to this effect: *Scot. Hist. Review*, XI, p. 173.

But in this Act, the principle of Crown right having been asserted, the grants already made to Lords of Erections, and of teinds to Titulars, were confirmed to the owners. Thereafter in the large domains that were left the King exercised his right of disposal, and in so doing service was rewarded, privilege indulged, and interest secured. Hitherto it had been customary to appoint Commendatorships, a type of possession which was not heritable. Powerful interests now contrived a method of more settled right and set the field for the acquisitive pursuit of landed property to be held heritably and hedged in with law.[1]

How definitely the campaign proceeded may be gathered from the fact that on Charles's accession in 1625 (which was scarcely forty years after the inception of James's policy) of the thirty abbeys in Scotland twenty-one had been erected into Temporal Lordships, six had been annexed to Bishoprics, and of the three remaining two were in the hands of Commendators. The only one retained by the Crown was Dunfermline and it was shorn of one large Lordship and two Baronies.[2] The same process had taken place in the lands of some fourteen Priories and eight Nunneries.[3]

Connell is no doubt correct in saying that "when Charles came to the throne he found the royal revenues in Scotland almost annihilated by the acts of his father, who had given away to his nobles nearly the whole of the benefices belonging to the church."[4]

It was in this situation that the Revocation by Charles of the foregoing bestowals was suddenly projected. The legal grounds supporting the recall made reference to the annexation of 1587: grants before that date were declared void inasmuch as the benefice belonged to the office and the beneficiaries had no power to make resignation; and after that date, because the consent of the legislature had not been given to their dissolution from the Crown.

An Edict announcing the royal decision was produced to the Council on 14th July by the Advocate, Sir William Oliphant, its full import being awaited with apprehension. As Dr Hill Burton has remarked, "It was the proclamation of a contest of which Charles was destined never to see the end".[5]

---

[1] Reg. P.C. 1625-1627, pp. cxv-cxvi, p. clix.
[2] Ibid., p. cxxxv.
[3] Ibid., p. cxlvi.
[4] Connell on Tithes (1815), I, p. 214.
[5] The Hist. of Scotland, Burton, 1897, VI, p. 75.

John Row has several references, and in one reporting the proclamation which was made in November at the Mercat Cross, Edinburgh, he says: "Quherin the King revoked all things done by his father, or his father's mother, in prejudice of the Crowne, causing this Revocation to pass through the Sealls, whilk bred a fear of great alteratione to come, as indeed the effect proved".[1]

The fears of the Council, where the influence of the Nobility held sway, were boldly voiced in a remonstrance made in the above month. They complained of secrecy: "That Revocation, whilk has been keeped so obscure that none as yett has seen the same"; and of "the feare whilk is generallie apprehendit thairupon by all your Majesteis subjects". It is something, they say, which "is heavily grudgit and murmurit at, and has possest the mynds of your goode subjectis with apprehensiones of the consequencies thairof, as if all thair former securities granted by your Majestie and your royall progenitours were thairby intendit to be annullit, and that no right made hierafter in the majoritie of Kings could be valid".

They also proceed to say with a stroke at the King's advisers: "Whatever project has been maid unto your Majestie of lawfull and great gain by this Revocation, we are of opinion that the gain sall not prove answeirable to the overture, and that the trouble is more than all that by law can follow".[2]

Professor Masson calls the above "a very bold letter of remonstrance",[3] but it appears to have been actuated by the self-interest of the Nobility, of whom eleven were present in the Council in a sederunt of thirteen. The ensuing negotiations proved that their fears were as well founded as their opposition was deep and enduring. From the first the King's recall was definitely aimed at the Lords of Erections and Titulars of Teinds, and was intended to do justice to the land-holding gentry, the clergy, and the Crown.

Charles made general proclamation of his purpose in January 1626, and issued the Edict for the appointment of a Commission in September, but meanwhile he was importuned to such a degree by deputations from the three chief classes concerned that action was withheld for further consideration, and it was in January 1627, that a great new Commission for the Surrender of

---

[1] *The Hist. of the Kirk of Scotland*, Row, Maitland Club, I, p. 133.
[2] Reg. P.C. 1625-1627, p. 193.
[3] *Ibid.*, p. xl.

Superiorities and Teinds was ready, being published early in the following month.[1] To meet the case of non-submitters a form of Summons for Reduction was prepared by Sir Thomas Hope so that the question could be tried at law.[2]

What Charles saw and aimed at doing is clearly stated in his accompanying letter:

"That everie heritour of the kingdom may have the tithes of his own lands upon reasonable conditions, by what title soever they may now be claimed or possessed by any other; that the churches may be providit of ministers and the ministers of competent stipends, and that We may have a reasonable increase of our revenue."[3]

The position of the Gentry was emphasised by the King, and quite possibly not only because they were actually subject to injustice, but for political considerations. In professed support of their right Charles explains that his desire is "To free the gentry of this kingdom from all these bonds which may force them to depend upon any other than his majesty: that the teinds may no longer be, as they have been heretofore, the cause of bloody oppressions, enmities, and of forced dependencies".[4]

Also in the Summons for Reduction which was framed by the Advocate, the stated object is:

"That the patrimony of the Crown may be restored: the kirks sufficiently planted; colleges, schools, and hospitals sufficiently maintained, and the Gentry of our kingdom relieved of the heavy burthens used against them in the leading of their teinds."[5]

The Revocation in the form in which it was published in February 1627 is usually described as *The Commission for the Surrender of Superiorities and Teinds*. The body appointed to give it effect numbered in all sixty-eight. It was representative of the Three Estates and included twenty Privy Councillors, and was in itself a small parliament. In contrast to their later reluctance and neglect the Commissioners sat regularly for the first four months and cited all who had interest to attend and arrange the terms of their submission. The expressed purpose was: "To treat with such as had right to erected benefices for a

[1] Reg. P.C. 1625-1627, p. 509.
[2] Note No. 61, p. 226.
[3] Reg. P.C. 1625-1627, p. clxxxvii.
[4] *Ibid.*, p. 228.
[5] *Ibid.*, p. 398.

surrender of those to the Crown on such terms as the Commission should suggest", subject to the Royal approval.[1]

But by the end of June only seven of the Lords of Erections, all of them Commissioners, made surrender, and that with reservation. Serious objections were raised by others: the Burghs also objected, and especially the Bishops, who fought tenaciously to retain their possessions, and in doing so won the King's displeasure.

At a certain stage Thomas Hamilton, the Secretary, was moved to vent his anger on Patrick Lindsay, Bishop of Ross, whom he failed to silence when in conference. "The whole Commission", he declared, "was wearie of his ignorance and impertinences, yet he impudently persisted"; and, betraying his sympathies towards his land-owning compeers, Hamilton added: "It is believed the Bishops' chief aim is to destroy the Erections grantit by blessed King James and ratified by the whole Estates of Parliament, and to encroach to themselffs all the teynds: which will be found too great a morsell for their greedie mouths".[2]

In the course of the following year, however, the business had so far progressed that Submissions were prepared and presented on behalf of the Lords and Titulars, the Clergy, the Burghs, and certain Tacksmen, and in September 1629 Charles answered these with four Decreets Arbitral designed to settle the problems and do justice to each of the classes mentioned.[3]

In a review of the action already taken Connell says: "By these proceedings was laid the foundation of that system which has proved so beneficial to the interests of Scotland. Instead of the old mode of drawing tithes in kind, which often led to disputes and sometimes to oppression, a mode was pointed out for separating and defining the interests of landholders, titulars, and ministers, in time to come. By this mode the clergy were in general secured in competent provisions, and there were preserved to landholde the quiet possession of their property, the full benefit of their improvements, and the exclusive right to all future rises in rent."

But the accomplishment of the desired end was by no means easy. The record shows that the work was exceedingly frustrating, and the years passed in a slow overtaking of the problems which

---

[1] Reg. P.C. 1625-1627, p. 352.
[2] *Ibid.*, p. cxcviii.
[3] *Connell on Tithes,* I, pp. 225-229.
[4] *Ibid.,* I., pp. 229-230.

were spread over all the country. Delay was caused not only by those who were laggard in complying but by the shirking of their duty by the Commissioners both clerical and secular.

Burnet the historian, echoing Sir John Scot's report made in *The Staggering State* (p. 142), says that the King's Advocate was also unhelpful, if not actually hostile to the change.

"Sir Thomas Hope, a subtle lawyer who was believed to understand that matter beyond all men of his profession, though in all respects he was a zealous puritan, was made King's Advocate upon his undertaking to bring all the church lands back to the Crown; yet he proceeded in the matter so slowly that it was believed he acted in concert with the party that opposed it."[1]

In June 1630 Charles had reason to write to the Commissioners saying he "was informed that there is ane great hindrance" in the progress of valuations, "occasioned by some indirect means".[2] The Commissioners for their part are found bitterly complaining of the delinquency of the sub-Commissioners. These sub-Commissions had been set up to conduct valuations in the parishes, and in January 1632 the parent body declared "that very few have as yet reported their diligence notwithstanding of the many dyets assigned unto thame for that errand"; and that "idle and impertinent excuses have been pretendit. Others did disdainfullie slight or refuse to go on, or to make anie excuse at all."[3]

In February 1632 twenty-seven Presbyteries, including Glasgow, are named as defaulting, and in March another twenty-two, including Dundee and Aberdeen.

The trouble was not confined to the sub-Commissioners, for as late as February 1633 the Privy Council was issuing exhortations to the chief Commissioners to be more attentive to their duty since their abstention "was hurtful to manie subjects who looked for an out-redd and dispatch of thair businesse"; and certain churchmen were such offenders that they were enjoined to appear before the Commission in Edinburgh in the month of March "under pain of rebellion".[4]

The neglect of their duty by the sub-commissioners was such that in March 1633 the Commissioners set a final date for reports,

---

[1] Quoted by Connell, III, p. 57.
[2] *Ibid.*, I, pp. 241-242.
[3] *Ibid.*, III, p. 242.
[4] Reg. P.C. 1633-1635, p. 32.

"with certification to them that shall neglect this favour that not only shall the sub-commissioners be punished and fined but the heritors and titulars shall be convened before the Lords of the great Commission at Holyroodhouse, there to see their valuations led and deduced before them".[1]

Nevertheless the minute of the date appointed for this final reckoning (15th June 1633) declares: "The sub-commissioners, titulars and heritors, being callit nane of them compeirit".[2]

In the succeeding years up to 1637 it was the same story: "Many tithes were unvalued and kirks unprovided".[3] When the King consulted the Commission as to the reasons causing delay and non-success, the Commission's summary of the various hindrances were: "Undervaluing: Exemption of some churches by royal warrant: Inequality of provision in churches of like worth: Delays due to the non-attendance of Commissioners: The long contests between Titulars and heritors".[4]

It was perhaps not surprising when in July of the above year the King wrote suspending the Commission. It is alleged that it was Traquair, who was then Treasurer, who brought the process to an abrupt termination because of some private quarrel with certain Commissioners.[5] Baillie, writing to William Spang in January 1637, reports that Traquair was guiding Scottish affairs "with the most absolute sovereignty that any subject among us this forty years did manifest".[6]

The civil commotion which accompanied the Revolution in 1638 obstructed further activity, but the necessity of the reform was not lost sight of, and the work of valuing teinds was renewed by Parliament in 1641, and in 1644, 1647 and 1649. Even during the usurpation of Cromwell there was a Commission for "Surrenders and Teinds". With the Restoration the process continued. In 1707 the powers of Commission were vested in the Court of Session and in 1874 *The Conveyancing (Scotland) Act* amended the law, re-defining terms and adjusting the relationship of parties.

In retrospect it is clear that Charles in this venture undertook a vast work of difficult but necessary reform, and his statements

---

[1] Connell, I, p. 247.
[2] *Ibid.*, I, p. 247.
[3] *Ibid.*, I, p. 248.
[4] *Ibid.*, III, p. 113, Appendix LII.
[5] *Ibid.*, II, p. 249.
[6] Baillie's *Journal*, I, p. 6.

and actions prove that he was actuated in the main by generous and fair motives. Nor is it denied that the scheme which he evolved and promulgated was in principle wise and just. Although requiring and receiving modification in the light of later social progress its essential rightness, as Connell has observed, has been well established, and Charles is worthy of being remembered gratefully in its connection.[1]

It is at the same time a strange reflection that in his initial step of seeking to resume the kirk lands as a possession of the Crown he was defeated by the Nobles, assisted it seems by the legal skill and astuteness of the Advocate.

It is on record, as has been stated, that the Lords of Erections made formal submission in obedience to the royal decree, nevertheless it is clear that they retained their lands and their superiority. How they were secured in their possessions is briefly referred to by Sir John Scot who reports of Sir Thomas Hope, that "He advised a way to the Lords of Erections to get all the Kirk livings back again, contrary to an Act of Parliament whereby they were for ever annexed to the Crown, by causing them to take a wadset of the same, and acknowledge in the writs that his Majesty was indebted (to them) in great sums of money, whereas indeed he was never owing any. This will not fail to be quarrelled by succeeding ages and those who have authority, and apparently for that reason will be reduced."[2]

That a legal procedure might be devised which would leave the Lords in the enjoyment of their lands and rents will not be thought an impossible accomplishment to lawyers with the skill of Sir Thomas Hope, the Earl of Haddington and other experienced statesmen. An outcome of this was that the Gentry and lesser land-holders had to deal with the Nobles as their superiors.

Charles's work of reform has been praised elsewhere. Professor Hume Brown called the Revocation "The outstanding event of Charles's reign as far as it has yet gone";[3] but a sombre fact connected with its history was the unrest and hostility which it bred. This was expressed, as has been illustrated, in a spirit of dogged non-co-operation and in the strife which was engendered among various classes of owners. Balfour in the *Annals* says it

[1] Note No. 62, p. 226.
[2] *The Staggering State*, p. 142.
[3] Reg. P.C. 1633-1635, p. viii.

122

was "The groundstone of all the mischief that followed after, both to the King's government and family".[1] Row sounded portents of trouble which he says were fulfilled.[2] Professor Masson has also reflected on the social disturbance which ensued, saying that the Revocation was "The most perturbing in its social consequences of all Charles's Scottish Acts".[3]

This whole matter, of which the foregoing gives briefly the official aspect, was dealt with by Sir John Scot in the *Trew Relation* because of the active part which he took in pleading the case of the Scottish Gentry, and because he himself belonged to that class. In distinction to the legalism of the official account we have in the *Trew Relation* an eager personal narrative, and a revelation of the rivalry and dangers that attended on the pursuit of party interests, with the significant appearance within the State of a group or class of influential people, the Gentry, who sought to achieve freedom in the tenure of their landed possessions.

The author frankly gives us as a useful preamble the "Petition of the Nobility" which was addressed to the King in December 1626. The petition is printed in full and presents an able statement of the position as it then appeared to the Nobles.

It recounts how the King's progenitors, especially Queen Mary and James, rewarded "The blood, means, and travails of us and our predecessors by investments, erections, grants of lands, teinds, patronages, offices, jurisdictions, privileges and free tenures". They emphasise the validity of their titles and their ratification by Parliament supported by many decisions of the Lords of Session. They are now affrighted at the large extent of the proposed recall, and point out that those who have purchased lands and teinds from them are so numerous that the action "may bring irreparable ruin to an infinite number of families of all qualities in every region of the land".[4]

This appeal along with others led as reported to a revision of terms and to a new Commission.

Scot says that having got intelligence of the above petition, and "meeting accidentally at Edinburgh with other seven he there penned the petition of the Gentry anent their teinds possessed by

---

[1] The *Annals*, II, p. 128.
[2] *Hist. of the Kirk of Scot.*, I, p. 133.
[3] Reg. P.C. 1625-1627, p. 82.
[4] *Scot. Hist. Review*, XI, pp. 187-189.

noblemen and Titulars of Kirk lands".[1] At this point he gives the names of four of his associates: Sir James Learmonth of Balcomie, Sir James Lockhart of Lee, Sir John Preston of Airdrie, and Sir William Baillie of Lamington, and says that "these four behoved to meet privately in the Cowgate for fear of being apprehended by the councillors and noblemen".[2] Later he gives the names of the other three, who were, Sir William Douglas of Cavers, Robert Forbes of Reres and Sir William Scott of Elie, "who had £1000 sterling of yearly rent subject to the slavery tithes of the Lord of Balcarres".[3]

The author says that he drew up the petition, "But although required by the rest to go therewith to his Majesty, he, having lately returned from London, desired Sir James Learmonth of Balcomie to supply his place, and the paper being subscribed was sent up and got a favourable answer".[4]

That the Gentry at this time were being threatened and denied the right of free assembly is clear from a letter which Charles sent to the Council, on which the latter took action in May 1627. Charles in this letter instructed the Council to permit the Gentry to meet freely and discuss their business, and he strengthened their representation on the Commission. An Act of Council of 1st May 1627 gave this effect, permitting the lesser barons and small-holders, "to come here, with ane or twa commissioners for ilk sherifdom, and attend this business".[5]

It has been noted that in July 1637, the King suspended the Commission. Up to this point the Gentry had not apparently devised any plan in their own interest, and the Revolution ensuing in 1638 must have temporarily obstructed all such activity. But Parliament resumed the work of valuing teinds in 1641, and in the very next year Sir John Scot appeared before the Commission of Exchequer on behalf of certain vassals. Again in 1647 he represented the cause of the Gentry when a report concerning, "The Settling of the Superiorities of the vassals of Kirk lands" was being considered by the Estates. The petition which he then sponsored led the Estates to suspend all transactions in landed

[1] *Scot. Hist. Review*, XI, p. 190.
[2] *Ibid.*
[3] *Ibid.*, XII, p. 76.
[4] *Scot. Hist. Review*, XI, p. 76.
[5] Reg. P.C. 1625-1627, pp. 594-595. In Scotland "baron" meant the owner of a freehold estate whether titled or not.

property by the Superiors, and remitted "All superiorities already passed by the Exchequer and the Great Seal since 1633 to the Lords of Session to be considered and judged by them."[1]

It was following upon this in the same year (1647) that Charles directed a remarkable "Summons of Reduction" to certain Lords of Erections with a statement of reasons justifying his action.

"Charles,

"Our will is that you peremptorily summons, warn, and charge our right trusty cousins and councillors, Charles Earl of Dunfermline, James Earl of Abercorn, Robert Earl of Roxburgh and John Earl of Lauderdale, To compear and answer at the instance of our Advocate for our entress (interest), who by divers laws and acts of Parliaments, and namely by divers acts of annexation, have good and undoubted right to all whatsoever Kirk Lands, teinds, superiorities, patronages, regalities pertaining of old to whatsoever abbeys, priories and other benefices erected in temporal lordships within our kingdom."

The royal right to pursue the cause of reduction includes the claim that he could receive these lands whenever he liked and without any process of law. He charges that the titles called for have been drawn "from him and his noble Father's hands by importunity, solicitation and indirect dealing". He relates the wrongs done to "our vassals" by "the hands of rigorous and crude persons, superiors, their fellow-subjects, in an infinite number of processes; many more than they ever suffered under prelates".[2] It is obvious that the wrongs suffered by land-holders persisted and was provoking protest and opposition.

The culmination of Scotstarvit's efforts was reached in 1648 in the Commission given to him by the Barons and Gentlemen Feuars. The statement shows the wide extent of the movement for reform and indicates the injustice which it sought to amend.

"We, Barons, Gentlemen, and Heritors of Kirk Lands, undersubscribing for ourselves and in the name of the rest of the Gentry of this Kingdom, being informed that albeit we have divers Acts of Parliament in our favour, making and constituting us his Majesty's vassals, yet the Lords of Erections are not ceasing daily to importune his Majesty to grant them new gifts of our superiorities and gifts of bailieries whereby we are forced to acknowledge them our superiors, contrary to equity and reason.

[1] Acts Parl. Scot. VI, pp. 774-776.
[2] Scot. Hist. Review, XII, pp. 81-83, 174-183, 408-411.

We have, therefore, made and constituted (our agent) the Lord Scotstarvit, giving and granting unto him to repair to his Sacred Majesty and to present a petition to him, and to argue the justice thereof by all lawful means and reasons he can devise; and humbly to crave his Majesty's answer thereupon, and to follow and attend the same until the procuring and obtaining thereof. And to hold all and whatsoever the foresaid Commissioner lawfully does or shall do in our names in the premises."[1]

In the petition which follows it is stated that there are 900 petitioners out of the Sheriffdoms of Fife, Stirling, Lothian, Roxburgh, Kincardine, Linlithgow, Dumfries, Selkirk, Renfrew, Berwick, Forfar, Ayr and Perth. Sir John says of this:

"In the year 1648 I got warrant from 14 shires to complain to the Parliament in their names and to urge the Act to be made in the Gentry's favour, and they commissioned some principal barons to second me in that business, being 80 persons in all at a meeting in the Tailors Hall,[2] where Sir John was president."[3]

The Gentry's Petition is a historic document and contains expressions of a spirit of independence not unworthy to be compared with some more celebrated utterances of that kind.

"The Petition of the Gentry given in by Sir John Scot, anno 1649, to the Parliament.

"That whereas sundry noblemen and others, taking advantage of the distempers and many difficulties of these times, having power and credit about his Majesty, have, contrary to many standing laws of the Kingdom, procured from his Majesty new gifts, grants and concessions, whereby his Majesty's immediate relations to us his vassals and subjects, the profits and emoluments of his crown, and our interest, are much prejudiced, especially by the new gifts of Kirk Lands, regalities and bailieries, for remeid whereof we have already made our humble address to the last session of Parliament. And being after long dependance delayed and frustrated we find it necessary again to have recourse to this honourable Parliament, so that our desires and grievances may by your wisdom and justice be immediately taken into consideration and brought to a speedy determination.

"Therefore we humbly beg that we may be freed of the great thraldom which has been brought upon us by the foresaid practice,

---

[1] *Scot. Hist. Review*, XII, pp. 79-80.
[2] Note No. 63, p. 226.
[3] *Scot. Hist. Review*, XII, pp. 79-80.

and that his Majesty and his successors may continue to be our superiors in all time coming. And that all such gifts of the superiorities of Kirk Lands, regalities, and bailieries, with power to enter vassals contrary to law, may be recalled and rescinded, and that we may enjoy our freedoms and liberties as freely as at any time heretofore. And that such acts and laws may be made and constituted as will serve to secure us and our posterity in the enjoyment of these freedoms and liberties in all times hereafter. All which, being consonant to good conscience and equity and the laws and liberties of this kingdom, we are sure your Lordships will grant."[1, 2]

The Petition of the Gentry was met by an Act of Parliament, but that it did not give full satisfaction to the pursuers may be gathered from Sir John's apologetic note in which he admits that he had made a compromise in the settlement. "It may be surmised that in procuring the said Act I exceeded my commission"; and he confesses that he was influenced by the persuasions of "The gentlemen of the Forest whereof nine were of the name of Scot."[3]

His conclusion to the whole matter has more than a touch of sardonic humour.

"But", he dryly narrates, "as it is written of Christopher Columbus that for all the good service he did to the crown of Spain in finding the Indies he was rewarded with a prison and irons on his legs, so was I little better treated by the Gentry of Fife, who in their Committee of 1650 summoned me to compear at Cupar in the midst of winter, under pain of plunder, and to bring with me the account of the hundred dollars sent to me to defray the charges of the lawyers who were employed to plead the cause of Reduction. Which forced me to send to Edinburgh a messenger when the passages were closed by the English, and bring from thence my servant, John Scot, who had received the money from Sir James Lumsden,[4] which was super expended."[5]

It is clear that Sir John, although in adventurous spirit not perhaps altogether unequal to the great discoverer, did not bring

[1] *Scot. Hist. Review*, XII, pp. 80-81.
[2] Note No. 64, p. 226.
[3] *Scot. Hist. Review*, XII, p. 75. "Forest" is a reference to Liddesdale.
[4] Note No. 65, p. 226.
[5] *Scot. Hist. Review*, XII, p. 78.

to his clients (the Scottish lairds) a wealth equal to the gold of the Indies. Rather it seems as if he had lightened their treasure kists of dollars to little or no good purpose.

The Act of 1649 was in truth marked "with many limitations and restrictions", and as a measure of compromise was regarded by the Scottish Gentry with dissatisfaction and protest. Their champion, having treated with ironical humour the complaint and fault which the gentlemen of Fife in particular had visited upon him, now proceeds to reveal the rigours to which he was put in his negotiations on their behalf. He says,

"At the time of the Parliament of 1649 when the Act in favour of the Gentry was made, the power of the Lords was so great with his Majesty—contrary to his own interest—that he wrote both to the Parliament and the Session in their favour, telling them to permit the noblemen to keep the power and servitude they had over the Gentry, being made to believe by them (the Lords) that the Gentry would that way be kept under, and as their vassals and followers be moved to act as pleased his Majesty."

Referring to the modifications made by himself as concessions to others, he says: "The reason was to get them (various corporations and persons) on our side to over-balance the power and opposition of the Lords". And he assures his fellow-barons that "when the supreme authority shall urge their right in law they undoubtedly will triumph in the cause".[1] The fact is that the forces of power and privilege, which lay with the nobles, and the vacillations of the King during the disturbed 40's were too much for the less influential figures who pleaded the rights of vassals and tenants.

Reverting to the passage above where Scot says: "At the time of the Parliament of 1649", etc.; it is evident that there are some doubtful implications as to persons and dates. Sir John was writing in 1660 and knew that Charles was executed on 30th January 1649. He could not therefore mean that the King had written to the Parliament in that year, although a brief interval may have been free to him early in January. Nor can Charles II be intended: it was too early for his involvement, and in any case Scot would scarcely dare to reflect publicly on the new ruling monarch.

But it cannot be forgotten that the Director of Chancery, as he then was, and the highly-placed advocate of the claims of the

[1] *Scot. Hist. Review*, XII, p. 78.

Gentry, was in a position to know the facts as to any correspondence the King may have had with his leading nobles during the period of his restricted life in England, which ran from early in 1647 to January 1649. This it happens was also the period of extreme agitation on the part of the Gentry against the continuing exactions of the Lords, their landed superiors.

In the circumstances we judge that Sir John was indulging a looseness of expression in his use of the phrase "at the time of". He definitely asserts that the King "wrote". As he could scarcely write in 1649, it must reasonably have been in 1647, or most probably in 1648, when the Gentry prepared their Petition and took parliamentary action. Charles knew all and plotted accordingly.

Not to assume some such explanation is to attribute to the author of the "Trew Relation" a mis-statement about facts which were well known to him. In 1660 he was 75 years old.

It was an ingenuous trait of this seventeenth-century statesman's character that he must plainly avow his personal reasons, howsoever private in kind, for making protest or taking action in public affairs, and his life was so linked with national events that the large affairs usually found him with personal stakes to assert or lose.

Firstly he indicates that in his business as Director of Chancery he had an obligation to serve his Majesty whose interest he found to be affected by the loss of Crown rents and the superiorities of vassals. In addition he points out that the income of his own office was being adversely affected, since fees which before passed into the Chancery were being uplifted by the bailies of the Lords of Erections. There was also the prejudice done to him, "as a heritor of five portions of land, all holden of Kirkmen", which would force him to seek entry from them and become their vassal.

Finally he repeats his charge against Lauderdale.

"I was also exasperated at a sentence obtained against me at my Lord Lauderdale's instance as Prior of Haddington, declaring him superior of some of my land holden of that Abbey."[1] Later he found a way to "elude Lauderdale", but the injustice continued to rankle. For these reasons he originally acted in 1627 and began a campaign of long years and no very evident success in which his protesting zeal was fanned "by minding the deadly hatred which the Lords of Erections had ever borne against him".

[1] *Scot. Hist. Review*, XII, p. 79.

Chapter IX

THE PRIVY COUNCIL

The record of the Privy Council, along with the Domestic State Papers, is probably the richest depository of the materials of Scottish history open to us in the period under review and, as Sir John Scot was for twenty years a Councillor, it may assist our study if we report the part he played in that capacity. As a preliminary it may be helpful to look at the origin and development of that important body and recount some of its functions and activities.

The editors of the official Register, a work of exhaustive volume and detail, give valuable assistance in essays of much critical research and scholarship which are presented as Introductions to different periods. Dr Hill Burton, Historiographer Royal, undertakes a brief account of origins, and the later editors and Historiographers, Professors David Masson and Peter Hume Brown, add illuminating notes as the record proceeds.

Although early records embodied in the existing collection of Scottish Acts make it difficult to distinguish between Parliaments or meetings of Estates, and Councils or meetings of the King's selected advisers, it appears certain that the Secret Council was virtually a State executive formed of particular statesmen who were probably nominated by the Estates and approved by the King. In the active part of the reign of David II (1341-1371), when State business began to be definitely minuted, the scribes are found making no distinction in style between the proceedings of Parliament and proceedings of Council. In both the monarch issued the Act or Resolution as his own, and the presence of Parliament or Council was either announced in the title or referred to in the narrative of the enactment. But one instance is noted where the Council restored a donation which Parliament had revoked, warranting the conclusion that a Council could do what a Parliament could do, and undo what a Parliament had done: this, however, was an exceptional occurrence.[1]

[1] Reg. P.C. 1545-1569, p. vi.

With respect to the activities of the Council in these early times it is shown that amongst other things it was concerned with the management and disposal of Crown lands, which involved dealing with lapsed estates and the feudal rights of subjects, and implies the functions of a Court of Justice. Very early, and perhaps in response to the need for uniform rules where community life was being extended, it is found exercising a power of municipal and domestic regulation. Common standards in the matter of weights and measures, the fixing of trons for the weighing of wool, land traffic involving the transit of merchandise, harbour fees, law and order, control of the menace of sturdy beggars, oversight of hostels and inns, came within its purview.

These activities among common concerns were, as we know, multiplied as time proceeded until there was almost no public aspect or department of national life which was not reviewed and controlled by the Council.[1] By the time of the early seventeenth century the most casual occurrences in remote places or the feuds and private differences of individuals could be the subject of its consideration and judgment. In one instance we find the Councillors discussing the case of a child injured by a cart at Culross, and in another they examine Sir John Scot's man-servant who has been brought before them for telling a lie. In many instances the Council seemed to have taken over much of the tribal interest and paternalism once exercised locally by feudal chieftancy which had waned as centralised government strengthened its hold over the whole country.[2]

It was in David II's reign that the practice was established of appointing Committees, "elected by the Commons and the other Estates", to do the business of Parliament in particular spheres of administration and so save the time and expense of the members. The historian Tytler says it is in the meeting of the great National Council in the autumn of 1367 that we find the earliest appearance of these Committees which probably gave rise to the later insti-tution of the Lords of the Articles, a body which framed legislative proposals for parliament and was subject to abuse by the crown or the dominant faction.[3] It became in time an object of offence and was finally abolished in the Revolution of 1688-89.

[1] Note No. 66, p. 226.
[2] Note No. 67, p. 226.
[3] Tytler's *Hist. Scot.*, II, p. 97, pp. 177-178. Burton's *Hist. Scot.*, III, pp. 390-392.

To one Committee, composed of six members selected from the clergy, fourteen from the barons and six from the burgesses, was committed the decision of all judicial pleas and complaints. To another, the Privy Council, which included in its number the clergy and the barons alone, was entrusted, in its original intention, consideration of all matters of special and secret import touching the sovereign particularly, and also the kingdom, before these matters came to the knowledge of the Great Council or Parliament of the nation. In 1371 the marriage of King Robert II and Elizabeth Mure presented itself as a constitutional problem of the highest moment. We are told that it was discussed in the Secret Council and adjusted by the Estates.

A Council to assist in government is next heard of in 1398 when King Robert III, being infirm and unable to attend to State affairs, appointed the Duke of Rothesay to act as his lieutenant, with the consent of Parliament. The arrangements contained provision that when the Estates were not in session the Duke was to be guided in his office by the Council. There is interest in the statement of terms: he was to act "with the Council General, (the Estates) and in the absence of them with the Council of wise men and leal, of the which these are the names of eighteen members of Estates". The Estates bound the selected group, "to put their proceedings in acts, with the day and place and names of the councillors in that deed, so that the Council being with him shall answer for his deed, and be punished through the sicht (oversight) of the Council General, as the cause requires".[1]

Further statutory references are casual and of little consequence until 1489 when there is an entry of importance as follows: "Anent the article of the election and choosing of certain Lords, spiritual and temporal, to be and remain of our Sovereign Lord's Secret Council for the ostension and forth-putting of the King's authority in the administration of justice, it is thought expedient that there be chosen to be the King's Secret Council, two Bishops, one Abbot or a Prior, six Barons, with my Lord Chancellor, Master of Household, Chamberlain, Privy Seal, Secretary, Treasurer, Clerk of Register; and these are the names of the said prelates and barons". The names, with four Earls included, follow: "these to be of Council when they are present or when our Sovereign Lord sends for them".[2]

[1] Acts Parl. Scot., I, pp. 210-211. Tytler's *Hist.*, II, p. 395.
[2] *Ibid.*, II, p. 220.

It was further decreed that the Council chosen in Parliament should be sworn in before the King and the Three Estates, and should remain as constituted until the next meeting of the Estates, "the members to be responsible and accusable to the King and his Estates, of their councils". Furthermore it was provided that all Acts of royal authority, especially those affecting the property and revenues of the Crown, should pass in the first place through the Council and then be sanctioned by the proper seals. This, says Dr Hill Burton, "was part of a continuous struggle, often revealed by the Register, with the object that the Sovereign, who in courtesy and theory was lord of all, should never be permitted to do any act of moment otherwise than under the sanction of the Estates or of some deputed body representing them".[1] It is clear that up to this time the Council was never a body subservient to the royal will or independent of Parliament.

About this time, that is to say in the early sixteenth century, parliament was reaching the stage of full development in the co-operation of its three great Committees, namely the Lords of the Articles, the Lords Auditors for Complaints and the Privy Council, sometimes called the Kings' Council and sometimes the Lords of Council.

As has been indicated, the original concern of the latter was King's business, and this from early times included what we would now call Home affairs, namely the framing and enforcing of regulations governing the country's domestic life and internal economy.

But it is on record that it also administered justice by hearing and pronouncing on litigations, and some difficulty is presented in seeking to draw a line between its judicial powers and those of the Committee for Complaints. It is suggested that the judicial exertions of both bodies—bodies answerable to the Estates— were to some extent inspired by jealousy of the King's justiciars and sheriffs whom they saw monopolising, or feared would monopolise, the administration of justice throughout the realm, and would thus promote the undivided power of the Crown. Later history indicates that these were not groundless fears.

An event of considerable magnitude occurred in the year 1532, when James V, advised it is thought by Dunbar the Bishop of Glasgow, instituted the College of Justice—"ane College of cunning and wise men"—a new Court intended to methodise and

---

[1] Reg. P.C. 1545-1569, p. XI.

correct the administration of justice in civil causes.[1] The practical aim was to overcome the delay and partiality which marked procedure in the courts of the feudal barons and to take the means of oppression out of the hands of the aristocracy. But it is worth noting that under the provisions of Parliament the Chancellor could preside over the Court when he pleased, and the king on occasions of importance or difficulty might send members of his Privy Council (three or four) who could influence the deliberations and sway the vote.

From a reference by Tytler to George Buchanan it seems that in these and other directions Parliament encroached upon the authority of the College and was not withstood, for which Buchanan blames the judges.[2] Indeed there appears to be truth in Hill Burton's assertion that the traditional idea of a "Committee" marked the conception of the College and affected its constitution. He quotes a significant instance of a somewhat later date, where, when it was proposed to appeal from the Court of Session to Parliament the suggestion was resisted as an illogicality, since, it was contended, the Court of Session was no other than a branch of the High Court of Parliament appointed for the administration of justice.[3]

We may perhaps at this point illustrate the difference of principle and the difference in the moral temper which developed and was manifested in the judicial Court during the earlier part of the reign of James VI. In 1598, sixty-six years after the institution of the College, arose the celebrated case of the King against Robert Bruce, minister of the High Kirk, Edinburgh. The King through his Council had deprived Bruce of his stipend and the latter sued the King before the Session. James, well assured of his right, and avid of debate, came to the Court and pleaded his cause with all the insistence of royal authority. He received the following answer from the Lord President Seton, a Roman Catholic:

"My Liege, it is my part to speak first in this court of which your Highness has made me head. You are our King, we, your subjects, bound and ready to obey you from the heart, and with all devotion to serve you with our lives and substance. But this is a matter of law, in which we are sworn to do justice according

---

[1] Acts Parl. Scot., II, pp. 335-336. Tytler's *Hist.*, IV, p. 212.
[2] Tytler's *Hist.*, IV, p. 213.
[3] Burton's *Hist.*, III, p. 395.

to our conscience and the statutes of the realm. Your Majesty may, indeed, command us to the contrary, in which case I, and every honest man on this bench, will either vote according to his conscience, or resign and not vote at all."

Lord Newbattle then rose and observed, "That it had been spoken in the city to his Majesty's great slander, and theirs who were his judges, that they dared not do justice to all classes, but were compelled to vote as the King commanded; a foul imputation to which the lie that day should be given, for they would now deliver a unanimous opinion against the Crown".

James was unprepared for this conduct and he persisted in reasoning the case, but in spite of persuasions, taunts, and threats, the judges, with two dissentient votes, pronounced their decision in favour of the Edinburgh minister. A letter in the State-paper Office declares that the King flung out of Court "muttering revenge and raging marvellously".[1]

This offers proof that the objection voiced by Buchanan against the compliance of judges where Parliament interfered with their decisions did not now obtain, and the integrity of principle is the more evident inasmuch as it was maintained against the Crown and the personal representations of the King. It is ironical but not surprising that James should endeavour personally to prejudice the course of justice in opposition to the obvious directions of his early tutor in letters and kingcraft.

We may reasonably assume that this respect for the sanctity of law was now increasingly cherished and that the later effort of Charles to separate the personnel of Law Court and high State office was actuated by a fear that the holding of dual office might disturb the balance of judicial administration.

Reverting to our narrative we may point out that with the advent of the College of Justice (1532) the existing Court of the Lords Auditors for Complaints ended, but, as is amply evident in the record, the Privy Council continued to retain its old judicial powers. There is in fact a tone throughout its proceedings as if the Court of Session was bound by the strict doctrines of the law, while the Council could administer justice by its innate prerogative and was bound to interfere if the strict application of law should impose a wrong on the subject. Secure in its position as a supreme Executive it could recognise the possible difference between law

[1] Tytler's *Hist.*, VII, pp. 376-377. MS. letter, State-paper Office: Nicholson to Cecil, 16th March 1598-9.

and equity and act accordingly. Thus we find that the Council assumed a position of relative superiority to the Court of Session, sometimes directing to it affairs not suitable for its own adjustment, and sometimes seeming to charge it to undertake disputed cases of litigation.[1]

The office and power of the Council was particularly emphasised at Mary Stuart's deposition in 1567, the situation showing that when the Estates were not sitting the Council governed the country. It so happened that the crisis occurred in June—the Estates having risen in April—and the proclamation was made in the name of the "Nobility and Council". It contained these terms: "We command and charge the Lords of Session, commissaries and other ministers of justice, to sit, proceed, and minister justice according to the laws of this realm, notwithstanding any tumult or bruit which may arise in the meantime of this enterprise".[2]

In its office as a judicial court the Council possessed the special virtue that it could grant a rapid administration of justice unencumbered by technicalities. The technicalities came later when its decrees fell to be implemented by the inferior ministers of justice, such as sheriffs and other officers of the Crown. It was "the supreme rectifier, going by law where there is law, and making law where there is none".[3]

Its early and long concern with Crown lands and feudal rights has been mentioned, and to its credit this appears to have led in time to the establishment of a uniform and secure system of land tenure in Scotland. The *Jus Feudale* (1603) of Sir Thomas Craig gave an important and systematic exposition of the history and principles involved in these transactions. It may be noted that between 1570 and 1612 the amount of private law business transacted by the Council had so accumulated that in 1610 legal cases began to be separately recorded in a book of Decreta as distinct from one of Acta.[4]

In pausing to survey the period back to David II it is interesting to distinguish in the activities of government the two notes of Authority and Harmony. Authority undoubtedly lay in the hands of the Estates with the Sovereign at their head. There was no rule by royal prerogative. The earlier firm and proud announce-

[1] Reg. P.C. 1545-1569, pp. xii-xiii.
[2] *Ibid.*, 1545-1569, pp. xiii-xiv.
[3] *Ibid.*, 1569-1578, p. xxvi.
[4] *Ibid.*, 1610-1613. Introd. p. 1.

ment of *The Declaration of Arbroath* contains the governing principle and makes the necessary distinction clear:

"By the Providence of God, the right of succession, these laws and customs which we are resolved to defend even with our lives, and by our own just consent, Robert is our King.

"Yet Robert himself, should he turn aside from the task that he has begun, and yield Scotland or us to the English King and people, we should cast out as the enemy of us all, as subverter of our rights and of his own, and should choose another King to defend our freedom."[1]

The persistence of this view leapt into sight when John Knox, having been asked by Mary Stuart if subjects having power might resist their princes, replied "If princes exceed their bounds, Madam, they may be resisted and even deposed". And the sturdy individualism of the Scot expressed itself when he was challenged by the Queen as to what his standing in the Commonwealth was which gave him the right to be her critic: the answer was—"A subject born within the same".[2]

The inner struggle between the Crown and the nation's representatives was, indeed, inevitable and continuous, but while the sovereign in courtesy and theory was lord of all, he was not permitted to do any act of moment otherwise than under the sanction of the Estates or of some deputed body responsible to them.

The Estates were supreme, and a long-continued harmony was effected by the willingness of the Sovereign on the one hand to recognise this fact, and the skill of the Executive on the other in giving to the agreed acts and resolutions the form and expression of the Royal will. Dr Hill Burton asserts that among the Stewarts there was an unbroken harmony in the relations of the Crown and the Estates which extended to the Privy Council, and that, "Until the deposition of Queen Mary and the raising of her son to the throne, there was nothing in the government of Scotland to represent royal prerogative on the one hand, with a constitutional opposition for the protection of popular or aristocratic privileges, on the other".[3]

The harmony of government to which we have referred was most apparent perhaps in the case of Mary where the requisite

[1] Tytler's *Hist.*, I, pp. 333-334.
[2] Knox's *Hist.*, II, p. 277 *et seq.* Calderwood's *Hist.*, II, p. 220.
[3] Reg. P.C. 1545-1569, p. xxxiv.

137

pressure on the monarch was concealed in carefully phrased resolutions excusing her conduct: and especially so in respect of the Reformation, which, in spite of the Queen's secret convictions, received her tacit consent.[1] It was this sovereignty of the national will, long maintained by statecraft in the agreed balance of monarch and state, which was later challenged by James and his successors and proved invincible to their doctrines of absolute kingship and their political intrigues and repeated assaults.

In a study of the Register it may be noted that the Third Volume opens with the year 1578 and the editorship is taken over by Professor David Masson, the Historiographer Royal, who handles the work until it reaches the year 1627, and therefore covers the whole period of the active rule of James VI. The notes show that when the Council was reconstituted in 1579 it had 27 members, but there were new admissions from time to time and extreme frequency of meetings. George Buchanan was a member and the young King began occasionally to take his seat. About three years later— in the sixteenth year of his age—James began to assert himself. By 1587 he had come of age, and in Parliament of that year an Act was passed reconstituting the Council. Sixteen members were appointed, "who were to be present when they chose or were sent for".[2]

A cautionary note now appears and was often justified in succeeding years: it is the note of protest at the frequent poor attendance of Councillors. Over this fault the King fell easily into an attitude of scolding rebuke. Here we have a suggestion of the malaise of a lessened sense of responsibility due perhaps to over-representation, or to a weakening in the conviction of national community, or the growing habit of government by committee, it being noticeable that this was now brought into the body of the Council itself. For in a revision of practice which marked the above act of reconstitution it was agreed that in civil actions the Council as a whole should not sit, all not being competent, and that the King should take counsel with those "who are most skilful in such affairs".[3]

With no great loss of time James now assumed supremacy and began to take arbitrary action or to send letters of command.

[1] The Proclamation, p. xxxvi, p. lxxvi, pp. 266-267.
[2] Reg. P.C. 1578-1585, p. 458.
[3] Ibid., 1585-1592, p. 160. Allowance must be made for the difficulty of travel.

When protests to this were made, he, according to the device so often revealed in his dealing with the Kirk and its leaders, yielded, only to insist later with greater force as the doctrine of royal power grew upon him.

The strugglings of protest are for some time evident. There is a Register note of December 1586 where a writing granted by the King without advice of the Council is declared null.[1] Notice is taken in 1587 that the King has granted letters "outwith the Council", and there is a resolution requiring his concurrence with whatsoever they conclude, on the ground that their conclusions have the force of law, "forasmeikle as the King's Majesty has committit the handling and ordering of the public affairs of his realm and estate to a certain number of persons nominated and chosen by his Highness to be his Privy Council and Officers of State".[2] But we may say that the expression, "nominated and chosen by his Highness", carries too fully an admission of dependence on the royal will, and permits the inference that the authority which chooses to delegate its power on one matter may logically withhold it on another, and may overrule the decisions of its temporary agents. The Stewart theory of monarchy was in fact in process of formulation and was provoking its earliest battles.[3]

On the occasion quoted James promised on the word of a Prince to support the decrees of the Council, but as the days passed he showed by his attendance that he intended to be his own premier. His increasing orders bore undoubted traces of his mood of sovereignty and self-assertion. He made a characteristic utterance in 1595 after the death of the Lord Chancellor Maitland of Thirlestane, when, having been spoken to about filling the vacancy, he replied that "he was resolved no more to use great men as his Chancellors but only such as he could correct and were hangable".[4] Maitland, an "Octavian", had held the King in check. James Melville says "He held the King upon twa grounds sure, nather to cast out with the Kirk nor with England".[5]

Professor Masson in his Introduction to the Register when it comes to the years 1604-1607 says: "We have noted in former volumes the gradual success of James in establishing in Scotland

[1] Reg. P.C. 1585-1592, p. 119, p. 224.
[2] *Ibid.*, p. 519.
[3] Note No. 68, p. 226.
[4] Reg. P.C. 1592-1599, pp. xxv-xxvi.
[5] Melville's *Diary*, Wodrow Soc., p. 271.

against all the opposition of the Scottish clergy those high notions of Kingship which he had held from his earliest manhood. At no previous time was he so much master of his native kingdom as in the last two or three years before his removal to England".[1]

The King left Edinburgh for London on 5th April 1603, to begin his long residence in the south. The future course of affairs showed that he exercised his mastery in absence as definitely as he did when present, and this despite the abortive effort at a Union of Kingdoms when, by his "royal prerogative", he discharged and discontinued the several names of England and Scotland in his title, and assumed "as his just and lawful style the title of King of Great Britain, France and Ireland, Defender of the Faith".

How he ruled the Scottish Council and over-ruled its affairs may be gathered from the steps he took early in 1610. In January of that year, writing from the Court at Royston, he re-cast the Council, reducing it from a large and loose body of about ninety persons to a compact body of thirty-five, all of whom he himself expressly nominated, decreeing "that the said number sall not be exceedit at anie tyme heerafter". He appointed seven a quorum and with characteristic fastidiousness prescribed rules for meeting and order:

"We have appointed the tymes of meeting for treatting of maters of estate and laying down of overtures for the good government of the commounwealth, and for keeping of peace and obedience in the countrie, to be weeklie upoun Tuisday afternoone, and for hearing of actiouns and calling of complaints competent to that judicatorie, weeklie upoun Thuirsday afternoone. And thair conveening ordinarlie to be at Edinburgh, or anie other place where thay sall thinke meete."[2]

Any Councillor absent for four days together from ordinary sittings was to be deprived of office, and there were other penalties calculated to correct the types of irregularity which had marked the past. His sense of religious decorum dictated the rigid necessity that Councillors should regularly communicate: "Whosoever sall not within sax moneths produce a testificat that he hes communicat and is willing to give all other due satisfactioun to the Churche, in that case sall *ipso facto* lose his place, as also if at least once everie yeere he do not communicat". Finally he asks for a regular

[1] Reg. P.C. 1604-1607, p. xxiv.
[2] *Ibid.*, pp. 815-816.

record of how the Councillors voted individually on important matters, "so that we may discern the goattis from the trew sheep".[1]

His domination of Scotland from the south was assured and persistent. In a speech to the English Parliament on 31st March 1607, having occasion to contrast the facility with which he continued to rule Scotland with the difficulties he experienced in England, he had used these astonishing words: "This I must say for Scotland, and may truly vaunt it; here I sit and govern it with my pen. And by a Clerk of the Council I govern Scotland now, which others could not do with the sword".[2]

Professor Masson remarks that when he died in 1625 he had for the last twenty-two years governed Scotland "through the post". The authority and harmony to which we referred was still operating but the authority had a new seat and the harmony was differently keyed. The latter was not now achieved by the politic submission of the monarch to the will of the Estates representing the nation, but by the uneasy compliance of the nation's leaders with the autocracy of the King. The old self-contained nationalism with its integrity of conviction and its single-sightedness was possibly weakening under the conception of a broader political unity, and also under the speculations and dialectic of a subtle theoriser who was also a powerful and patronising sovereign.

When we pass to the reign of Charles I we find the Council struggling against the same kingly lordship. Charles was young and was more inflexible than his father. The old King's autocracy was shrewdly tempered by his native sense: he knew the Scottish nobles intimately and knew how far he could go. This was precisely what his son did not know, and his ignorance of it was a deadly defect which accompanied him throughout his reign.

The Council was reconstituted early in 1626, forty-seven members being nominated. Three Englishmen were added to it, one being the Earl of Pembroke, friend of Shakespeare, dead ten years earlier; and it was no accident that Archbishop Spottiswoode of St Andrews was named first in the Commission, although the editor tells us that the Chancellor always took precedency in actual fact.

With reference to the King's invidious action in naming the Archbishop first in the new Commission, we may offer two notes

[1] Reg. P.C. 1604-1607, p. 97.
[2] *Ibid.*, p. xxv.

of lively comment both from the *Annals*. They relate to Chancellor Hay and prove that even Charles could not always effect his imperious will. The first reports that in a letter to the Council of 12th July 1626, the King,

"Commandes that the Archbishope of St Andrewes, Primat and Metropolitane of Scotland, may have place of precedency befor the Lord Chanceler, and so consequently befor all others; wich notwithstanding, the Lord Chanceler Hay, a gallant stout man, wold never condescend to, nor ever suffer him to have place of him, doe quhat he could, all the dayes of his lyfetyme."[1]

The other is in the nature of a personal memory of the annalist, and a very amusing one, of the date of the Coronation in June 1633. It may well explain some of the stiffness of the King's manner on that occasion. He says: "I remember that King Charles sent me to the Lord Chancellor in the morning on the day of his coronation to show him that it was his pleasure—bot onlie for that day—that he wold cede and give way to the Archbishop. But he returned by me to his Majestie a very bruske answer, which was: That he was readie in all humility to lay his office down at his Majesteis feet; but since it was his royal will that he should enjoy it with the known privileges of the same, never a stoled priest in Scotland should sett a foot before him so long as his blood was hot."

"When I related this answer to the King he said: 'Weel, Lyone, let's goe to businesse. I will not medle farther with that cankered goatish old man, at whose hand there is nothing to be gained but soure words' ".[2, 3]

The reconstitution to which we have referred was inevitable at the opening of a new reign, and there is a suggestion that the Lords hoped for a relaxation of autocratic control and even dared to challenge it, not yet having assessed the young King's temper. Indeed one almost sees the train being laid for the future policy and conduct of the leaders who had to do with Charles, for since he suffered no one to compel his judgment how could statesmen attain their ends save by counsels of craft and flattery.

---

[1] The *Annals*, II, p. 141. Quoted by Balfour, not entered in the Register. Discussed in a footnote by Professor Masson, Reg. P.C. 1625-1627, pp. 344-345.

[2] *Ibid.*, p. 141. S. R. Gardiner reads *goutish* for *goatish*. *The Personal Government of Charles I*, p. 373.

[3] Note No. 69, p. 226.

In his Introduction to the period covering January 1629 to July 1630, Professor P. Hume Brown, who assumed the editorship of the Register after Professor Masson, says that "not even during the last days of James VI did the Council more completely dominate the life of the nation than in the opening years of the reign of his son": but he adds that its deliberations and doings were inspired and directed, as formerly by James, so now by the personal mandate of Charles. No Parliament met and there was no General Assembly: "Bishops, judges, Privy Councillors, and high officers of State all retained their positions on the terms of unconditional submission to the royal authority".[1]

In the immediately succeeding years—during which Charles was substituting personal for parliamentary government in England, with Laud dominating ecclesiastical affairs—another unexpected reconstruction of the Council took place: this was done by mandate of the King in March 1630.

To the question as to why this was done there is no answer, save that the young monarch wished to remind his councillors that they held their office solely at his pleasure and on condition of deferring to his will: a principle that has already been illustrated by the account given of the debates at Whitehall in 1625.

During the royal visit for the Coronation in 1633 nine Englishmen—including Laud—were added, and Archbishop Spottiswoode was made Lord Chancellor in place of Sir George Hay, Earl of Kinnoull. This was the first time since the Reformation that an ecclesiastic held that high office. The trend and weight of Charles's church policy was also made evident by the addition of two more Scottish bishops.[2]

The period April 1635, to December 1637, which occupies Volume III in the Second Series of the Register, marked what was possibly the most inglorious and unhappy epoch in the Council's history. Those attending (amongst others Sir John Scot was uniformly absent) were willing agents of the King's policy, and through the Council he issued those edicts regarding the Scottish Church which occasioned the great revolt and were finally so disastrous both to King and country.

The Parliament of 1633 saw the passing of certain offensive Acts which had been prepared by the Lords of the Articles. One

---

[1] Reg. P.C. 1629-1639. Introduction, Professor P. Hume Brown, p. i.
[2] *Bishop Guthrie's Memoirs.* Crawfurd, 1748, p. 16. Burton's *Hist.*, VII, p. 141.

of these renewed a statute of James VI declaring the King to be supreme over all causes and persons, and gave him power to prescribe the apparel of churchmen. A second ratified all previous Acts establishing Episcopacy in Scotland.[1] These aroused keen opposition, the chief spokesmen of protest being John, Earl of Rothes, and John Elphinstone, Lord Balmerino. It was in this connection in the following year that the latter was charged with a treasonable act, when Hope pressed for a conviction, and "the prelates raged like a tempestuous sea".[2]

The sequence in the action was that in 1635 Charles sent down the Book of Canons to displace the Book of Discipline. In May 1637 the Service Book, somewhat misleadingly known as "Laud's Liturgy", was introduced in place of Knox's Book of Common Order. The riot in St Giles occurred two months later.[3] By September petitions against Charles's innovations began to pour in to the Council. In that body, which now included ten Bishops,[4] a formal and submissive attitude was adopted. But when popular opposition became widespread and violent, prudence suggested modifications of the official policy, and at a session with a more varied attendance than usual the Councillors having reasoned upon "the causes of the present combustion within the countrie", declared "in one voice", that "the imposition of the Service Book, Book of Canons, and the High Commission[5], are the causes".[6]

Archbishop Spottiswoode the Chancellor was absent when these things were debated and decided, but following upon the meeting he declared his advice by letter, which was, "To lay aside the Service Booke and not to press the subjects with anie more, rather than to bring it in with such trouble of church and kingdom, as we see".[7]

It was now evident that a party within the Council was venturing to assert itself and was assuming a more independent attitude, for when Hamilton of Orbiston was sent to communicate this finding to Charles, amongst his instructions was one declaring that the afore-mentioned impositions "were contrary to, or without

---

[1] The *Annals*, II, p. 216.
[2] *Ibid.*, p. 219.
[3] Reg. P.C. 1635-1637, p. 483.
[4] *Ibid.*, pp. vi-vii.
[5] Note No. 70, p. 226.
[6] Reg. P.C. 1638-1643, p. 7, pp. 8-9.
[7] *Ibid.*, p. viii.

warrant of, the laws of the kingdom".[1]   The report when conveyed caused royal astonishment, and the accompanying advice provoked the King's extreme resentment.   To give effect would, he said, "hazard the overthrow of that church government which our deare father of blessed memorie hath established".   His unfortunate response was to appoint as Royal Commissioner in Scotland the Marquis of Hamilton, whose policy was declared in a Proclamation of 4th July 1638.[2]

Amid the threats and concessions which ensued the Council bowed as hitherto towards the official policy and became a passive instrument by which the various declarations were made.   On the 22nd September 1638, it was instructed to secure the people's subscription to the King's Confession in place of the National Covenant, a demand attached as a fatal condition to all the accompanying concessions.   Charles's attitude to the National Covenant was that it infringed his prerogative: it left him, he said, "with no more power in Scotland than the Duke of Venice".[3]

On the day on which the above autocratic and repressive direction was received the thirty members of Council present signed it and appointed Commissioners to every part of the kingdom with power to exact subscription from all the lieges. We have already described the refusal registered by leading personalities, amongst them Lord Scotstarvit and other Senators, and the special steps taken by Scotstarvit to elucidate and secure the grounds of refusal.

As is well-known at this stage the General Assembly was called, as a conciliatory measure, to meet in Glasgow in November, with a Parliament to follow in Edinburgh in May of the ensuing year. This shift, designed as a means of subjection, with the Assembly cowed into obedience, was defeated by the official failure to understand the strength of the opposition now inflamed by the extreme unwisdom of the latest decree.

The Assembly met and with a leadership prompted to extreme action by its Presbyterian convictions, by popular support, and by the inept extravagance of the King, it demolished in a four week's sitting the whole ecclesiastical edifice erected by Charles and his father.   The Council looked on in helpless dismay, and its declaration on 18th September that the Assembly's acts were

---

[1] Reg. P.C. 1638-1643, p. ix, pp. 9-12.
[2] *Ibid.*, p. x.
[3] *Ibid.*, p. xii, pp. 64-77.

null and void was its last, and too late, effort in responsible government and pronouncement.[1]

The Revolution ensued, with war, the death of Charles, and the Cromwellian Occupation. After the Restoration of Charles II Scotland was treated as a satrapy. Only minor matters were left to the direction of the Councillors, who met at Holyrood House. In 1669 Lauderdale was able to boast with truth in Scotland: "The King is now master here in all causes and over all persons". And so it remained until the end of the Stewart rule in 1688.

[1] Reg. P.C. 1638-1643, pp. 95-102.

Chapter X

THE PRIVY COUNCILLOR

There are several references to Sir John Scot in the Register which are of earlier date than his admission to office. In two instances he is associated with his brother-in-law, William Drummond, in the diverse affairs of love and finance. Drummond entered on his lairdship in 1610, and Scot married the poet's eldest sister probably in 1608. As he had become, according to Nisbet, a member of the Scottish Bar in 1606 it is likely that he would be willing, if not indeed eager, to place his legal knowledge and budding skill at the disposal of his relative, should occasion arise. Occasion apparently did arise in 1610 when Drummond entered on a law-suit with his mother, Susannah Fowler, over the disposition of the family estate.[1]

It is probable that the lawyer took a part in this dispute, for, as if in its connection, we find the lady denying posesssion of an assignation of marriage made out by Mr John Scot between Sir John Drummond—the poet's father—and the Laird of Maners, with respect to a ward of the latter. The law-suit between mother and son was happily settled in July 1611.[2]

If his action in the foregoing was in the nature of a probability, there is no doubt as to the professional part he took in a further litigation about eighteen months later when he made, possibly, his first appearance as a pleader before the Council. His name, linked with his office, had of course already come before its notice, for in March 1611 the resignation to him of the Directorship of Chancery by William Scott of Elie is minuted in the record;[3] and in August 1612, the Council ordered his brother, in his absence, to see that precepts of Chancery for the Parliament were expedited with all diligence.[4] But the matter of the litigation was definitely a case where he would have occasion to exercise the gifts which

---

[1] Reg. P.C. 1610-1613, p. 686. Susannah Fowler was sister to William Fowler, the courtier poet.

[2] *Ibid.*, pp. 704-705.

[3] *Ibid.*, p. 153.

[4] *Ibid.*, p. 452.

undoubtedly brought him into prominence and favoured his later promotion to high office of legal and administrative importance.

The case, dated 14th January 1613, was one of debt, where William Drummond complained against Edward McMath, merchant, burgess of Edinburgh, and his cautioner, Sir James Crichton of Ruthven. A horning[1] had been issued against them on 25th November for not paying the complainer £10,800 as principal, and £2,000 of liquidate expenses, and it had not been met, nor had they on that occasion appeared. The procurator for the pursuer was Mr John Scot, and permission was given to issue letters of caption. We hear nothing further of the case, and presumably the lawyer succeeded in reaching a settlement satisfactory to his client.[2]

Two years later there is a resolution where Mr John Scot of Scotstarvit and Mr William Drummond of Hawthornden receive licence "to eat flesh at all times when they shall think expedient during this forbidden time of Lent, from 21st day of February last bypast to the feast of Pasche next-to-come".[3] Professor Masson suggests with some plausibility that the brothers-in-law intended a visit to Fife to Scot's house at Tarvit, or more likely at Thirdpart, where they might have freedom for festivities. This he thinks would suit Drummond's purpose of courtship with Mary Cunningham of Barns, an adjoining estate. There can be no question that the wooing was pursued, and how ecstatic it was may be judged from the poems which followed when Drummond's lover died in the same year, and after marriage had been arranged.[4]

On 25th August 1619, Scot had leave to travel "To Flanders and other foreign parts for one year,"[5] and on the same date it is recorded that Prince Charles appointed him his Director of Chancery: "He always behaving himself dutifully and respectively to the Heich Chancellour in all things concerning his place and charge"[6]. This in all likelihood was the first occasion on which the name of Sir John Scot came officially before the notice of the future King, who was then a youth of eighteen years.

[1] Note No. 71, p. 226.
[2] Reg. P.C. 1610-1613, p. 153.
[3] *Ibid.*, 1613-1616, p. xc.
[4] In 1616 (the year of Shakespeare's death) appeared *Poems: Amorous, Funerall, Divine, Pastorall*, the story of Drummond's love.
[5] Reg. P.C. 1619-1622, p. 78.
[6] *Ibid.*, p. 138.

He was made a Privy Councillor on 22nd March 1622. The King's letter of authorisation dated 14th March, reads: "Being credibly informed of the sufficiencie of our beloved Sir John Scot of Scotstarvit, and of his earnest affection to our service, we",[1] etc. The minute of admission is to the following effect: "The Secreit Council by warrant and writ of his Majesty, received and admitted Sir John Scot to be ane of the ordinary number of his Majesty's Privy Council, and to enjoy all freedoms, dignities, privileges and immunities", etc. "Likewyse, the said Sir John being personally present, he with all due reverence upon his knees, his hand lyand upon the holy evangel, made and gave his solemne oath of allegiance, and the oath of a Privy Councillour." His name appears on a sederunt for the first time on 1st April 1622. He was thirty-seven years old.[2]

The expression "ordinary" member in the above minute attracts attention, and it was not long until Sir John made an appeal and endeavoured with shrewd purpose to alter that classification. This, it would appear, raised at this juncture the whole important question of the order of honour in the Council, for we find the somewhat blunt rejection of his request set at the end of a statement which declares afresh the Council's rule of precedence. The date was 18th February 1623, less than a year after his admission.

"The Lordis of Secreit Councell, according to the Actes and Ordinances formerlie made anent the ordour to be keeped in his Majesteis Counsell Hous, and conforme to ane missive letter written by his Majestie to Sir George Hay of Kinfauns, knight, Lord High Chancellour of this kingdome, ordains nane be suffered to remaine in the Counsell Hous during sittings but onlie the Clerk, and that the macers sall attend thair office outwith the Counsell Hous doore. And that the Lordis tak thair places according to thair rankis, to witt:

"The Lord Chancellour and Theasurer to have the first places, and nixt unto thame the two Archbishops, and after thame the Earles and Viscountis according to thair rankes, and after thame suche of the Bishops as are on the Counsell, and then the Lordis according to thair rankes; and immediatelie after thame the officers of Estate, to witt: the Lord Privie Seale, Secretar, Clerk Register, Advocat, Justice Clerk, and Theasurer Depute: and nixt to the Officers of Estate suche of the Sessioun as are upon the

[1] Reg. P.C. 1619-1622, p. 702.
[2] Ibid., p. 702.

Counsell, according to thair admissiouns; and then the barons and gentlemen being of the Counsell to have thair places according to thair admissiouns.[1]

"Anent the motioun made by Sir Johne Scot, that he might be ranked amongst the Officers of Estate as Directour of Chancellourie, the Lordis find that he has not a place in Counsell as Directour of Chancellourie, and therefore ordaines him to tak his place amongst the barons."[2]

This has been called a rebuff, and the ambitious knight certainly risked something in the nature of a rebuff in putting forward his motion, but the rejection, like the application, rested entirely on the status of the Chancery Directorship which required definition, and precedent Acts were apparently quoted to show that this office was not ranked as one of State. There is not the slightest doubt that Sir John wished it to be classified as such. His own observation about the office, made at the end of *The Staggering State* with reference to his later dismissal, was to this effect: "Albeit in all times bypast it has been an Office of State and at his Majesty's disposal, yet partly by malice but chiefly by ignorance, it was at the English coming to Scotland in 1650 holden and reputed an office subservient to the College of Justice".[3]

In the introduction to an authoritative version of the above work published by Walter Ruddiman in 1754, a short account of the Offices of State is given, in which the editor says that in the Act 31, Parliament II, James VI, the following were enumerated as Crown Offices: The Treasurer, Secretary, Collector, Justice General, Justice Clerk, Advocate, Master of Requests, Clerk of Register, Director of the Chancery and Director of the Rolls. But he adds that in 1617, when Parliament met, the King in Privy Council declared "That in that and all other Parliaments eight only should sit as Officers of State, and these he ranked as follows: Treasurer, Privy Seal, Secretary, Clerk Register, Advocate, Justice Clerk, Treasurer Depute, Master of Requests": from which it will be seen that, amongst others, the Director of Chancery is excluded.[4] It was probably to the declaration of James in 1617 that the Lords referred in their reply.

---

[1] Note No. 72, p. 227.
[2] Reg. P.C. 1622-1625, pp. 175-176.
[3] *The Staggering State* (1754), p. 160.
[4] Acts of Parl., Vol. IV, 1593-1625, pp. 526-527. At the time the point at issue was the voting right of Officers of State in Parliament.

Sir John Scot's place in the Council was, therefore, despite the earlier usage to which he obviously refers in the note quoted, and on which he no doubt founded his plea, simply according to his rank as a baron. It is likely that this effort marked an aspiration after honour rather than power. Greater power than he very soon wielded could have come only through admission to that select few who were entrusted with consideration of the King's most weighty and intimate affairs.

This is amply revealed in the record. His lower classification did not affect his activity in the Council where in keeping with his force of character, his professional ability, and his readiness in debate, he was one of the most alert and valuable of members, and for ten years undertook a vast amount of executive responsibility and labour: we are here referring to ten years of exceptional service: he was a Lord of Council for almost twenty years.

Nevertheless it remains clear that he retained a jealous estimate of his office and was pertinacious in asserting his rights. This was evident a few years later on the occasion of the funeral of James VI in 1625, when he found himself ranking in the procession after Sir George Elphinstone, the Justice Clerk. On that occasion being in a "vehement fume" he forthwith "took instruments and protested before the Council that it should not prejudge him in the right and privilege of his place".[1] This was reported by Gilbert Primrose to his father as an interesting piece of gossip. Somewhat curiously the note presented the scrupulous Sir John in a rather unfavourable light, although at the same time it praised Spottiswoode, the Bishop of St Andrews, who, as the Scottish Primate, claimed equality with the Bishop of Canterbury, and was granted it. But being refused the right of going in the attire used in Scotland he absented himself from the funeral. "He would never", he said, "do that scandal to the Church of Scotland as to assume English apparel and forego his own".[2, 3]

Rivalry in office was by no means rare and there was an apposite case in 1628 when Sir Thomas Hope, the Advocate, engaged in a dispute with the Justice Clerk on the same question of precedence. By a coincidence, probably accounted for by the temper of the Justice Clerk, this was the same Sir George Elphinstone with whom Sir John had a brush in 1625. How keen and personal the

[1] Reg. P.C. 1625-1627, p. xiii, p. 650.
[2] *Ibid.*, p. 650.
[3] Note No. 73, p. 227.

difference was may be judged by the appointment of the President (Menteith), the Secretary (Sir William Alexander), the Clerk of Register (Sir John Hamilton, Haddington's brother), and Sir John Scot, whose commission was, "to travail for mediating and agreement between them."[1] Even within this small and ruling group we see how agitated were the currents of self-interest and antagonism, and already Hope had squabbled about precedency with Sir James Galloway, the Master of Requests.[2]

For the first ten years of his councillorship Scotstarvit was most regular in attendance and incessantly busy in Council affairs. The later withdrawal of his interest, which when it happened was incisive and sustained, corresponded with the troubles of 1632, and with the reconstruction of the Council in 1633 when Archbishop Spottiswood was appointed Chancellor. A fair estimate of his diligence is provided by figures of attendance in the periods in which the Register is reviewed.

In the Introduction to the period extending from 1622 to 1625 the editor comments on the frequency of his presence, saying that he appeared at considerably more than half of all the sessions.[3]

From March 1625 to June 1627 he was present 81 times and signed Acts of Council 5 times. The Advocate was then Sir William Oliphant who made 66 attendances and signed Acts of Council and missives 51 times. From July 1627 to December 1628 Sir John Scot was present 83 times and signed Acts and missives 66 times. The height of his interest was reached in the period January 1629 to July 1630. The following is a comparative statement of leading attendances. The Advocate Hope's record was 117 attendances and he signed Acts 69 times. The Clerk of Register was present on 105 occasions and signed Acts 65 times. Sir John Scot had 103 attendances and 61 signatures. Attendances indicate days and there were usually two sessions.

A decline of activity is now in evidence. In the period August 1630 to December 1632 the Advocate was present 148 times and supplied 63 signatures. The Clerk of Register was second with 94 attendances and 24 signatures. Sir John was again third with 76 attendances and 24 signatures. But in the following period from January 1633 to February 1635 he was significantly absent from all sessions. The Advocate was present on 154 occasions, and the

[1] Reg. P.C. 1627-1628, pp. 490-491.
[2] *The Lord Advocates of Scotland*, Omond, Vol. I, p. 107.
[3] Reg. P.C. 1622-1625, p. xi.

new Clerk of Register, Sir John Hay (one of the so-called Incendiaries) was much in evidence, being present on 137 occasions. On his last attendance which was on 16th August 1632, there was a small sederunt made up of the Treasurer, Privy Seal, Winton, Traquair, Sir Archibald Acheson, Sir John Scot and Sir James Baillie.

We cannot avoid the conclusion that Scotstarvit's withdrawal from participation in the affairs of the Council was, at least to begin with, associated with the crisis in the history of Menteith. His last regular appearance was in August 1632, and he must in September have sent his *Reasons* to the King by the hand of Robin Dalzell, for it was on 2nd October that Charles despatched his urgent demand for proof of the allegations made. At the end of December Scot rode to London. Charles was dealing with the charges in the early months of 1633, and after a lull Menteith was finally set down in November of that year.

Remembering how, and by whom, the Earl was supported, and Sir John's active dis-service—in the changing of the Session and the Revocation—to the powerful nobles who formed the inner core of the Council, we can see that his presence in the Chamber would be practically impossible, and his appearance in the streets during that winter may not have been without danger. The facts which followed and dictated his continuing absence were no doubt political and religious, and linked with Charles's policy and the changing character of the Council personnel. He continued to be a Councillor until 1641 but does not appear again until 11 April 1639 when the Council was making almost its last effort to bring Charles to reason. On this occasion it was decided to visit the King in a body and "deprecate his wrath". We find Sir John scrupling to attend: his earlier personal encounters with Charles may have wakened a fear of unpleasant contrasts, but his objection was adroitly overcome, as the following minute shows:

"Edinburgh, 11th April 1639.

"Forasmeikle as the Lords of Privie Council and Session have resolved to take journey towards his Majesty anent the calamitous estate of this Kirk and Kingdom, and whereas Sir John Scot of Scotstarvit, one of the said Lords of Session, has represented that, in respect of his public place as Director of the Chancellary, he is unwilling to be absent from his charge in attending his Majesty's service therein, without special warrant from the said Lords, therefore the Lords declare that his absence from the charge on the occasion aforesaid shall no ways be prejudicial to him; especially seeing the time of his absence is to be short, and that there is no great appearance of business at his office by reason of the not sitting of the Exchequer."[1]

Again he was present on 10th May when it was agreed to petition the Marquis of Hamilton, the King's Commissioner, to receive some of their number to confer with him "concerning the evils hanging over this countrie, and to advise if any fair way can be found out for the accomodation of the same". Sir John signed the petition.[2] Noticeably on this occasion the Chancellor Spottiswood and the Bishops were absent, the sederunt consisting of Argyll, Mar, Perth, Wigtown, Galloway, Lauderdale, Southesk, Napier, Sir Thomas Hope, James Carmichael, Sir R. Graham, Sir A. Gibson, Sir A. Fletcher, J. Balcomie, Sir J. Halyburton, Cranston Riddell, Sir J. Scot, Sir Pa. Nisbet. This completed the sum of his attendances and his active participation in the deliberations and affairs of the Council.

Before leaving this phase of his history we may describe the serious and prolonged suit which brought his conduct into judgment not only before the Lords but before Parliament. This was the case where he was accused of charging exorbitant fees in the business of Chancery.

As a preface there is the following resolution made at Edinburgh on 4th February 1606.

"The Lords of Secret Council, considering the great extortion used by the Writers and Clerks of all the judicatories within this realm, in extorting frae the subjects sic unreasonable and exorbitent prices for the writs as ocht not to be sufferit in ane weill-governed commonwealth, provoking thairby not only private grudge but public exclamation against the libertie and with-gait (toleration) grantit to sic shameful scafferie and extortion, heichly to his Majesty's offence, the hurt and prejudice of guid subjects, and the reproach and slander of the judges under whose judicatorie the said Writers and Clerks serve, Have therefore set doun the prices of all letters, writs, etc. of the signet, privy and great Seals, so that the subjects may know what price they ought to give."[3] At this time, in keeping with the above resolution, a scale of charges was drawn up for all departments under Chancery.

[1] Reg. P.C. 1638-1643, p. 117.
[2] *Ibid.*, p. 117-118.
[3] Reg. P.C. 1604-1607, pp. 164-165.

The complaint against Sir John was precisely one of "scafferie", or the illegal exaction of fees due to his office, which we first hear of from an Act of Parliament in November 1625. The charge was renewed at different times and it was long before the whole matter was satisfactorily explained and settled. On the above occasion the complaint was from the barons, and the Estates admonished the Director, "to conform himself in his prices to the book made and set down anent prices of writs and seals and ratification thereof made in Parliament, with warning that if he fail he shall forfeit his place to his Majesty".[1]

This severe reprimand and threat of drastic penalty involved serious questions of right on Sir John's part, and of authority on the part of Parliament, and it is curious to note than when the matter was dealt with by the Privy Council the action and stricture of the Estates is not mentioned.[2]

Professor Masson in his introduction to Vol. I of the Second Series of the Register, when remarking that Sir John was present in the Council on 23rd February 1626, says "That crusty knight had not till then had courage to show his face again at the Council Board after the rebuke he had received from the Convention of Estates".[3] In this the editor miscalculates the spirit of Scotstarvit, and must also be speaking in error as to the facts, because, as has been shown, Sir John, not long after the close of the Convention in November, was called to London and was there in the beginning of 1626, and apparently until the middle of February, for when there he speaks of the King's new Commission affecting the Council and the Session which was dated 14th February 1626.[4] Nor, although he could perhaps truthfully be called a "crusty knight", was he a faint-hearted one, as his duel with the redoubtable Melrose, his senior in years and experience, in the presence of the Duke of Buckingham and the English Council, amply proves.[5]

Moreover the sequel shows that the Estates had by no means spoken the last word where his conduct and tenure of office were concerned. It has been recorded that the Estates in the Convention

[1] Reg. P.C. 1625-1627, p. 180.
[2] Ibid., p. xxxiii.
[3] Ibid., pp. xliv-xlv.
[4] Trew Relation; Scot. Hist. Review, vol. XI, p. 186.
[5] In reflecting on his temper we must not forget the occasion when he entertained the General Assembly "with a world of merry tales".

of 1625, "showed a considerable spirit of independence" in dealing with his Majesty's proposals. But in the case of Sir John Scot they may have been exceeding their powers in threatening to terminate an appointment which was at the disposal of the Crown. The following is a complete history of this matter which for a considerable period reflected adversely on the character of Scotstarvit.

On 6th February 1627 a Council minute shows that the Commissioners for Burghs charged Sir John with obtaining, "by some private moyen (means) and sinistrous information", a signature,[1] the effect of which was to increase a common charge of 40 shillings to 50 or 60 pounds.[2] Moreover they alleged that he was acting on the signature without first submitting the matter to the Council to allow or disprove it.

"The Lords, with the consent of Sir John, ordained the signature to be stayed and in no case to pass the Register of Seals until it be heard, cognosed, and allowed in Parliament."[3] This matter in spite of the above ruling was re-opened at a sitting of the Council on 4th September 1629:

"Complaint of the Commissioners of Burghs that Sir John Scot has procured a signature from his Majestie prohibiting any bailie of burgh from giving sasine to persons succeeding as heirs in any wise until such persons are first retoured and served in Chancery. This novatioun (innovation) is regarded as a heavy oppressioun on the poor inhabitants of Burghs, obliging them to pay 50 or 60 pounds for what by the loveable custome of hesp and stapple they wer accustomed to receive for 40 shillings."[4, 5]

Here we have the same complaint as before, the complainants observing that they had already tendered it in February 1627 when their Lordships had decreed that the signature under which the Director had acted should not be "exped" until it was heard and allowed in Parliament: but Sir John, they allege, had actually passed it through the seals and intended to seek letters and publication of it. When in the Council he was challenged to answer this charge he said he had not been warned that it would be raised and was unprepared to answer. He was thereupon warned

---

[1] "Signature" implies a missive signed by the King.
[2] The pound Scots was (in 1707) equal to 1/8d.
[3] Reg. P.C. 1625-1627, pp. 517-518.
[4] Ibid., 1629-1630, pp. 283-284.
[5] Note No. 74, p. 227.

to be ready to answer next Council day, and meanwhile the signature was to be stayed.[1]

It is not until four years later that we have a final statement and decision. This occurred on 11th February 1634, under an entry which reads: "Ane Act in favor of Sir Johne Scot anent the prices of his Office".[2]

Here we find the "crusty knight" exhibiting a vigorous power of defence and taking every occasion to berate his "umquhill uncle" for his neglect of the interests of the Chancery office while holding the Directorship: "he did not so muche as once opin his mouth in that errand".

The position now was that towards the end of 1633 he had made a supplication to have the question cleared, and the Earl of Haddington and some others were appointed to meet and confer with him and to report to the Lords. This committee was now reporting and in doing so it introduces his Supplication and quotes it in full:

"Anent the supplication presented to the Lords of Secreit Counsell by Sir Johne Scot of Scottistarvet, knight, Director of our soverane Lord's Chancellarie, makand mention that in the year of God when the supplicant was minor (1606) and his umquhill uncle exercised the directorie of the Chancellarie, the Lords of Privie Counsell set down a booke of rates conteaning the prices of all writs and seales that sould be tane from the lieges in all tyme thereafter: and the Clerkes of the Session, writters to the signet, and other clerkes and keepers of seales wer warned as to the setting down of these prices. Bot the supplicant's said uncle, knowing that as soon as the supplicant came to his majoritie he would clame the right of his awne place and office, he being thairfoir carelesse what sould become of the same, never solicited the Lords thairin, nor did so muche as once opin his mouth in that errand, and so by his silence and negligent connivance the Lords set down the prices of all writs passing the Chancellarie in a farre lower measure than formerlie was payed for the same. And as soon as it pleased God that the supplicant acquired the right of his awne office and was possest thairin, and finding a sensible prejudice done to him anent the prices by the silence and negligence of his uncle, the supplicant petitioned the Kingis Majestie in the moneth of February 1626 (when in London) so that a commission

---

[1] Reg. P.C. 1629-1630, p. 284.
[2] *Ibid.*, 1633-1635, p. 193, p. 200.

157

and reference might be given to the Commissioners for Grievances to take to thair consideratioun the prejudice done to the supplicant on the said prices. Also at that same tyme his Majestie by his letter directed to his Excheker declared that it was his royall pleasure that the said prices should be settled by the Commissioners, and that meantyme he should be suffered to take the accustomed prices. Bot since the Commissioners for Grievances had never met in judgement, and until occasion thereof, the supplicant still lyes under the censur of the Act of Counsell made in his minoritie.

"Whereupon Sir John petitioned his Majestie and his Estates in the late Parliament (June 1633)[1] who remitted the matter to the Lords of Counsell, declaring that thair (the Council's) determination should stand as ane constant modification in all tyme hereafter, and sould have the force of ane Act of Parliament; he pointing out that he has never broken the rule that the half of the price of writts passing the Great Seale, and the double the price of writts passing the Privie Seale, should be the prices of writts passing from the Chancellarie."[2]

The minute shows that Sir John in his supplication proceeded to set down prices for other writs, of which he carefully quotes the particular cases and transactions: "These being the prices whairby the supplicant rules his office, which are so moderate that he persuades himself that no subject can or will oppose himself thairto".[3]

All this having been considered the following was the finding of the Council.

"The Lords, having conferred thereupon, finds and declares that thair has beene no materiall change in the prices of the Chancellarie tane by Sir John since his entry to that office, but that he has keeped a good mediocrite and behaved himself discreetly and respectivelie therein. And to the intent that all matter of question and contestation be removed, and that no persons take occasion to scandall and reproche Sir John," etc., the Council then proceeded to fix the fees in the scale and order scrupulously supplied by the supplicant, accepting his figures practically in their entirety.[4]

[1] Acts Parl. Scot., Vol. V, p. 53.
[2] Reg. P.C. 1633-1635, pp. 201-203.
[3] Ibid., p. 202.
[4] Ibid., p. 203.

It will be seen from this that Sir John had opened the matter with the King in February 1626 and that the King's directive had permitted him to take the "accustomed prices" until the question could be dealt with by the Commission for Grievances, a body which was notoriously remiss in sitting. It was presumably to this recourse to the King that the Burghs referred, saying that he had employed "private influence and sinistrous information."

If the phrase "accustomed prices" means the fees as they obtained in his grandfather's day, then he was undoubtedly entitled to make charges higher than the revised scale allowed. His disturbance of "the loveable custom of hesp and stapple" has been explained, and we see him accepting the authority of "the royall pleasure" where it overrides an Act passed by the Lords of Council in 1606 and maintained by Parliament in 1625. As the matter does not arise again it may be assumed that the new Act of Council prevailed and that Sir John persuaded others as well as himself of the moderation of his fees of office.

Professor Masson makes an interesting reference to the rebuke and threat which was served to Sir John by the Estates in the Convention of November 1625. He says that Parliament before ending had instructed the Privy Council to send a report of its proceedings to his Majesty. This was done accurately save in one particular, namely, that no mention of the rebuke was included.[1] Did the Lords fear that the Estates were presuming to exercise a power which entrenched on the Royal prerogative and that it was wise to omit the matter from the report? The conclusion is reasonably possible, since the conduct of this Parliament in some other respects had already considerably provoked the King's displeasure.

Up to the year 1632 there were few questions great or small which came before the Council where Scotstarvit's judgment and capacity for work were not employed. Among many passing matters we find him (along with Sir Thomas Hope) examining witches; inspecting the state of repair of the royal houses and castles of Edinburgh, Holyrood, Linlithgow, Stirling, Dunfermline, and Falkland in view of the approaching coronation; executing a Commission against Jesuits; intimating to the Lords of Session the death of the Prince of Bohemia;[2] regulating the fishing in the river Eden, Fife; consulting with the Advocate and the Justice

---

[1] Reg. P.C. 1625-1627, p. xxxiii.
[2] Note No. 75, p. 227.

Clerk over the case of a sea captain whose ship had been robbed by the sea-rovers of Hamburg, and many other affairs of private and public interest. His activities in fact offer an index to the wide variety of matters, legal, economic and social which came under the purview and control of the Privy Council at that day.

As an illustration of his personal relations with the State Secretary, and his curious and delicate association with Menteith, the President of Council, two matters may be mentioned. In the first as a Commissioner for the Nova Scotia colonisation scheme he was authorised by Sir William Alexander in July 1626 to act in his stead. In the letter of warrant, the Secretary, "Heritable lieutenant of New Scotland to his Majestie" says:

"Because I cannot weele attend in persone to give my testimonie in so far as I haif interest for the passing of signatouris, Thairfore witt ye me to haif maid and constitut my verie honourable freind, Sir Johnne Scott of Scottistarbett, Directour of the Chancellarie, and Williame Alexander my eldest sone, or ather of thame in my place, giving thame full power to do, performe, and approve concerning the passing of the signatouris."

Sir John asked that this letter "be insert and registrat in the Bookes of the Privie Counsell, thairin to remayne *ad futuram rei memoriam*; which the Lords agreed to do in the maner and to the effect abone writtin".[1]

In the case of Menteith interest lies firstly in the presence of both men in the small attendance of members in the following instance, which was not an exceptional case. When in July 1628 a Commission was appointed to examine and revise the whole body of Scottish laws, the sederunt of Council consisted of Menteith, Haddington, Winton, Linlithgow, Perth, Lorne, Hope, Hamilton and Scotstarvit.[2] It may be said in passing that to read the direction sent by Charles concerning this undertaking is to feel sincere admiration for a great conception which was most eloquently expressed. This revision was linked with the changes already made in Session and Council, and is seen as part of a corrective and beneficent law reform animated with a spirit of humanity and justice.[3]

In order that the laws might be administered freely to the whole commonweal Charles proceeded to revive the ancient custom of

---

[1] Reg. P.C. 1625-1627, p. 339.
[2] Note No. 76, p. 227.
[3] Reg. P.C. 1625-1627, pp. 365-366.

Circuit Courts in every shire, and it is noticeable that in October 1629 the Judges appointed to hold Courts in Haddington, Duns, Selkirk and Peebles, were Menteith, Thomas Henderson of Chesters, and Scotstarvit.[1]

He would be a grudging critic who would not admit that Charles at the opening of his reign and in respect of the foregoing measures had generous intentions to improve the well-being of his Scottish subjects.

But perhaps the most significant and intriguing instance of Scot's active Councillorship belongs to the part he played in connection with the choice of a Latin Grammar for the Schools in 1630. In July of that year the King gave warrant for a Commission to sit and settle the matter, and the cause thereafter became one of nation-wide interest, the King, the Burghs, the Schoolmasters and the Universities all being involved, and the Committee spending two busy years in reaching a solution. The prize for the successful author was a considerable one, not only of scholarly prestige but of the sole printing rights and profits covering the entire supply of text-books for 21 years. In a scholarly and influential Committee of eleven the Bishop of Dunblane was Convener with Sir John Scot to act in his absence: this was probably a tribute to the latter's well-established Latin scholarship.[2]

The Grammar in use was one composed by Alexander Home, Schoolmaster at Dunbar. It had become the subject of criticism, some of which was clearly due to the ambitions of rival dominies. The Committee however was also dissatisfied and after much labour and consultation with the leading teachers of the country, choice was made of a new Grammar composed by David Wedderburn, Schoolmaster at Aberdeen.[3]

The record shows that the final report was prepared and submitted to the Council by the Bishop of Dunblane and Sir John Scot. In recommending Wedderburn's Grammar the report says it was designed: "For the weale of the youth and gayning of much tyme in the progress of thair studies and learning of good authors. Whilk being offered to the whole Maisters of Schooles of best

---

[1] Reg. P.C. 1629-1630, p. 226.
[2] *Ibid.*, p. 596.
[3] Reg. P.C. 1630-1632, p. 163. A well-known scholar and Latin poet (1580-1646). Poet-Laureate of Aberdeen in 1620 and friend of Arthur Johnston.

mark, and also to all Colledges and Universities within the Kingdome, they have given thair approbatioun thairto".[1]

The national excitement provoked by this matter almost suggests that in that day the Scots were a nation of schoolmasters. Also it is clear that where culture and scholarship were concerned ecclesiastical and political differences could be forgotten, inasmuch as the Committee agreeably fulfilled its task although its Convener and Vice-Convener were respectively a Bishop, and a Presbyterian who was later a staunch supporter of the Covenanting party.

[1] Reg. P.C. 1630-1632, pp. 454-455.

CHAPTER XI

THE CORONATION OF CHARLES I

The record of this important and often-delayed event is in a variety
of ways of considerable historic importance, the matter being
handled by the small active group of Councillors. Scotstarvit
was charged with urgent duties in its connection, although, due
to repeated postponements and the change latterly in the political
complexion of the Executive, he was not officially in evidence at
the closing stage. Other passages in this work show how engaged
he then was with the serious business concerning the Earl of
Menteith, a business which was brought to a crisis on the actual
occurrence of the long-delayed royal visit. On that occasion, with
his brother-in-law as Master of the Pageants, the testy knight did
not ruffle the proceedings with any question of honour and
precedency in the order.

The entries in the record referring to the Coronation begin with
Charles's letter of 5th July, 1628, where he intimates his intended
visit, "for receiving the crown and keeping of a Parliament".[1]
The proposed date was 15th September of that year, so that he
was giving his Councillors a very short time to prepare for the important event. Actually he did not come to Scotland, and Parliament did not meet with himself in attendance, until June 1633.

Consequent upon this intimation a hurried survey was made of
the Royal Houses and steps were taken for their repair. Somewhat
prominent precautionary orders were also issued with a view to
the King's recreation and outdoor pastime.[2]

Although these preliminary steps were taken, the notice nevertheless caused consternation among the leaders, and on 18th July
the Council lamented the lack of funds to entertain the King's
coming, and despatched a frank and reproachful letter to the
ministers at Court, that is to the Scottish nobles who were there
in the King's attendance. The Council (skilfully mingling loyal
congratulation with actual indignation) said,

[1] Reg. P.C. 1627-1628, p. 367.
[2] Note No. 77, p. 227.

163

"Albeit this is the joyfullest news which could happen unto us in this world, yitt we cannot conceal our just grief in expostulating with your Lordships, that you, knowing the state of the Kingdome, should not opin your mouth to represent unto his Majestie the impossibilitie to have preparatiouns for so great a work upon so short advertisement. You know that there is no money in his Majesteis coffers: rents and customs are spent, and places and houses are ruinous and decayed. And, lastly, we wonder that your Lordships did not remember the seasoun of harvest in the middes quhairof his Majesteis dyet is appointed."[1] The Councillors at Court were told plainly that since they advised the venture they must supply the means to finance it.

This protest was subscribed by the "Bishop of St Andrews, Mar, Haddington, Glasgow, Wintoun, Lauderdaill, Seaforte, Lorne, Areskine, Dunkeld, Aberdein, Dunblane, Melvil, Carnegie, the Master of Elphinstoun, Hamilton and Scottistarvett."[2]

It received at an early date an adroit and troublesome reply from the King. In it he pointed out that a great part of the taxation granted to him in October 1625 was still unpaid and would be useful for his intended visit, and instructed the Councillors to call before them all defaulters, and inquire the cause, and name delinquents and prosecute any who were denounced as rebels for their contempt.[3] The Council determined to give effect to this unexpected instruction, and six persons were appointed to carry it out, their sense of duty being encouraged by the promise of £2000 to be granted jointly for their service.[4]

At the same initial meeting "The Lyoun Herauld (Sir Gerome Lindsay) was instructed to informe himself what had beine the ancient form of coronatioun of the Kings of this kingdome, and was adverteist to be heir the morne to gif his advyse anent the mater".[5]

The register shows how very diligent and frequent in assembly the Council was in the following two months and how many matters were attended to. Among the first of their considerations was the place of the ceremony, and the immediate choice was the Kirk of St Giles:

"The Lords haveing conferred and reasouned at length upon

---

[1] Reg. P.C. 1627-1628, p. 387.
[2] Note No. 78, p. 227.
[3] Reg. P.C. 1627-1628, pp. 395-396.
[4] *Ibid.*, p. 427.
[5] *Ibid.*, p. 385, p. 387.

the most convenient plaice for his Majesteis coronatoiun, hes concluded that the Church of Sanct Giles in Edinburgh is the most conspicuous plaice for that solempnitie, and ordanis ane missive to be written to his Majestie for that purpois: and hes appointed to meete after noone in the Counsel Hous of Edinburgh and thairfra to goe and sight the Kirk of St Giles, and ordanis the proveist and baillies to be wairned to attend. . . . Haveing sightit and considderit it they thinke it fitt and expedient for the great solempnitie, and suggests that the partitioun wall betwix the great kirk and the east, or little kirk, be tane doun and removed. And remits this to the proveist and baillies, to returne ane answere the morne."[1]

On the following day (22nd July) a letter to the King was prepared stating that "the Kirk of St Giles was the most proper plaice for so glorious ane actioun", and proceeding to intimate the Lord Lyon's report.[2] It is to be noted that the form submitted, which we may assume was carefully studied in the ancient style, did not agree with that finally chosen by the King. That Charles might not accept it in its entirety seems to have been anticipated by the Council, in view of the following letter:

"Touching the solempnitie of the coronatioun of your royall progenitours, we callit befoir us the Lyoun King at Armes, fra whome we ressaved the forme and modell heerwith inclosed as the ancient forme of the coronatioun of this kingdom, the expediencie whairof to be followed we remit to your royal consideratioun, and what your Majestie will have to be altered thairin it sall be performed."[3]

The letter proceeds to say that warning has been given both by proclamation and missive to the whole Nobility to attend both the Coronation and the Parliament, and how they were to be robed: "The Marqueisses, Erles, and Viscounts, with thair creatioun robes of crimson velvett enermyned and with their crounes: the Lords with thair scarlett robes, and the whole to attend Parliament in thair scarlett robes. And quhat forder may concerne the honnour and credite of these solempnities sall, upon notice of your Majesteis pleasure, be carefullie furthered and advanced."[4]

When these various resolutions were taken fourteen Councillors

[1] Reg. P.C. 1627-1628, p. 389.
[2] Ibid., p. 392.
[3] Note No. 79, p. 227.
[4] Reg. P.C. 1627-1628, p. 393.

were present, and there can be little doubt that they cherished a sincere expectancy that the King would fulfil his engagement. Professor Masson in the Introduction to the Register for 1627-28 refers to the form of Coronation provided by Sir Gerome Lindsay as "perhaps the most interesting document in the volume".[1]

At a Council meeting prior to that at which the form was submitted, the Edinburgh Provost and Baillies made their report on the Kirk of St Giles: it was highly practical. They declared that in the opinion of men of judgment and experience to take down the partition between the Great and Little Kirks, "is a worke impossible to be perfyted betwix this and the appointed tyme for the coronatioun, and they consider that the Great Kirk is a pairt and plaice conspicuous eneugh for such ane solempnitie".[2]

An interesting point was raised about the orientation of the King during the ceremony, and the Scottish Secretary was written to at Whitehall.

"Haveing designed the Church of St Gyles in Edinburgh as the fittest plaice for his Majesteis coronatioun, we have sensyne caused sight the same and considerit in what pairt his Majesteis throne and stage may be most convenientlie erected. But our resolution concerning this point has been affected by a receaved opinion that thair is a necessitie that his Majesteis face during the solempnities must be directed towards the east, on which, if it be a formall and unchangeable ceremonie, we sall rule our proceedings accordinglie.

"But if his Majestie may indifferentlie looke to the south—whilk we hope may be—it will greatly aid the credit and beautie of the actioun, which cannot with so great a show and luster be performed if the throne sall be plaiced with a reference to the east, in respect of the situation of the church and disposal of the windows within the same.

"Whairwith desyring your Lordship to acquaint his Majestie at some fitt opportunitie, and to certifie backe with all possible diligence his Majesteis pleasure and resolution, we sall conforme ourselffes."[3]

At this meeting held in the height of the emergency the number attending had shrunk to nine Councillors, the faithful group that

[1] Reg. P.C. 1627-1628, p. xxxix. Printed in full, pp. 393-395.
[2] *Ibid.*, p. 391.
[3] *Ibid.*, p. 405.

met responsibly for serious deliberation and all necessary action. However, the rush of activity and flush of expectation—stimulated by the shortness of time—was brought to a sudden and early end by a royal missive postponing the visit from September 1628 until April 1629, "because of manie great impediments and difficulties". It was actually 28th August when the King's warrant halted everything and gave the hard-pressed Council some well-merited relief.

In the period 1629-1630 there was announcement on three several occasions that Charles was coming north to consummate his accession to sovereignty, and in each case postponement ensued. During this time the Council had a variety of matters to consider, and on certain points it discloses its anxiety.

On the 19th February 1629 the minutes show that no answer had been returned from Whitehall as to the suitability of the form of Coronation service which had been submitted. Also the question as to the orientation of the ceremony had not been answered.

The Lyon King at this point caused cogitation over several matters in which he was officially interested. One was whether the coats-of-arms of himself and his pursuivants should be renewed? This was decided in the negative. He also advanced a cautious proposition as to whether or not at the Coronation he should carry the single arms of Scotland or the arms quartered. The answer given by the Council was emphatic and was unquestionably politic in the circumstances:

"The Lords of Secreit Counsell having heard the propositioun and doubt moved by the Lyoun Herald whether or not at his Majesteis coronatioun he sould carie the single armes of Scotland or the armes quartered as now is used, the Lordes thinkes that the herauld must carie the armes quartered and mixt with those of England, France, and Ireland, according as has beene heertofore observed in all publict solemnities both in Scotland and England."[1]

As this minute is of date 19th February 1629, and Sir James Balfour was not appointed Lyon until June of the next year, it is clear that it was his predecessor who raised the "doubt" about what Arms should be carried: the Index to the Register errs on this point. And since, according to the statement of the Council, the use of the arms quartered had heretofore been observed in all

[1] Reg. P.C. 1629-1630, p. 50.

public solemnities, his query appears to have been both awkward and unnecessary, and may suggest reasons as to why his demission of office occurred.

There was now a proposal that the Kirk of Holyrood, despite its "defects and ruines", should be considered as the setting for the historic ceremony, and the Bishop of Dunblane, Sir John Scot, Sir James Baillie, and James Murray, the Master of Works, were directed to study the possibilities. Their report gives evidence of a very thorough survey and understanding of what was needed for "decoreing and beautifing" this royal sanctuary. The main proposal was that three galleries be removed, "whairby the kirk sall be better lighted and aired and the people heare God's word more commodiously".[1]

Other interesting items of alteration were that, "ane window would be stricken out upon the laigh north east gavill, which will wonderfullie decore and beautifie the kirk"; four other windows were to be opened on the south side under his Majesty's lofts for lighting and airing that quarter, and the pulpit was to be moved one pillar toward the west.

Acknowledging themselves to have been "ripelie advised" by the report, the Lords allowed the removal of "the three lafts foregainst his Majesteis seate, and the building of a great laft on the east gavill", but reserved consideration of the other points to a more fit time. The work was "to be performit by the baillies of Edinburgh and the Sessioun of the Kirk of the Canongait, and upon thair charges".[2] The inspection of both buildings continued, and so in spite of the early prepossession in favour of St Giles the Kirk of Holyrood was finally chosen.

At this point further action was taken on behalf of the Lord Lyon. The introduction of this matter which is entered in the minute of 17th March 1630, shows that the King had already appointed Sir James Balfour and that it only remained for him to receive the gift formally and to be officially inaugurated in office. At the above date the reference is to his supplication, "that whereas it has pleased his Majestie to appoint him Lyoun King of Armes", steps should be taken for his installation, and in particular that a crown be made and provided for his use. The Councillors agreed that he "be provided with ane croune of gold", and with a native sense of economy decided "to bargane for the same at the easiest

---

[1] Reg. P.C. 1629-1630, p. 493.
[2] *Ibid.*, pp. 106-107.

rate and pryce they can".[1] A letter from Charles warranting the necessary steps to complete the appointment was received in the month of April by the Lord Chancellor:

"Charles R., Right trustie and weilbelovit cousine and counsellour, we greit yow weill. Having preferred our trustie and weill belovit Sir James Balfour of Kynnard, knight, to be our King of Armes in that our kingdome, and being willing that no honnour belonging to that place and office should be diminished and impaired, it is our royal pleasure and will that yow, with all convenient diligence, inaugurat him with all ceremonie dew and requisite, in as goodlie forme and maner and as solemnlie in all respects as ever anie Lyoun King has beene crouned heirtofore in that our said kingdome. For doing whairof these presents sall be to yow a sufficient warrand. So we bid yow fareweill.

"From our Court at Whitehall the 20 day of Apryle 1630."[2]

A note consisting of two lines shows that Sir James Balfour received the formal gift of office on 8th June 1630.[3] On 2nd May he had been knighted at the hand of the King's Commissioner, George, Viscount of Dupplin, and in the month of June there is a minute showing that his inauguration was shortly to follow, thus: "The Lords ordanes the Maister of Workes to supplee the absence of the Maister of Ceremonyis at the creatioun of the Lyoun King of Armes upon Sonday nixt". The date was 15 June 1630.[4]

"The 15 June this yeare, being Sonday, Sir James Balfour of Kynaird, knight, was with grate solemnity crouned Lyone King of Armes by George, Viscount of Dupleine, Lord Chanceler of Scotland, his Majesteis Commissioner, in the Chappel Royal at Holyrudhouse; and after the ceremony was endit the Lyone feasted the Lord Commissioner, the Lordes of his Majesteis Privy Counsaill, and Senators of the Colledge of Justice, in the Earl of Linlithgows housse adjoining the palace."[5]

On the 3rd August 1630 the Council intimated to the Commissioners of Parliament that the King had deferred his coming until 1st April 1631, when he would receive the crown "for the peace and security of our native and ancient kingdom".[6] But

[1] Reg. P.C. 1629-1630, pp. 491-192.
[2] *Ibid.*, p. 531.
[3] *Ibid.*, p. 561.
[4] Reg. P.C. 1629-1630, p. 613.
[5] Balfour's *Annals*, Vol. II, p. 179.
[6] Reg. P.C. 1630-1632, pp. 1-2.

when this day arrived Parliament was postponed to 4th August, and on that date a further shuffle—"until his Majesty have more time and leisure"—was made to 13th April 1632[1] In November there was a confirmation that the great event would actually take place on the latter date and for the eighth time the Council addressed itself to its preparatory task, at least to whatever steps yet remained to be taken. Nevertheless in the Spring of 1632 Charles wrote delaying his visit for another twelvemonth, in view of "foreign affairs, the state whereof is sufficiently known to be very considerable"; and he appointed the 18th day of June 1633 as the Coronation date.[2]

It was now generally rumoured that the King never intended to come for his Scottish coronation. Not unnaturally there was widespread dissatisfaction and complaint. He was treating his "native and ancient kingdom" with scant respect and was ruling it as a King not yet crowned.

Among the provisions which were finally studied by the harassed Lords was the interesting one of song at the church service, and there is the following note of a somewhat naïve character set down on 17th January 1632.

"The whilk day the quiristers of the Chappel Royal compeirand personallie before the Lords of Privie Counsell, and being demanded if they were able and would undertake to serve his Majestie both in the daylie service and at the coronatioun, they declared and affirmed by the mouth of Andro Sinclaire thair speechman, that they had both skill and abilitie to discharge that service to his Majesteis contentment and the credite of the countrie."[3]

This single note does not settle the question of who were the choristers at the Coronation, but there is every likelihood that the individuals interviewed by the Lords were employed even if others came north to take part.

In 1629 Edward Kellie was appointed Receiver of Chapel rents and Director of Music at the Chapel Royal at Holyrood.[4] In January 1631 he was at Whitehall and supplied the King with a detailed account of how he ordered the music of the Chapel and

[1] Reg. P.C. 1630-1632, p. 315. England was busy with troubles abroad.
[2] Ibid., p. 468. The Coronation took place on this date.
[3] Ibid., p. 408.
[4] Reg. of Presentation to Benefices V, p. 45. Quoted by C. Rogers in his History of the Chapel Royal, p. clxii.

how he selected the musicians. He stated that in his chamber at Holyrood he had set up, "An organ, two flutes, two pandores with viols and other instruments, with all sorts of English, French, Spanish, Latin, Italian and old Scotch music." He claimed that he had received the hearty approval of the Lords of Council and quotes the extreme terms of their commendation. In addition he assures the King that while in London, and for the period of five months, he had fully studied the music and praise of the Coronation of 1626, and says that he is ready upon command to undertake with the means aforesaid at the forthcoming Scottish event.[1]

It seems clear that Kellie had gone south to solicit the honour of directing the orchestral and vocal offices on the great occasion and that he had prepared himself for the task: in his report he says he could do it better "than could be done by strangers". He probably succeeded in his plea, as he continued to be Director of Music at Holyrood until February 1635 when his successor was appointed.[2, 3]

The appearance of the choristers before the Council with their "speechman Andro Sinclair" in January 1632 suggests that the matter was still open at that date: Kellie was possibly then in London. Nevertheless English performers, both instrumentalists and vocalists, came north in the King's train, sixteen men with eight boys and two organists, all to wait on his Majesty on his Scottish journey.

About the month of March 1632 Lord Traquair, Sir John Hamilton, Sir George Elphinstone, and Sir James Baillie, with the Master Householder, were commanded to arrange lodgings in Edinburgh for the King's retinue; and the Committee formerly appointed was ordered to re-visit the Royal Houses and report if the work contracted had been satisfactorily completed. All this was afoot when as already stated the meeting of Parliament was prorogued.

Sir John Scot made his last regular appearance at the Council on 12th August 1632 when the sederunt numbered seven: he therefore shared almost to the end the protracted and vexatious planning for the great event.

It had been decided with the King's consent to hold the

[1] *Ancient Scottish Melodies*—W. Dauney (Edin. 1837), pp. 365-367.
[2] Reg. of Presentations to Benefices, VII, p. 24.
[3] Note No. 80, p. 227.

ceremony in Holyrood Kirk and the Masters of Works were ordered to begin with diligence and make certain specific repairs. Notable features in this were the placing of a peal of bells in the north-west steeple, renewing the great west door, and repairing and thacking in good order the two turnpike stairs.[1]

On 26th March 1633, the Council received through James Maxwell of Innerwick, one of his Majesty's bedchamber and earlier mentioned in connection with Sir John Scot's hurried visit to London, "a booke conteaning the forme of his Majesteis coronatioun". In an accompanying letter the King said, "Having perused and approved this forme we send it heerwith to the effect that all may be prepared accordinglie in dew tyme".[2]

This reference to a "booke", prepared presumably by the new Lyon, and perused and approved by the King, is of considerable interest, for it implies that the version supplied by Sir Gerome Lindsay had been rejected, and it may be that a deficiency in this respect affected the change of appointment. Balfour had already established an acquaintance with English scholars of kindred interests and revealed those gifts which made him a distinguished annalist and antiquarian. But even so the Order was not completely satisfactory, for William Hay, Earl of Errol, the High Constable, complained of its omissions in respect of his office, and the King asked the Council to consider his claims, and, "if they find his allegations just", to authorise him to carry out the appropriate offices.[3]

We learn that medals to celebrate the occasion were to be struck by Mr Nicholas Briot: "Ane hundred peeces of gold at the worth of 20 shillings sterline the peece, and twa thousand peeces of silver at twelffe pence the peece, of the weight and fynenesse of his Majesteis standard".[4, 5]

The Committee charged with the care of the Royal residences had reported that the King's houses required "present and tymous reparation", and they added that the tapestry at Holyrood was "verie evil worne, and eaten and spoyled with rattouns." It was decided that the tapestry should be cut and portions of it used in

[1] Reg. P.C. 1633-1635, pp. 12-13.
[2] Ibid., pp. 55-56.
[3] Ibid., p. 106.
[4] Ibid., p. 108.
[5] Note No. 81, p. 227.

patching. James Liddell, a famous baker of James VI, was brought out of retirement to officiate in the Royal Bakehouse.[1]

It was perhaps partly from pride of country or an eye to the picturesque that the Council decided that Chieftains from the West Highlands were to be present "in their best order, and make a display before the English".[2]

In connection with the King's progress through the country it was ordered that roads were to be made passable on a parish basis: towns *en route* were to be well-furnished "with all kynde of vivers and provision for men and horse, with lodgings cleane, handsome, and neat. Bedding and naperie to be cleane and weill smelled. Pewter vessels to be large, and no middins or beggars to be seene in the streets."[3]

On the 1st of May the Council had commanded Sir John Scot the Director of Chancery, and his deputes, to give out precepts warning the whole nobility, prelates, and commissioners for the small barons and burghs, to attend his Majesty's Parliament which was to be held in Edinburgh, and to begin, God willing, on the 18th June. Anent the doing of this the Act to be to them a sufficient warrant.[4]

The Lords were naturally much exercised over the question of order in the King's entry to the city and in the Coronation procession. On 4th June they agreed "to advyse with the King if the English sall ryde together after his Majestie or if they sall ryde promiscuouslie with the natives"; and also the question touching the order of the Bishops' riding. And as late as 12th June they dealt with the final disposition of all parties concerned:—

"It is thought meit that the Scottish nobilitie sall preceed and ryde immediatelie before his Majestie, and that the English nobilitie sall ryde behind his Majestie, and that the nobilitie sall keepe thair rankes without mixing up with the gentrie: and that the Lord Mairshell sall have ane care that they ryde in order without presse or confusion.

"The Lords thinkes fitt that his Majestie, about the west end of the long gait neere to St Cuthbert's church, sall take his great

[1] Reg. P.C. 1633-1635, p. 52.
[2] *Ibid.*, p. 106. Carlyle assumes that the political reason was that their presence would indicate the loyal and dutiful affection of his Majesty's most remote subjects. *Cromwell's Letters and Speeches* (1850) III, p. 108.
[3] Reg. P.C. 1633-1635, p. 5.
[4] *Ibid.*, p. 81.

horse whairupon he is to enter into the toun, and that the heritour and tennent of the ground sall be satisfied of the skaith whilk they sall susteane upon that occasioun.

"Anent the carying of the cannopie during the tyme of his Majesteis Coronatioun, it is thought meit that there be ane list of twelffe nobelmen's sones presentit to his Majestie to the intent his Majestie may out of these mak choise of sax for the service foresaid.

"It is thought meit that the haill nobelmen and bishops, with sax commissiouners for the gentrie and sax for the burrows, sall on the morning of the coronatioun go to the King's presence (which was at Edinburgh Castle) and thair tender their deutie in the name of the Estaits, in the words sett doun in the booke of the coronatioun, whilk speeche sall be delyvered by the Lord Chancellor.

"That his Majestie be consulted anent the order and place to be keeped by the Lords Chancellor and Constable in thair ryding at the tyme of the entrie, coronatioun and parliament; as lykewayes anent the place and order of ryding of the bishops at the tymes forsaid."[1]

On 15th June the magistrates of Edinburgh were instructed "to have ane standing guarde on either side of thair street on the day of his Majesteis coronatioun, and nane of the said town sall stirre or remove".[2]

These and other matters were finally arranged no doubt in consultation with the Lyon King, who presents the precise Order in the *Annals*. One unrehearsed item which he reports is that at a certain point the King's progress was held up by an unfortunate difference on procedure which arose between the eldest sons of Earls and the Lords of Parliament. Charles had to resolve this on the spot and gave orders that the sons of Earls should have precedence.[3]

As already reported it was on this historic occasion that Sir James Balfour was sent to the Lord Chancellor to say it was his Majesty's pleasure that he would give place to Archbishop Spottiswoode in the procession: on which Kinnoull replied brusquely that in right of his office "never stoled priest in Scotland should set foot before him so long as his blood was hot". It was

---

[1] Reg. P.C. 1633-1635, pp. 112-113.
[2] *Ibid.*, p. 117.
[3] The *Annals* (1824), IV, p. 371.

perhaps a rash response to make to the imperious Charles, who characterised Hay as "a cankered goatish old man",[1] and in the following year appointed the Archbishop as Chancellor in his place.

The note of 15th June is the last in the Register about the event which took place in Holyrood Kirk on 18th June 1633. Charles was crowned by Archbishop Spottiswoode, and Laud, who came north for the occasion, probably had something to do with the ceremony being in full Anglican order, a fact which gave hurt to many of the King's loyal subjects and aroused the hostility of Parliament.[2]

There were other signs of daring innovation; for example, the Bishop of Moray preached before Charles in his rochet, the first instance of its use since the Reformation, and this innovation was followed by a royal warrant directing all ministers to use the surplice in divine worship.[3]

At the end of the *Annals* the account of the royal entry to Edinburgh is succeeded by the Lyon's account of the Coronation. In contrast to the bald and antique outline presented by the late Lyon this is a refined and elaborate direction, and is remarkable for its detail, its orderly arrangement, and its dignity throughout. An idea of the fullness of the report may be gathered from the volume of the text, where there are approximately 5,000 words as against 800 in the earlier version.

The colour of the scene is sometimes suggested: there is a note of a table cover "of green velvet laced and fringed with gold", and, "On the southe syde of the Communion Table was ther a trawersse of crimpsone tafty placed werey conveniently, quher his Majestie did reposse and disrobe himselfe".[4]

The choir was in evidence with anthems on seven occasions: *Behold, O Lord our Protector, and look upon the face of thine anointed; Firmetur manus tua; Misericordias Dei; Veni Creator Spiritus; Zadoc the priest and Nathan the prophet; Be strong and of good courage; Te Deum laudamus.* The Litany was sung and read by the Bishops of Moray and Ross.

It is noticeable that in his vows the King promises "to maintain

[1] Note No. 82, p. 227.
[2] Balfour says of Laud: "Laud, the over-ruling Bishop of London, a prime actor in all the following tragedies". The *Annals*, II, p. 192. James had warned Laud about the tough "stomach" of the Scottish people.
[3] Acts Parl. Scot., V, p. 21.
[4] The *Annals*, IV, p. 384.

the trew religioun of Christ now preached and professed within this realm", and avoids any ecclesiastical distinction, but the episcopal interest was present in the fourth item in the Vows:

"We also beseech you to grant and preserve unto us of the clergy, and to the churches committed to our charge, all canonical privileges, and to defend and protect us as every good King in his kingdom ought to defend his bishops and the churches under their government."[1]

It is seen that in this later and accepted form the Lyon King's office is more subdued: he does not appear almost as a rival majesty as he did in the other, being crowned, and surrendering his crown, and commanding the King to be crowned; nor did he repeat "sax generatiouns" of Charles's descent. Apart from carrying the ampule of oil he acts his part as herald and summoner. Although the essential actions were otherwise the same, yet it is evident that what may have been deemed more rude usages had been eliminated. But Charles was invested with the robes royal of King James IV, and the Nobility came kneeling as of old and swore, "So mott God helpe me as I shall support thee", touching the crown and holding up their hands.[2]

In an editorial footnote to the *Annals*, possibly inserted by Haig, it is rightly said that the ordering of this ceremonial occasion reflects great credit on the professional exertions of Sir James Balfour; but it is obvious from the choral items and the liturgical features that other minds and hands were also engaged in completing a form so extended and various.

Before the account closes we learn the reason for the fabrication of "medals" by Nicholas Briot. These gold and silver "coynes", as they are now called, were to be thrown freely amongst the people when the King went in procession from the Kirk to the Palace. Balfour says "This coyne had the Kingis face on the one syde, with the circumscriptione: *Carolus, Die Gratia Scotiae Angl: Fran: et Hyb: Rex Coronat*, 18 June 1633. And on the reverse a thisell, floured full in 3 grate stemes, and maney small branches issewing from it: with the devisse: *Hinc nostrae cruor Rosae*".

Having received Communion "with grate reverence", and the blessing being given,

"The King, with the crown on his head, in his robes, and the

---

[1] The *Annals*, IV, pp. 392-393.
[2] *Ibid.*, p. 399.

Sir James Balfour, Lord Lyon
1600-1657
Reproduced by permission of the Scottish National Portrait Gallery

John Spottiswoode, Archbishop of St Andrews
1565-1639
Reproduced by permission of the Faculty of Advocates

sceptre in his hand, returned with his whole train in solemne maner to his palace. Then were the pieces of gold and silver flunge all the way as he went by the almoner, the Bishop of Moray." Meanwhile "the trumpetts sounded" and "were answered by the Castell of Edinburgh with the thundering of great ordinance".[1]

As a social event the Coronation was a success. The English invasion put a big tax on a small nation, but native sense, and no doubt pride, assisted by official warnings, were equal to the occasion, and Clarendon says of the Scots that "the whole behaviour of that nation towards the English was as obliging and generous as could be expected".[2]

It is worth remembering that the pageantry was in the charge of William Drummond, Scot's brother-in-law: his scenario for the occasion is to be found among his writings. We are told that Parnassus Hill was presented in an entablature where Scotland had a footing in the characters of Duns Scotus, Hector Boece, John Major, Gavin Douglas, George Buchanan, Sir David Lyndsay and other "worthies". The national note was also sounded by a procession of 107 Scottish kings and the Genius of Caledonia. The Genius of Edinburgh, a nymph with Religion on her right hand and Justice on her left, delivered the keys of the City to the King in a silver basin.[3]

We make no doubt that Sir John Scot discussed with his relative the fancies and meanings of the varied pageant, and cast his eye critically over the dedicatory verse, but we are not told that he himself was stimulated to make any congratulatory offering to his sovereign.

It is a sad reflection that the royal enthronement in all its religious solemnity and pomp, and the gay and colourful public processions and fashionable gatherings which were its social accompaniment, were enacted in a capital where the leaders of church and nation knew that the foundations of the national life were being troubled and shaken by the royal policies; and, if we are to believe Sir James Balfour in his character of annotator, the King personally made an impression which bred antipathy, although it must be

[1] The *Annals*, IV, 403-404.
[2] *Hist. of the Rebellion and Civil Wars in England* (1705), I, p. 62. Clarendon makes interesting reflections on Scotland at the time of the King's Coronation, pp. 62-66.
[3] *The Poems of William Drummond* (1832), The Maitland Club, pp. 257-280.

remembered that both in English and Scottish affairs he had heavy and unpleasant cares of State resting upon him. Indeed in his procrastination, and perhaps partly by it, Charles had timed his crowning to coincide with the beginnings of his decline and downfall in Scotland.

Chapter XII

THE COMMON FISHING

In March 1629 a note in the Privy Council Register confronts us with practical industry and technical process: "The Lords nominate the Clerk of Register, Sir John Scot, and Sir James Baillie to convene togidder and call before them such skilful and honnest men as they think fitt for trying the sufficiencie of the new tanned hides, and to report to the Counsall what they find thairin".[1]

This refers to the venture of Lord Erskine who claimed to have invented a new process of tanning.

Here we have an illustration—amid the amazing variety of business submitted to the Council's judgment and control—of its vigilant oversight of national industry and commerce. In the excitement of the seventeenth century's political and religious turmoil we are prone to neglect the field of economic affairs. This of course was in ceaseless operation, and in the official record we frequently find the Council taking steps to promote native crafts and the country's commercial prosperity. Of this interest there was an outstanding example during the reign of James when that Monarch in the middle of 1623 delivered to his Councillors a wide and stimulating trade review containing a number of directives which are remarkable for their searching reference to prevalent conditions and needs, and for an urgent sense of the importance of the issues involved. Despite his kingly theories and pedantic displays the King employed considerable shrewdness when dealing with plans of a practical kind. A Commission having been appointed it resolved in terms of a minute of 12th July 1623, as follows:

"The which day it was found that his Majesty's proposition anent manufactures was most princely and honourable and necessary to be undertaken and followed out as a work which will probably import credit and benefit to the country."

It was agreed that the following propositions, conceived in a

[1] Reg. P.C. 1629-1630, p. 85.

spirit of modern alertness, should be considered at an early meeting:

"What manufactures are presently within the kingdom and how they may be entertained. If the country stands in need of other manufactures: and how and from whence the practice thereof shall be brought in. What manufactures are fitted for the country and what for exportation. If the manufactures presently within the kingdom shall be holden forward according to the present working, or if they shall be reformed and reduced to a more profitable form. If there be a sufficient number of skilled workmen within the country for the manufacture of wool both to serve for the use of the country and for exportation. And if the number be not sufficient what further number is requisite, and where shall they be had. If notice shall be taken as near as conveniently what may be the quality of wool within the country. Whether it is more expedient that one or two societies shall be joined, and what places are fitted for erecting the works. If it be not expedient that commission be given to certain persons to set down rules and ordinances for keeping the workmen and their helpers and prentices in order and obedience."[1]

The terms of this last proposition cast their own light on the labour background where restiveness and rabbling reflected harsh conditions and the absence of effective supervision.

Following upon this review a Standing Commission on Manufactures was appointed, its importance being emphasised by its representative character; in its composition it drew on the Nobility, the Gentry, and the Burghs. Sir John Scot was a member, and reports appear occasionally in the Register in future years.[2]

In the succeeding reign of Charles concern for the country's industry continued but it became largely engrossed with the native fishing, a primary source of national subsistence and profit. Here too in the course of lengthy and difficult negotiation the serious and patriotic spirit of the Lords of Council was conspicuously in evidence. In this connection we have the almost incredible story of the Common Fishing.

The commercial venture which was entitled as above was designed on grandiose lines and its originators quite deliberately set it forth as a "British" scheme. The King was so much its

[1] Reg. P.C. 1622-1625, p. 291. Wool, specially noted above, was as in England, a staple product of great value in the industry of weaving and the export of cloth.   [2] Ibid., pp. 299-302.

inspirer, or at anyrate took it so definitely under his personal patronage, and the plan involved to such an extent the collectivisation of private effort and means under a Corporation set up by the State, that it might truthfully be described in modern terms as a royal venture in nationalised industry.

As a common merger of the fishing trade of England, Scotland, and Ireland, it tended to disturb the standing of the separate kingdoms, for the ambition of the speculators, who hoped for profit on a most extensive scale and proposed to exploit the seas which lapped all shores alike, led to the inclusion of laws of mutual citizenship and tended to blur and efface the outlines of individual sovereignty.

This vast trading scheme, conceived and launched as a business of State, has its history engrossed in the records of England and Scotland, and in some measure it involved official collaboration between the two countries, but in respect of the enactments required to give effect to its proposals it was dealt with necessarily by the separate legislatures, and the English connection centres in Whitehall only because the scheme emanated thence where the King had his court with his advisers at hand. Common Fishing it may have been but it was a problem particularly applying to Scotland, although it could never have originated in Scotland. The fact that Charles with his kingly theories, his character, and his financial needs, was England's king affected and coloured the whole of the negotiations.

Here we have an action whose consequences were deeper in implication and wider in scope than anything involved in a coronation ceremonial or in any other measures relating to the country's domestic trade or manufacture. Scotland to a far greater degree than England lived on its fishing industry, and representative interests brought into the picture the title to superiorities possessed by landowners around the coasts, the rights and interests of the Free Burghs, and the ancient privileges of the fishing population: three vital matters which demanded the most serious and particular care on the part of the Estates and the Privy Council.

In the record of these critical proposals, which were keenly studied and debated in all their aspects, we have a valuable insight not only into the concerns of a most important national activity, but into the temper and manner in which these concerns were weighed and handled by the statesmen of the time.

We review it in these pages not because Sir John Scot was outstanding in its promotion. The fact is that the scheme, being officially inspired and its problems studied in common by the nation's leaders, at first by the Estates and later by the Privy Council, no individual could be specially identified with its progress and completion. But it will be appreciated that the importance of the venture was such that not to consider it along with the other issues raised in this work would leave our survey of the period historically impaired and incomplete. As to Sir John's personal interest in this matter there can be no question. At a later date he owned the fishings of the island of Inchkeith. Here, too, it is the Scottish story that we present as that story is reported fully and clearly in the National records.

The business opened in the following circumstances.

In the months of July and August 1630, the first great National Convention of Charles's reign was held in Edinburgh. Its chief purpose was to vote supplies and make provision for the King's promised coronation visit. Parliament took steps in this direction by fixing an annual tax of 30 shillings on "everie pund land of old extent" for four years.[1] It was while this assembly was sitting that the royal communication was received concerning a General or Common Fishing. The matter it will be seen originated in the English Council and took process in this way:

"At Halyrudhous, 30 July 1630.

"The whilk day Sir Williame Alexander, his Majesteis principall Secretarie in this kingdome, exhibited to the Estaits his Majesteis missive letter underwrittin, togidder with the instructiouns given by his Majestie about the erection of a General Fishing. Of whilk missive and instructiouns the tennour follows.

"Charles R.

"Right trustie and weil belovit cousines and counsellours, We greit yow weill. Having with the advice of our Counsell heere in England maturelie considered that, as weill in thankfulnesse to Almightie God as for the benefit of our loving subjects, we ought no longer to neglect that blessing offered unto us in the great abundance of fish upon all the coasts of these isllands, that we may enjoy with more honnour these rights which properlie belong to our imperiall crowne and are usurped by strangers, We have

[1] Acts Parl. Scot., V, pp. 209-210.

182

thairfoir considered of a way which in tyme by God's favour may produce this good effect, and also increase our navigatioun and trade. And because this worke concerneth equallie all our three kingdomes and must thairfoir be undertaken and ordoured by commoun counsell and assistance, We have taken this opportunitie of your conventioun at Edinborrow to send our instructiouns to Sir Williame Alexander our Secretarie for Scotland. And we require yow to give him hearing at large, and freelie to treate with him on everie point in whatsoever may be found expedient for the furtherance of so good and great a worke. And with-all we expect that yow proceid not onlie to a resolutioun upon such articles as fall to be agreed upon, bot that yow also endeavoure to putt thame in executioun, so that by him we may speedilie understand how yow take it to heart and how farre yow concurre in the worke: Whairin you may expect from us suche priviledges and powers as sall be as convenient and reasonable as yow can desyre. And also be assured that we sall gratiouslie accept your extraordinarie care and forwardnesse in a bussines which with extraordinarie earnestnesse we recommend unto yow. Given at our Palace of Westminster the 12 day of July 1630.

By his Majesteis commandment
John Coke."[1]

It will be found that the reference in the letter to "rights usurped by strangers"—a state of things which is quoted as justifying the new official scheme—was treated somewhat sceptically later on by the spokesmen of the Free Burghs. The reference to strangers implied the Dutch fishing fleets which had customarily been active in the northern waters around the Scottish coast and had by the early seventeenth century organised and enormously increased their trade.[2]

James VI in return for compensation and on certain conditions granted rights of fishing in Scottish seas to the Dutch: but an important provision was that they had to keep "ane kenning" (14 miles) from the land, and the shore and loch fishings were reserved for the natives. The territorial waters appear never to have been invaded by others.[3]

---

[1] Acts Parl. Scot., V, pp. 220-223.
[2] *Trade and Fishing of Great Britain* (1661), J. Smith, pp. 11-12.
[3] *History of the Outer Hebrides*, W. C. Mackenzie, p. 295.

The reference therefore in Charles's letter to "rights usurped by strangers" had no strict application to the staple native industry which we will find repeatedly described as "the land fishing". Yet the allegation was used as a justification for the State venture which actually took over almost all the native waters. It is more than possible that emulation of the profitable Dutch success was the prime motive for the commercial measures now being initiated.

At this time Charles was harassed with financial difficulties. His long efforts to gain supply from the English Parliament had been frustrated and he was now ruling England without a Parliament and with a scarcity of means. We cannot therefore altogether dismiss the suspicion that the project of the General Fishing—"so good and great a worke", which he "recommended with extraordinarie earnestnesse"—was intended to give some replenishment to the royal coffers; and certainly the forecast of profits was distinctly dazzling.

The character of the State Secretary, Sir John Coke, supports this view. It was he, an unpopular figure, who had been employed to introduce to Parliament the King's frequent requests for money. Clarendon said of him, "His cardinal perfection was industry and his most eminent infirmity covetousness".[1] It was from this background that the fishing proposals emerged and became a subject of long and stubborn debate to the Scottish Estates, the Privy Council, and the Free Burghs, the representatives of the latter being particularly shrewd and dogged in the contest.

A letter almost in the terms of the foregoing was at the same time addressed to the Council. It included the good phrase and plan that the Fishing might become "a nursery of seamen", and pressed the point that, "a great stock (of capital) would require to be raised by contributions of the adventurers"—a term of English usage implying the shareholders—"who will not be drawn into it but by the hope of great and present gain".[2]

When we examine the plan it is seen to comprise an orderly scheme considerable in conception and highly optimistic in outlook. With cool elaboration and calculation it describes the steps by which the right of private fishing may be taken from the lieges and the fruit of their labours be multiplied with advantage

---

[1] *History of the Rebellion* (1836), Clarendon, III, p. 114. He estimated that the profits on the Lewis fishing alone would amount in one year to £18,270. *Hist. of the Outer Hebrides*, W. C. Mackenzie, pp. 221-222.
[2] Acts Parl. Scot., V, p. 221.

to the "adventurers", among whom Charles, chiefly by an expenditure of his royal rights, was prominent.

In the prospectus the costs are swiftly estimated on the basis of a fleet of boats two hundred in number, each of forty tons burthen and with a crew of sixteen men. The cost of the hulls, the fittings, the nets, the wages, and the victualling is precisely stated. The fishing seasons are said to be from June to September and October to January for herring, with the month of March for ling and cod. The catches are closely enumerated: in the March fishing, for example, "Everie vessel may catch 6,000 fish"; and the total annual profit, with the capital charges met, is reckoned at £165,414. The second last clause in the tabulation reads: "And so these three fishings in one yeare will repay all the disbursements, and yeeld in cleere profit all the shippes and netts with thair furniture to serve againe for manie yeeres, and beside, in money to be shared among the adventurers, £165,414."[1]

The Privy Council was instructed to enquire as to the number of vessels that might be furnished and the proportion of money that might be raised in Scotland, and "to consult with the nobilitie and gentrie, and speciallie with the free burrows", on the whole question. This note of solicitude concerning the Burghs was certainly not misplaced.

When, however, the originators proceeded to set down the governing conditions as distinct from the framework of the practical system they soon reached serious questions of sovereignty and citizenship and common right. Making the observation that the herring fishing was carried on all the year about the Hebrides and Ireland, they proposed that "the adventurers should fishe freelie in all plaices and at all tymes, yitt so as the lawes and freedome of everie kingdome may be preserved, whilk is our gratious resolutioun".[2] Nevertheless (in spite of the cautionary clause) here obviously was an intention to invade coastal waters, the preserves of the fishing population of the several nations, and the intention, it may be said, was fulfilled in the royal decisions made later.

It was a logical step from the proposition that "all adventurers should fishe freelie in all plaices", to the resolution that "they should be naturalised respectively in either kingdome both to obey the lawes and to enjoy the liberties thairin".[3] This mutual

[1] Acts Parl. Scot., V, pp. 221-223.
[2] Ibid., p. 222.
[3] Ibid.

exchange and enjoyment of citizenship was more easily proposed than accepted.

In a concluding note at this point it was baldly intimated that in view of the desirability of Lewis as a fishing centre the King had resolved to take it into his own hand as adherent to his crown, "yitt purposing to give such satisfaction to the Erle of Seafort as sall be honourable and just".

Colin, Earl of Seaforth,[1] who is here mentioned had received a Charter of Lewis in 1628 and hoped to have Stornoway erected into a Free Royal Port with the rights of trading in fish. But the Burghs when consulted made objection and Charles withheld his consent. Now, when the Common Fishing was anticipating a rich harvest, the King cancelled Seaforth's patent and took Lewis and its fishing to himself, an Act of Parliament being passed to this effect.

The royal letter, with its reasons, anticipations and requests, having been laid before the Convention of Estates, steps were immediately taken to appoint a Commission representative of the nobles, gentry, and burghs. Fifty-four commissioners were named and were instructed "to meete the morne at seven of the clock to conferre, reason, and treate upon the propositioun".[2] At an assembly a few days later Commissioners (27 out of 54) were instructed to meet with "the burrows" and to report on a fixed date. Throughout all the subsequent negotiations the Burghs were constantly consulted, and constituted the chief bargaining agent.

The result of this initial conference with those who represented the country's fishing interests was submitted to the Convention on 7th August 1630. The Commissioners' report was an uncompromising document to this effect:

"Halyrudhous, 7th August 1630.

"They fand the associatioun with England to be verie inconvenient. Touching the land fishing—which consists in fishing within loches and isles and *twentie aucht myles* from the land coast, whilk is proper to the natives and whairof they have been in continuall possession and never interrupted by the Hollanders— they fand that the Burrowes were able and content to undertake it by thamselffes without communicating with anie other natioun.

[1] Note No. 83, p. 227.
[2] Acts Parl. Scot., V, p. 223.

"It being demanded (a question apparently put by the Commission to the Burghs) if Englishmen, being permitted by his Majestie to fish in the loches, might bring thair fish to Free Ports and sell thame to the lieges? It was answered that they may not by the lawes of the Kingdom".[1, 2]

At this point the Convention adjourned to allow the Commission and Burghs to meet and consider certain propositions which if answered would clear the way for further action.

"The Estaits ordains the Committee to meet at twa of the clocke, and to confer, reasoun, and report thair resolutiouns to the public meeting at three of the clocke", on the following points:

"If they will enter into ane associatioun with the English for undertaking the Commoun Fishing indistinctlie without exception?

Or if they will joyne thairin with reservatioun of the land fishing?

Or if they will absolutlie refuise the associatioun?

And that they sett down the reasouns of thair desyres, or refusall, to be considered by the Table.

Eodem die post meridiem.

The Burrowes declared as above and the Estaits renewed the Commission to meit on the first Privie Counsell day of November."[3]

The bearing of this appears to be that the Burghs adhered to the points made in the earlier report, namely: the inconvenience of the Association, the native right to the land fishing, and the law prohibiting Englishmen from selling fish in Free Ports.

The answers at this early stage contained a plainly intended negative, but the King's manner of negotiation brought about later a kind of superficial compliance which throughout future proceedings cloaked the native inertia that finally defeated the whole ambitious scheme.

The Convention, inasmuch as it must perforce conclude its sittings, had committed the business to the Privy Council which was due to meet on 3rd November. Meanwhile the Commission prepared its report for the King, wherein certain "Observations" resting on the contention of the Burghs contained the essential objections and difficulties.

This was sent and on 12th October Charles made reply in two

1 Acts Parl. Scot., V, p. 226.
2 Note No. 84, p. 228.
3 Acts Parl. Scot., V, pp. 226-227.

letters, one directed to the Estates and the other to the Council, both being in their tone pacific and conciliatory. At the same time the English Council replied to the Observations of the Commission.

Charles in his letter acknowledged the steps already taken and urged the final completion of arrangements He gave assurances that no right would be invaded and that only benefit was intended. The Estates were asked what support and contribution might be expected, and were requested to send a delegation to England, "with absolute power to conclude thairin without anie restrictioun". In an urgent postscript in his "own hand" he said:

"This is a worke of so great good to both my kingdomes that I have thought good by these few lines of my owne hand seriouslie to recommend it unto yow. The furthering or hindering of which will either oblige or disoblige me more than anie one business that has happened in my time. C.R."

The letter to the Council was almost alike, and of the project it said: "Which speciallie recommending to your care we bid yow fareweill. From our honnour of Hampton Court the 12 day of October, 1630."[1]

The matter had now passed from the Estates to the Privy Council, and when that body met at Holyroodhouse on 3rd November 1630, the attendance numbered 13 Councillors and 21 Commissioners out of the whole number who had been individually notified. The President, William Earl of Menteith, outlined the proceedings up to date. First, the royal instructions in the King's original letter. Second, the Observations made by the Scottish Commission in the light of their discussions both in the Convention and with the Burgh representatives. Third, the rejoinder made by the English Council to which these Observations had been submitted in the interval. Copies of Menteith's report were issued to all present, "to be considered by thame, and they to offer their opinion and judgment concerning the same on Mononday nixt at ten of the clocke", which was 8th November.[2]

The second item in the above order, namely the Observations, which skilfully supported and amplified the position taken by the Burghs, are of considerable interest. They read:

"Whereas from the instructiouns sent by his Majestie to his Secretarie of Scotland concerning the erectioun of a Generall Fishing, it would appeare that the said fishing is understood of

---

[1] Acts Parl. Scot., V, pp. 229-230.
[2] Ibid., p. 228.

these fishings whairof the benefite is onlie reaped by strangers, and doth no way touche these fishings which are enjoyed by natives, it is necessarie that the particular fishings within everie Kingdome be made known, so that the lawes and freedoms of everie Kingdome may be preserved.

"It is desyred that it may be cleared what these fishings are which are called commoun benefits and cannot be separately enjoyed.

"It is desyred to understand what the severall undertakings will be for this Generall Fishing in England and Ireland.

"It is desyred that the Scottish adventurers be naturalized in England, seeing that the denization whiche the Englishe are to have in Scotland is equivalent to naturalization in England.

"It would be considered in what maner the returne for the fish exported out of each kingdome sall be made to the kingdome whairin they are takin.

"As to the government of the Associatioun; it is fitt before being treatted of, that the preceding articles be cleered and the severall undertakings condiscended upon, so that all the undertakers may joyne togidder for the perfyting thairof.[1]

"As to the article for building one or more Free Burrowes in the isle of Lewes; there can be no answer given thairunto till the nixt meeting of the Estaits, in regarde that it would be against the standing right of Regall Burrowes and of others having interest, who, in reasoun, must be heard before anie opinioun be given thairin.

Sic subscribitur. W. Alexander."[2]

To these shrewd queries and observations the English Council made the following politic answers.

"With respect to the first and second foregoing articles, his Majesteis royall and just intentioun is, as we conceave, most cleere, not to take away or derogat frome the particular and personall grants and rights of anie of his subjects, whose lawes and liberties he purposeth to mainteane. But that in all his kingdome where commoun fishing is or may be used by anie of his people, that everie brother of this companie, made capable according to the respective lawes of each kingdome, may freelie

[1] It is to be noted how Charles dealt with this suggestion of popular control.
[2] Acts Parl. Scot., V, p. 228.

fish there. This mutual participatioun being the bond of union and sole means to recover his Majesteis right and power at sea, and to enriche all his subjects, and these chieflie where the greatest fishings are.

"For the third, they are assured that in England and Ireland the proportioun (of capital contributed) sall be answerable to the abilities of either kingdome and the greatnesse of the worke.

"Fourth The difference betuix naturalizing and free endenizing is not important in the mater of fishing, which is the onlie use the companie will make of them. When a parliament sall be callit the brothers of this companie will probablie finde no difficultie to obteane what they desyre.

"Fifth. Touching the (financial) returns, his Majestie will provide according to his wisdome for his owne indemnitie and interest: and it cannot be doubted that, for the public profit, thair returnes will respectivelie increase according to the increase of trade."

The reply concludes with a warning note against any idea that a work like the Fishing could be ruled by "popular agreement", and states plainly the principle of the monarch's absolute control.

"The government of the companies can have no reference to a popular agreatioun (agreement) of all the undertakers, inasmuch as thair liberteis and powers depend whollie upon the king's grace and gift, which is the more to be respected for that he hath expressed his gratious purpose to admit advice from his counsell in eache kingdome in anie thing that may require further consideratioun. We doubt not that the lords and estates in Scotland will concurre with suche a government as sall be most conformable to the crowne we live under and obey."[1]

Of the proposal to erect new Royal Burghs, a matter which excited the acute jealousy of the existing burghs, it says:

"Though we are perswaded that his Majestie will not straine his prerogative royall, nor exercise other powers than the lawes of that kingdome have putt into his hands, yitt we will not take upon us to answere yow in this point but referre yow to his Majestie for full satisfactioun. Onlie wishing that his Majesteis most royall, just, and cleere intentiouns may prevaile with yours, *not to questioun* but unanimouslie to advance so profitable a worke: as we are confident yow will endeavoure."[2]

[1] Acts Parl. Scot., V, p. 229.
[2] *Ibid.*

On "Mononday nixt at ten of the clocke", as arranged, the Council (11) and Commissioners (22) duly met at "Halyrudhous" to give their opinion and judgment concerning the foregoing, and their decision was to continue the matter "till Wedensday nixt at twa of the clocke, and ordanes every Estait[1] to consider how the Generall Fishing may be undertaken and ordoured with the least harme and greatest benefite to this State, and what instructiouns are fitt to be given to the Commissioners who sall be directed to treate anent it".[2]

On the 10th, when there were 14 Councillors and 9 Commissioners present, the discussion was delayed "till the morne in the afternoone". There were now present the same number of Councillors with two more Commissioners, and the special delegation to go to London was appointed. The paucity of numbers in the sederunt is significant.

"At Halyrudhous, 11th November 1630.

"The whilk day the Lords and Commissioun agreed and voted that ane commission sall be granted to the Erle of Mortoun, Treasurer, the Erle of Menteith, president, the Marquess of Hamiltoun, the Erles of Roxburgh and Carrick, Sir Williame Alexander, Secretar, Mr Johne Hay and Mr George Fletcher, or anie five of thame, to convene and meet with the English Commissioners and to conferre and treat upon everie thing that may concerne the intendit Associatioun, and with absolut power to conclude thairin, having his Majesteis approbatioun thairto; with provisioun that nothing be done nor concluded prejudiciall to the priviledges of this kingdome and crowne thairof." Also, "Certane articles were sett down by the meiting whairupon the Instructions to be given (to the Commissioners) sall be formed and drawn up".[3]

"At Halyrudhous, 12th November 1630". There were present 14 Councillors and 7 Commissioners. The Commission and its Instructions were officially allowed in the general terms already quoted and were subscribed by the Chancellor, the Bishops of St Andrews, Dunkeld, and Dunblane, Haddington, Winton, Melville, Hamilton, and Sir Thomas Hope. Sir John Scot as Director of Chancery was given warrant to "exped" the Commission and to append the Great Seal thereto.

[1] Note No. 85, p. 228.
[2] Acts Parl. Scot., V, p. 230.
[3] Ibid., p. 231.

The Instructions reveal the anxiety of the Scottish Council and indicate the resolution of the Burghs that no national right in fishing shall be surrendered. This of course was the whole field of dispute. Fishing beyond the "twentie aucht myle" limit (the figure used by the Burghs)[1] was presumably always open to anyone whatever his nationality. This made the King's claim "to enjoy rights which are usurped by strangers" rather extravagant, and, as has been noted, elicited from the Burghs the assertion that "no Hollander had ever invaded the land fishing". It also provoked their query about, "what these fishings are whilk are called commoun benefits and cannot be separately enjoyed?"

The following are the Instructions which were given to the special delegation, the strict exceptions being noteworthy.

"Instructions givin for the Kingdome of Scotland (to the Commissioners) authorized by warrant under the great seale to treate with the Commissioners for the Kingdome of England anent the erecting of a Commoun Fishing.

"1. Yow are warned carefully to advert to the provisioun that nothing be done derogatory to the libertie and privileges of the kingdome, crowne, and lawes thairof.

"2. Yow are to have ane speciall care that by ane article of the treatie it be enacted that the natives of this kingdome be preferred in the choice of the most commodious and opportune places for erecting thair magazens;[2] and yow are lykewayes to advert and provyde that suche places be desyned and appointed to the English as may be without manifest prejudice to the land fishing here.

"3. Yow are to have the lyke care that it be declared by ane article that the seas foreanent the coasts of this kingdome and about the isles thairof and all that is interjected betuix thame and that mid-lyne in the seas whilk is equallie distant from the opposite land, are Scotish seas, properlie belonging to the crown of Scotland, and that the English has no right nor libertie to fishe thairin, nor no part thairof, but by vertew of the Associatioun, and not otherwayes.

"4. That it be declared that these of the Associatioun sall be permitted to fishe in all the Scotish seas, excepting alwayes and reserving to the Scotishmen thair trade of fishing within thair loches, firthes, and bayes within the mayne land and isles of this

---

[1] The protected limit is afterwards stated as 14 miles.
[2] A "magazine" was a storehouse.

kingdome, and in the seas within fourteene myles of the coasts of the said mayne lands and islands.

"5. That it be provided that these of the Scotish Associatioun have and injoy the lyke priviledges and immunities of custome, and erecting of magazens, in England and Ireland, as the English doe injoy heere in Scotland. And that for this effect it be declared and provided that naturalizatioun sall import no forder priviledge to the English in Scotland than the Scotish doe injoy of thair denizatioun in England.

"6. That it be declared and provided that these of the English Associatioun who sall settle thameselffes upon Scotish land sall be debarred during thair abode in these places from all fishing within the reserved waters, except onlie for taking of freshe fishe for thair present use and interteanment allanerlie, and that they buy no fishe upon the sea nor land from the natives but for thair interteanment, as said is. And that they, nor nane of the English Associatioun, sall be suffered to have commerce, nor to make merchantdise, except onlie of victualls and uther necessars for thair present use and consumption: and that they export no commodities furth of the kingdome, nor import anie to be sauld within the same, except fish taken by thair awne vessellis.

"7. That it be declared and provided that these of the English Associatioun sall be liable to the payment of custome, bulyeon, and other duties for the fish which they sall make[1] on the Scotish land and export furth of the same.

"8. That the fish to be taken by vertew of the Associatioun sall be free to be inbrought and sauld in all his Majesteis thrie dominiouns.

"9. That these of the English Associatioun who sall bring and make fish upon the Scotish ground sall be equallie subject with the natives to rateablie contribute towards the furnishing and provisioun of this countrie as occasioun sall require and conforme to the lawes of the kingdome made in this behalfe.

"10. Yow are to have ane speciall care, and to foresee, that the proportioun of the Scotish undertaking be not limited nor defynned, and that it be not exclusive of what we may afterwards contribute, according as our abilities sall fra tyme to tyme increase.

"11. It is lykewayes to be provided that no privilege granted to the brethrein of the Associatioun sall be prejudiciall to the liberties

---

[1] The word "make" as here used means to salt or cure.

which the natives of this kingdome formerlie injoyed for selling thair fish in England.

"12. If anie question arise betuix the persons of the Associatioun concerning the fishing in Scotland, the mater sall be determined before the Commoun Counsells to be erected in either kingdome for this purpose, without appeale to be made thairfra.

"13. That no strangers (foreigners) be admitted to the Associatioun otherwayes than as servants, except they transport thameselffes to his Majesteis domininouns, take the oathe of alledgeance and be indenizened: and that they trade with thair owne stocks, and subject to the lawes of the kingdome anent trade."[1]

At this point a protest was registered against the substitution of the title "Britain" for "Scotland" in the articles of the Association. The protest is included as article 14, and the Lords requested the Commission to give expression to it when they went south. The Privy Council on 9th November prefaces the Commission's instructions with the following mandate to Sir John Scot:

"14. Forasmeikle as there is ane commissioun ordained to be passed and exped under his Majesteis great seale to some speciall and selectit persons of this kingdome for conferring, treating, and concluding with the commissioners to be nominat and authorised of his Majestie under the great seale of England, toward ane associatioun and erecting of ane Commoun Fishing; and whereas this matter is nationall betuix Scotland and England, whilk are twa free and distinct estates and kingdomes, and should be differenced by thair particular names and not confoundit under the name of Great Britane: and whereas lykewayes the great seale of this kingdome in the circumscriptioun thairof bears the particular names of Scotland, England, France and Ireland, thairfoir the Lords of Secreit Counsell ordains and commands Sir John Scot of Scottistarvet, Director of the Chancellarie, to write the said commissioun in these termes: *Carolus Dei gratia Scotiae, Angliae, Franciae* et *Hiberniae rex, fidei defensor;* anent the doing whairof the extract of this act sall be unto the said Sir John ane warrant."[2, 3]

The direction to the delegation proceeds to broaden the basis of protest by pointing out that there has been "no union as yitt

[1] Acts Parl. Scot., V, p. 232-233.
[2] Reg. P.C. 1630-1632, pp. 56-57.
[3] Note No. 86, p. 228.

with England", and that "the style Great Britane" is not received nor employed there. They were asked to report to the King himself the prejudice done to Scotland by this practice.[1, 2]

This concluded the Instructions, but in spite of the many stiff and angular propositions contained therein, the giving with one hand and taking back with the other, the Council also enclosed a congratulatory and obsequious message intended as a song of "placebo", which referred to "the great and glorious worke of the fishing in which we have bended our whole endeavours to give your Majestie content and satisfactioun".[3]

The diplomatic covering note (which did not deceive the King) ran as follows:

"Most Sacred Soverane,

"Upon receipt of your Majesteis letter of the twelfe of October last, and upon our perusall of the postscript thairof writtin with your Majesteis owne hand, we wer exceedinglie overjoyed to perceave your Majesteis gratious approbatioun of our weake endeavoures in your Majesteis service, and of your Majesteis princelie care of this your Hienes' ancient kingdome and libertie thairof, and of your royall intentions and directions for advanceing all things whiche may tend to the credit of the same; and especiallie in that great and glorious worke of the fishing, in which we have bended our whole endeavoures to give your Majestie such content and satisfactioun as becometh your Majesteis most humble and loyall subjects and servants.

"We have lykewayes heard the report of suche as your Majestie did formerlie trust to treate with your other commissioners, and are so hopeful and confident of a finall and happie conclusion in that business that we have, with instructions, dispatched newe commissioners with absolute power to conclude that great worke whairof both the trade, shipping, strength, and glorie of your Majesteis kingdome may be advanced, your subjects employed, and your kingdomes and subjects secured from all feare of anie forraine invasioun, being confident of strength, substance, and maintenance at home under your Majesteis princelie government and protectioun."

The Commissioners, as men "of eminent qualitie and place",

1 Acts Parl. Scot., V, p. 233.
2 Note No. 87, p. 228.
3 Note No. 88, p. 228.

were then recommended to the King's approbation and favour so that others by their example "may hereafter be encouraged with all alacritie to execute anie other of your Majesteis services and commandements, as becometh dewtifull and loyall subjects. All which we doe humblie leave into your Majesteis own princelie consideratioun". The missive is subscribed at Halyrudhous, 23 Decembre, 1630, by "Duplin, Hadintoun, Seafort, Lauderdaill, Melvill, Carnegie, Bishop of Dumblane, Master of Elphinstoun, Archd. Achesone, Hamiltoun, Sir Thomas Hope, Sir G. Elphinstoun".[1]

The foregoing steps were taken on 12th November and 23rd December, 1630, respectively, and three months elapsed before the matter re-appeared in the Council, as it did on the last day of March 1631. The sederunt was much larger—26 in all—and Scotstarvit was now present and continued to be regularly present until the practical conclusion of the business.

Why he should not up to this time have shared the discussions is not made clear, but it was probably due to his disturbed relations with Menteith. By November 1630 the Fishing business had passed into the hands of the Privy Council, and Menteith, as President, was prominent at the few meetings that were held before the special Commission of which he was a member went south. There is reason for thinking that close association may have been judged inadvisable. The trouble which began early in 1629 had continued. Sir John had quarrelled openly with the President in Council and with Sir Thomas Hope at the Exchequer, and the threat of the former to have him displaced as an Extraordinary Lord of Session had been realised in this very month of November 1630. Exactly a year later Hope, recalling this quarrel, was inciting Menteith to discountenance Scot in a new contest for legal office. Possibly in view of what was at stake Sir John decided to play for safety, and he may be assumed to have consolidated his position for he was appointed an Ordinary Lord of Session in July 1632. When Menteith had gone to London Sir John re-appeared in the Council.

In the Fishing negotiations a stage had been reached where a progress report—in point of fact a request for guidance—sent home by the delegation was being heard. The burden of it was that in the opinion of the English Commission there was an element of "too muche" in the Scottish reservations.

[1] Acts Parl. Scot., V, p. 233.

"May it please your lordships, We have had some meetings with the English commissioners, and having demanded all firthes, loches, bayes and isles, with some distance to be reserved for the natives, it is thought too muche, except we condiscend upon particulars, whairby we may show thame that we intend onlie to reserve that without which the natives cannot subsist. And thairfoir we ourselffes not knowing the name of everie ane of these places do intreate that your lordships would be pleased to informe yourselffes particularlie of thame, and to acquaint us with the same, and of your opinion thairin. And be assured that as we will be willing to do all things reasonable that tend to the advancement of that great and good worke, so we will omit nothing that doth concerne the good of our native kingdome whairwith we are entrusted and are in duetie bound.

> Whitehall the 25 Marche 1631. Subscribitur Morton, Menteith, Roxburgh, Lorne, W. Alexander, Johne Hay, G. Fletcher."[1]

The uncompromising demand of the Burghs had been for the whole of the land fishing, which consisted of the fishing within "the loches, firthes, and bayes of the mayne land and isles, and in the seas within fourteen myles of the coasts thairof". This claim was now rejected, and Charles and his Council were forcing upon the Burghs, through the Commissioners, a policy of reduction, the limit of which was expressed in the hard phrase, "that without which the natives cannot subsist". The Scottish Council decided to pass this request back to the Burghs.

The first step in the reference was to summon the Provost and Bailies of Edinburgh, who compeared in the persons of their procurators, Nicoll Udwart and Alexander Guthrie. These legal agents pointed out that this was a matter common to all the Burghs and declared that all should be consulted. The Council agreed and "assigned unto thame the twentie day of Apryle nixtocome for giving in ane perfyte answere and report in writt concerning the particulars mentioned in the said letter".[2]

When the 20th April arrived there was a sederunt of thirteen Councillors. The Bishops of Ross and of the Isles were included, and it can be assumed that they represented both a regional and

---

[1] Acts Parl. Scot., V, p. 234.
[2] Reg. P.C. 1630-1632, p. 196.

197

a personal interest in the matter. Dues were exacted for the shipping of herrings within a diocese.

Commissioners from Edinburgh and the Burghs requested a delay until the next morning inasmuch as the question, "Whether the English sall be permitted to fishe in reserved waters", was so serious. This extension was granted and they were again instructed "To give a perfyte report in writt of the particular firthes, loches, bayes, and isles, whilk they desyre to be reserved".[1]

On the following morning it was found that "the perfyte report" described the whole Scottish coastline with its firths, and included the islands of Orkney and Shetland with all the Western Islands and the waters between the islands and mainland, with fourteen miles outward, "as being necessar for the haill lieges living upon the coasts and isles".[2]

This question of the fishings to be reserved for the natives was the crux of the whole matter, and it will be found that the King and his Councillors began and pursued a whittling process until they had reduced the reserved area of Scottish waters to such small limits as conversely enlarged the area for the Fishing Company and gave to it the hope of generous and satisfactory returns.

The Scottish Councillors themselves however judged the claims of the Burghs to be too extreme and made a gesture of concession by abolishing the fourteen mile limit save, "for suche coasts as are weill peopled, where countrie people live most by fishing, without whilk they could not possiblie subsist nor yitt be able to pay thair maisters thair fermes and dewteis".[3]

Having come to an understanding on these lines the Council conveyed the proposals to the Commissioners at Whitehall. In doing so it explained that the spokesmen of the Burghs "had stood very punctuallie upon the article of your Instructions whairby there is to be a reservation of all fishings within fourteen myles aff the land, whilk includes all loches, firthes and bayes: and thought it needlesse to condiscend upon particulars where all was includit".[4]

Why indeed should they trouble about particulars when the whole of these shoreward waters was claimed as their just right? But the Councillors proceed to state that they themselves had called

[1] Acts Parl. Scot., V, p. 234.
[2] Ibid., p. 235.
[3] Ibid.
[4] Ibid., p. 236.

for "retrinchments". They add a note that "It cannot be qualified that ever any Hollander or stranger fished in these waters", and conclude by intimating that they had aimed at getting the willing assent of the Burgh Commissioners, "and would be laithe to have thame hurt in that whilk they conceave to touch the bodie and commons of the countrie so nearly".

At this point an affecting tone of seriousness enters into the farewell and warms the ancient record: "Resting assured", it says, "that nothing will be wanting in your lordships that may tend to the preservation of the liberties of your native kingdom, we commit your lordships to God".[1]

This communication, which marked an important but by no means final stage in the negotiations, was subscribed at Holyrood by Hay the Chancellor, Wigtown, Lauderdaill, Gordoun, the Bishops of Rosse and of the Isles, Sir Thomas Hope, Sir G. Elphinstoun, Scottistarvet and Sir James Baillie.

Three months later there came a shattering royal rejoinder:

"Charles R.

"Having considderit that letter which you wrote unto us, We cannot conceave what necessitie can be for reserving so manie places, and lykewayes fourteen myles distant from everie shoar. It would seem that as these of the Associatioun have libertie to land in anie place, so they should be free to fishe wherever they are to pass. As we are willing to reserve for the natives suche fishings without which they cannot weill subsist, so we will not reserve anie thing to thame which may be a hindrance to this generall worke."[2]

Of this letter, typical of Charles's manner where the royal will was being frustrated, the Council makes the following brief minute:

"Whilk being read, heard, and considderit, the lords ordains ane copie thairof to be given to the Burrows, and that they give ane answer thairto upon Thursday nixt."

Meeting two days later (28th July 1631) the Burghs craved a delay, and the next assembly was an important one held at Perth on 22nd September of the above year. The delay of almost two months suggests an agitation on a national scale. Twenty

[1] Acts Parl. Scot., V, p. 236.
[2] Ibid., pp. 236-237.

Councillors were present and this proved to be the final and critical act of bargaining on the Scottish side. The city of Perth was probably chosen to suit the convenience of those dwelling in the north and west. We are told that "some of the nobilitie, gentrie, and commissioners for the burrows compeared and gave in the declaratioun underwrittin".[1]

It may be said that the submissive and respectful tone of this declaration, and the concessions made, show that the King's autocratic manner and his threat were having effect, but it must still remain very doubtful if men of practical experience really accepted the scheme as being justly conceived and possible of fulfilment.

In general the reservations were now limited to the Firths of Forth and Moray on the east, and the Firth of Clyde and the waters between the inner side of the Western Isles and the mainland.

There was insistence however that on the east coast, from the Red Head to Buchan Ness, there was "absolut necessitie of reservatioun of fourtein myles, both for the daylie use of the inhabitants for their sustentatioun, as lykewayes for the good of the salmond fishing in the rivers Dee, Don, Ithan and both the Eskes, whilk by the encroaching of the busses (the herring trawlers) may be altogidder undone to the great prejudice of the whole kingdome, it (salmon) being one of the most pryme native commodities of this land".[2] It was also claimed that Orkney and Shetland must be reserved, the question of the fourteen mile limit being left, as it was elsewere to "his Majesteis gratious will and pleasure".

At the Perth meeting, which occupied two days, Scot being present, the Council supported these proposals and commended the exceptions, pointing out that it was for his Majesty's satisfaction that "the Burrowes had been moved to relinquish the universalitie of their former claims", and because they were "confidentlie persuadit that your Majestie will proceed with that accustomed tender regard towards the weal of this your ancient and native kingdome which in the whole course of bussines you have beine pleased favourablie to expresse".[3]

This ended the record of negotiations as far as the Scottish

[1] Acts Parl. Scot., V, p. 237.
[2] Ibid.
[3] Ibid., pp. 238-239.

Register is concerned, and it must be admitted that the executive body of the Council had acted throughout with a serious sense of statesmanship and with great understanding and tact. It was almost exactly a year later, 7th September 1632, that the Earl of Strathern (Menteith's new title) as President produced before the Council at Holyrood the Charter for the Association of Fishing, which the minute says, "had been concluded agreeably by the Commissioners of both kingdomes".[1, 2]

The main features of the Charter were as follows: The Association would be governed by a Council twelve in number, six of the Scottish nation and six of the English or Irish. These would be "nominated and constituted in all time to come by his Majesty, his heirs and successors, and be removed at his Majesty's will and pleasure". The nominees on the Scottish side were William, Earl of Morton, William, Earl of Strathern, Robert, Earl of Roxburgh, William, Viscount of Stirling,[3] John Hay and George Fletcher. On the English side they were Richard, Lord Weston, Thomas, Earl of Arundel, Philip, Earl of Pembroke, Thomas, Viscount Savage, Francis, Lord Cottington and Sir John Coke.

The Council was to frame laws for the government of the Society, and was given judicial powers (subject to State laws) in respect of the conduct of its members and servants: in purely Association matters the Civil Courts had no standing. Courts of Judges to deal with disputes were to be set up in every province and in large towns, and to visit the fishing fleets at sea, appointments to be on a national basis equally.

The members of the Society were free to fish wherever they pleased (excepting in the area to be reserved). They could salt, dry, load and barrel their fish freely within any Burgh or outside it: they had liberty to choose sites for stages and storehouses, reasonable prices having been paid. And a clause which compelled support for the Society and severe penalties to private parties was that all non-members were strictly prohibited from trading in sea fish in any part of the King's dominions.

The Warrant for Sealing the Charter said:

"Forasmeikle as the treatie for a generall associatioun for the

---

[1] Acts Parl. Scot., V, The Charter, pp. 239-244.
[2] Note No. 89, p. 228.
[3] The Secretary, Sir William Alexander, was elevated to the peerage in 1630.

fishing, wherein his Majestie was oftymes present, is now concluded by the commissioners of both kingdomes to his Majesteis great contentment, and to the evident good of both, thairfoir the Lords of Secreit Counsell according to his Majesteis warrant ordains and commands Sir John Scot, knight, director of our soverane lord's Chancellarie, to pas and exped the said twa chartours throw the Chancellarie, and ordains George, Viscount of Dupline, Lord high Chanceller, to append his Majesteis great seale to the said twa chartours, putting the great seale of Scotland in the first place to the chartour whilk his Majestie has given as King of Scotland, England and Ireland, and to append the great seale to the other chartour whilk his Majestie has given as King of England, Scotland and Ireland in the second place: and ordains the directour of Chancellarie to dait the said twa chartours of the dait of which the chartours of the Kingdome of England are, which are dated at Westminster the nyneteenth day of July 1632.[1] Anent the doing of whilk this act sall be unto the Lord Chanceller and Directour of Chancellarie, and to either of thame, ane warrand."[2]

Charles, it should be said, had condescended to prescribe the reserved fishings to which there was only an allusion in the Charter. These were, the area of the Forth estuary with the outward boundaries of St Abb's Head (always called St Tabb's Head) and the Red Head near Lunan Bay: and the Firth of Clyde with the outward bounds of the Mulls of Galloway and Kintyre. There is no mention of any other area in this letter which was specifically written about reservations and is dated at Oatlands the last day of July 1632. An Act of Parliament was passed later reserving the Lewis fishing for the King. One can see how ineffectual were the strivings of the Burghs and the Council, and how illusory was the King's "tender regard" for his ancient kingdom and the subsistence of its toiling people.

On this whole business as recorded in the Acts of Parliament the Clerk now inscribes the concluding note: "Heere ends the Acts of the Convention and all that hes past in the treatie anent the Fishing. Jacobus Prymrois".[3]

The subsequent history of this ambitious effort in national trade shows that it was almost completely abortive, and that, too,

[1] Note No. 90, p. 228.
[2] Acts Parl. Scot., V, pp. 243-244.
[3] Ibid., p. 246.

at an early date. Misselden in 1623 had said that a Society of Fishing would be "a mine of gold of extent unlimited".[1] But the verdict passed on the practical venture was that it was "the chief failure of the epoch before the Civil War".[2]

There were two causes of this. The first was the ludicrously insufficient supply of capital. Although the original computation of fishing vessels was in hundreds, actually there was no more capital than could build and equip twenty herring busses. Another cause was that the fish taken could not be salted in a sufficient manner to stand long transit to the markets abroad, a defect suggesting the use of inferior materials, due probably to the tax imposed on the better salt imported from overseas.[3] But behind everything there must have been the drag and opposition of the fishing populace and of the Free Burghs who obviously could not be forcibly recruited into such a scheme. Charles and his Society had invaded the sphere of a basic means of livelihood for the whole fishing fraternity and had attempted to compel conformity against native interests and long-standing rights.[4]

We hear of a new "Royal Company" in 1677: it too was endowed with special privileges and provoked popular defiance of its regulations.[5] How this Company was finally regarded may be seen in the legislation which sought to redress the state of the industry in 1690.

"The Act Annulling the Gift of Erection of the Royal Company of Fishing.

"Our Soveraigne Lord and Lady, with the consent of the Estates convened in Parliament, considering that the late Royall Company erected for Fishing is now dissolved by reteiring their stocks and quitting the prosecution of that trade . . . and considering that they yet continue to exact six punds Scots per last of all herrings exported furth the Kingdom to the hurt and prejudice of his Majesteis lieges, Therefore their Majesties, with the advice and consent of the Estates of Parliament, Do rescind, reduce, and

---

[1] *The Balance of Trade* (1623), Edward Misselden, pp. 140-141.

[2] "An unbroken record of failure and loss." *Royal Fishery Companies of the Seventeenth Century*, Elder, p. 81.

[3] *Joint Stock Companies to 1720.* W. R. Scott, II, p. 366. He says that by 1638 the whole subscribed capital of the parent Society was lost. Hume Brown comments: "We seem to have here the very temper that issued in the disasters of Darien". Reg. P.C. 1630-1632, p. xix.

[4] Note No. 91, p. 228.

[5] *History of the Outer Hebrides*, W. C. Mackenzie, p. 327.

annull the forsaid gift of Erection, with the haill priviledges and immunities belonging thereto, together with all Acts, confirmations, and ratifications thereof. And declares the forsaid Company to be dissolved: Discharging heirby and strictly prohibiting the exacting of the six punds Scots for the last of herrings, or any other imposition or exaction upon herrings or any other fishes on account of the forsaid Company, or of any having their rights, from the takers or exporters of herrings, salmond, white fishes, or any other fishes in all tyme coming.

"And for the further encouragement of the trade of fishing, their Majesties, with the advice and consent forsaid, Do allow, invite, and encourage the Merchants of the Royall Burroughs, and others of their good subjects, to employ their stocks and industry in the trade of fishing and curing of herring. In which they shall enjoy all the freedoms and advantages competent to them before the Erection of the forsaid Company. And, particularly, the forraigne salt imported and employed for the curing of fishes shall be free of Excise or other duty.

"It is also hereby expressly provided and declared that, albeit the taking of fishes is allowed to all the lieges without prejudice of men's particular proportions, yet the exportation of fish doth belong to the Merchants of the Royall Burroughs, conform to the Act of Parliament of this present Parliament."[1]

A scrutiny of the above Act shows how complete was the recognition of the injustice done to the lieges by the Royal Company of Charles II and by the earlier Erections of 1632 and 1661. The Annulling Act of 1690 discloses a widely different attitude. Here was a re-orientation of policy which departed from autocracy and privilege and embodied in a remarkable degree the modern conceptions of popular right and the responsibilities of the State to a vital basic industry.

[1] Acts Parl. Scot., IX, p. 224.

CHAPTER XIII

THE STAGGERING STATE OF SCOTS STATESMEN

The above alliterative title may have pleased Sir John's sense of humour but there is little humour in the underlying conception of his work. The period of its review covers fairly nearly the years 1560 to 1660. These hundred years contained not only remarkable political misfortunes and vicissitudes for the nation, but offered in the wealth represented by church lands, endowments, and proscribed estates, an unprecedented field for the acquisition of property by those noblemen in power who combined desire with the means of possession. Ethical standards in spite of the Reformation were much invaded by worldliness and greed, and, where possession was achieved, the national upheavals and the uncertainty of life were such that retention could not long be guaranteed.

It was in this vexed scene of varying fortune that Scot of Scotstarvit lived long years at the centre of affairs and in a position of official advantage, whereby he was able to make intimate observation of events and their sequel, and of individuals and their histories. So long did he live that he saw not only the beginning but the conclusion of many ambitious careers. His minutes and observations thereanent constitute the book which in its reflections on individuals and their conduct has sometimes provoked severe adverse comment.

In the authoritative version which was first published by Walter Ruddiman, junior, in 1754 under the editorship of Walter Goodall, the producers claim to have studied not only several later manuscripts but one very old copy which contained additions, and even "whole lives" written in the author's own hand, and was therefore judged to be an original. Sir John, whose literary method was to make anecdotes illustrate history and indicate character, contented himself usually as to the time of events by the reference of the context. The publishers therefore took advantage of the labours of "Dr Mackenzie, a very learned Scots antiquarian", who with fastidious zeal had furnished his own copy of *The Staggering State* with precise dates in the margin, and had also supplied a few footnotes.[1] To these the editor added other notes which are invariably short amplifications of matters baldly referred to by the author. As evidence of the latter's historical accuracy it may be said that in these footnotes there are scarcely more than a dozen proffered corrections, and few or none of a serious character, although there are sometimes heated confutations of partisan statements made by George Buchanan and John Knox on whom Scot occasionally founds his charges.

Sir John's compilation merits examination for several reasons. For one thing its papers comprise an ordered catalogue of cases classified according to office. The author himself calls it, "This catalogue of Statesmen", and again, "This short catalogue". Although mere sketchy summaries the papers profess to carry the essence of the matter in the reported instances, and can be accepted as a magazine of trustworthy information on certain features of conduct which are not likely to appear in the standard records. For the historian they contribute some curious and valuable information about the social conditions and customs of the time.

The Staggering State must also be accepted as a treatise containing a serious theme, although the writer never pauses to say so or to rationalise expressly upon the matter: the theme is in fact implicit, and is amply and vividly illustrated in a long succession of concrete examples. Its underlying proposition, which forms a linking principle to its pages, is a conviction drawn from many instances to the effect that a law of retribution operates inevitably in the affairs of human society. It is indubitable from the insistence with which he draws attention to it that the book was penned in order to illuminate this rule. He also admits in a related fashion the conception of the Mosaic Law where it teaches that the ill-doing of the fathers is visited upon the children. Repeatedly at the end of his notes he pronounces upon the family disasters which have followed from the greedy initial conquest of lands and riches. There is a frequent refrain that the race, or family, "is like to cease", and he sees the ill-gotten wealth "evanishing and melting like snow off a dyke". Carlyle in his *Cromwell* calls *The Staggering State* "a strange little book, not a

[1] This was probably George Mackenzie, M.D., 1669-1728, of the Seaforth family. His chief work was *Lives and Characters of the most Eminent Writers of the Scottish Nation*.

satire but a Homily on Life's nothingness enforced by examples: it gives in brief compass the cream of Scotch Biographic History in that age".[1] This is a recommendation of some worth coming from such an authority.

In a way the work may be regarded as a Memoir which not only says something directly about the matters handled but something indirectly about the author, as Carlyle notes. From it we can deduce his sharp habit of observation, and possibly his ready ear for news and even for gossip, for although historical sources are at his command and quoted as required, yet he writes rather as one who draws upon the recollections stored up in his retentive memory: much of it is the harvest of things heard or noted in the passing in a day when public report was the readiest agency of the nation's domestic history. He has the lawyer's detachment which leaves his expression composed even when he is making serious allegations. In common with his contemporaries he shared, but not to a pronounced extent, a proneness to credulity and superstition and this may occasionally have disturbed his judgment. But his moral standards, although perhaps more robust than refined, are consistent and worthy, and no one can miss the genuine ring of his indignation over wrong and oppression. He possessed a deep and active sense of a divine rule operating in the life of man.

With respect to the adverse charges which have been levelled against him a note of apology is required. In the first place it has to be admitted that in a number of instances the character of the report casts grave reflections on the private life of the persons concerned. But it can at least be said that there is no attempt at embellishment and no love of scandal for its own sake; also a suggestion of malignancy is scarcely justified and is not likely to have invaded the mind of a man whose affections were sound, as is shown by his friendships, and who was accustomed to the impartial verdicts of law and justice. What has been called malignancy is really an aspect of the habit of frankness and insensitivity of taste which undoubtedly marked the whole temper of that day.[2] Sir James Balfour could say of Scotstarvit himself that he was "a busie man in foul weather and one whose covetousness far exceeded his honesty", a remark made, Masson thinks, in a spirit

[1] *Cromwell's Letters and Speeches* (1850), Footnote II, p. 70-71. Another Footnote III, p. 138.
[2] Note No. 92, p. 228.

of personal rancour. Baillie could refer harshly to "blind Milton and that maleficent crew". Lord Napier's *Diary* contains extremely grave charges against contemporary statesmen, and Gordon of Rothiemay is ironical and severe. It was not the commentator's fault that the characters dealt with were often unfit to sustain a frank assessment based on ethical principles. These were, as Sir John and other leading men of his day confessed, "unhappy times", when worldly opportunism was imperfectly restrained by moral prohibitions.

Perhaps occasionally he is affected by political and ecclesiastical prejudices. We feel this in the case of the house of Hamilton—so justly respected to-day—where his narrative of the fortunes of the family in the times of James V and Mary Stuart is founded on the hard reviews and criticisms of Buchanan and Knox. His adoption of these severe reflections may possibly have been influenced by the existing sorrows of Scotland in which James, the 1st Duke of Hamilton, played so unfortunate but not a dishonourable part. And yet Sir John with unhesitating magnanimity tells the fine story of the founder of the family in James II's time, who, in the disaffection of the Earl of Douglas, told the Earl, "To fight a battle with the King, and either there to win honestly or die gloriously".[1]

In the pronouncement of censure he is quietly impersonal and his brief judgments seem to be chastened with a spirit of regret. He does to some extent take his stand as a deliberate censor of morals, but it is fairer to regard him as a spectator of life whose objective style and strict standards of conduct happen to be exercised in a scene of history marked by rude deeds and avaricious passions.

A point of interest which may have some bearing upon the gloomy aspect of the work is that the instances are actually a selection from the whole possible number involved. For example in the hundred years mentioned, although there were some seventeen Chancellors, Scot deals only with twelve. There were sixteen Secretaries, he presents nine. Of twelve Advocates he reports upon six; on five of these he gives adverse reports, but finds it difficult to set the engine of retribution into action against his old neighbour and adversary Sir Thomas Hope of Craighall. Although by no means omitting earlier Officers of State he nevertheless deals mostly with contemporaries, and there need

[1] *The Staggering State* (1754), p. 78.

be little doubt that he is fully conversant with the facts which he records.

In view of the foregoing selected figures, and the prevailing pattern of misfortune which is presented, we may assume that he chose those individuals who exhibited in their conduct a haste to be rich succeeded by a stumbling fall into ruin, and that the book is therefore of a specialised character. The word "staggering" is to be taken with an almost literal significance. As he saw it many Scottish statesmen in their pursuit of gain had lost their balance and were being precipitated towards a final calamity for themselves and their offspring.

The question of the author's age is pertinent to the subject, and there is evidence indicating that he began about 1650 when he was 65, and kept on writing or revising until as late as 1663. His way of referring to incidents dates his observations. For example, speaking of the Earl of Traquair who was taken prisoner at Preston in 1648 he says that "he has been detained since" in England. Traquair was released in 1654 and Sir John was therefore writing after 1648 and before 1654.[1] In a reference to John Maitland, the later Duke of Lauderdale, who was captured at Worcester in 1651 and held until 1660, he mentions "the Tower, where he lies at this present". The limit hereby indicated is extended with exactness in the note on Sir William Kerr, in which he dwells on the curious deaths of several servants of the family, the last, that of Andrew Learmont, occurring "in May 1662". An added paragraph on the history of Sir Archibald Johnston, Lord Warriston, gives evidence of yet later activity: "He was the last Clerk Register and a Lord of Session, and being in England was taken prisoner and sent home to Scotland, and for crimes contained in his dittay was publicly executed at Edinburgh at the Market Cross, anno 1663".[2]

At this time our author was seventy-eight years old and was apparently keeping the catalogue up-to-date. If he began the compilation say in 1650, that would mark the inception of Cromwell's usurpation with the accompanying suppression of Scottish rule and sovereignty, and Sir John's own departure from all active office. Even at this disastrous juncture he was considerably

---

[1] He also speaks of "the late King" showing that he wrote shortly after 1649. *The Staggering State*, p. 42.
[2] The expression means he was the last who combined the two offices. *Ibid.*, p. 128.

o   209

advanced in years, and his reflections upon misfortunes national and personal which were numerous and harrowing may have led him to see a dark and forbidding pattern in the history of many of his fellow statesmen. But it is noticeable that very much earlier, in the Latin poem which Drummond set out in English, this busy and resolute lawyer betrayed a strong sense of life's frustrations and vanity. The marked reiteration of calamity in the work we are discussing suggests that the intrusion of fate in human lives had become an acute conviction and almost an obsession with the author.

Readers of the narrative will notice the frequent use of the word "conquest" i.e. conquessed, in relation to the possession of lands. It implies something acquired in distinction to something inherited, and, as Sir John employs it, conveys suggestions of the exploitation of power or office for personal aggrandisement. Almost, you would think, he reveals a reluctant admiration for those who successfully practise it, but he recognises that without the stability of sound character it is finally fruitless.[1]

The following is a specimen of his style of paper, written about his associate in office, Traquair. It lends some support to Carlyle's opinion that *The Staggering State* contained "The cream of Scotch Biographical History in that age."[2]

"Sir John Stewart of Traquair, knight, thereafter created earl of Traquair, was first brought in by the Earl of Morton to be Treasurer Depute to him[3] but within a few years he displaced the principal and got full possession of the Treasury to himself; which place he managed so nimbly that he conquest many lands in the space that he enjoyed it, to wit: the baronies of Drochils, Linton, Horsbrugh, Henderland, Dryhope, and many others. He was, as Lucan said, *impatiens consortis*, for, finding himself opposed in judicatories by the kirkmen, called Bishops, he rested not until he got them undermined and by Act of Parliament expelled from the kingdom. Their own insolence, pride, and avarice gave him good ground to do so, for they could not be content with their bishoprics but urged also to have all the rest

---

[1] Note No. 93, p. 228.

[2] The spelling in the standard edition (1754) of *The Staggering State* has evidently been modernised.

[3] Depute Treasurer from 1630 to 1636, and Treasurer from the latter year until 1641. The Latin quotation implies that he was averse to a colleague or unable to brook a rival.

of the Kirk livings, as abbacies, priories etc., which exasperated the whole kingdom against them."[1]

"In these times the said lord Traquair, after subscribing the Covenant, went up to Court and there in open council declared against the public resolutions of the kingdom of Scotland, which was the first ground that moved the English to levy an army against this nation: with which army the King himself came down to the border. But matters being then pacified, the said Earl of Traquair was made the King's commissioner to the Parliament, but after that, was declared incapable of government and an Incendiary, and behoved to retire to England. There, being with the King, and having dealt for the releasing of the Earl of Lothian, then prisoner, he obtained such favour and respect of the said Earl that by his means he was brought in again to the Parliament wherein the Engagement against England was concluded. With which army he went himself and was taken prisoner at Preston, where he has been detained since" (i.e. in England). He then goes on to say:

"One, Mr George Nicol, a writer, gave in a paper to the King against Traquair's dealings when he was in his grandeur, but he got no other thanks nor reward from his Majesty save that he remitted him to the censure of the Council, who decerned him to be scourged, a paper put on his head, and to stand a forenoon at the Cross of Edinburgh; which made the poor young man fly the country, and terrified all other persons from informing his Majesty of anything that was done to his prejudice in the kingdom." After briefly reporting some gossip about Traquair and describing his deplorable decline into poverty in his latter days, Scot concludes by saying: "It is likely his family will not be of long subsistence."[2]

The perception of the working of retribution is most ironically exhibited in the case of James, Earl of Morton, where Scot concludes a brief summary of the Earl's doings by saying: "He caused bring home that heading instrument out of Halifax called *The Maiden*, wherewith he was first himself beheaded, 2nd June 1581."[3]

In this, his very first note, he seems to keep readers in view by stating in a parenthesis that Morton's actions are set down in full

[1] Note No. 94, p. 228.
[2] *The Staggering State*, p. 42-45.
[3] *Ibid.*, p. 3.

in the histories of Buchanan and Knox, and in Home's history of the family of Douglas.

His references to Archbishop Spottiswoode, whose appearance in the Council as Chancellor coincided with his own retiral, are not complimentary. On the other hand of his son Sir Robert, the President of Session, he says, "he was an able scholar and no ways evil inclined". He quotes a prophecy of Welsh concerning the Archbishop and reports the loss of lands which he had conquessed for his family, and also the execution of the above Sir Robert, and the grandson John, both for assisting James Graham: "so that Mr Welsh's prophecy is very likely to take effect".[1]

He has a similar tale to tell of John, Earl of Mar: "He sold many lands in his time, as the Lordship of Brechin and Navarre, the barony of Walstoun, the barony of Coldingham, the whole spiritualities and tiends of the Abbacies of Dryburgh, Cambuskenneth and Inchmaholm: yet was his estate nothing bettered thereby". It was of the vast substance of these conquests that Sir John observed, "It evanished and melted like snow off a dyke".[2]

In speaking of George Earl of Huntly he mentions his son George, first Marquis of Huntly, who slew the Earl of Murray and burnt his house at Donibristle in September 1591;[3] then, having recounted several family misfortunes, proceeds to say that the late Marquis's second brother, "the Lord Aboyne, and four others with him, as by a divine providence revenging the fact of Dinnibirstle, were burnt alive in the house of Frendraught in *anno* 1630". He sees the family "very near extinct and going to decay".[4] The reader may sometimes feel that the forces of retribution have taken sides with Sir John and his friends, and that calamity is in danger of being confused with judgment.

In addition there are situations in which the conception of divine justice is reduced almost to the ridiculous by the nature of the judgments preferred. It scarcely seems to be any reflection on Sir Thomas Hope that a ship bearing a part cargo of lead ore belonging to his son (from the Leadhills mine) should sink with all its crew. And we cannot think that Sir John is recording an act of divine disfavour when he concludes a dirge on Sir George Elphinstone of Blythswood, Justice Clerk and a troublesome

[1] *The Staggering State*, pp. 22-23.
[2] *Ibid.*, p. 37.
[3] Note No. 95, p. 228.
[4] *The Staggering State*, pp. 3-4.

colleague, by saying, "He left only one son behind him, who had two thumbs on each hand". Nevertheless as Sir John was bound to have at his command the whole tale of the disposal of estates, we may rest assured that the bewildering fluctuations of fortune as reported were historical; and probably never before, nor again in our history was worldly prosperity so readily attained and so lightly lost.

The chronicle has its dry humour—Carlyle calls it "laconic geniality"—and that it should predominate in the following case is to Scotstarvit's credit, for had he wished to tell a sensational story no career would have exemplified it more strikingly than that of James Stewart, the son of Lord Ochiltree. That Scot did not do so may have been because in his view Stewart's brief rise and fall had about it the air of something at once shallow and preposterous.

This soldier and courtier returning from Holland in 1579 gained favour almost at once by accusing the Earl of Morton of treason in the King's presence, and thus effected his ruin and execution. James VI, then a youth seventeen years old, thereafter gave him exceptional and rapid advancement. In 1581 he was made a member of the Privy Council: he was granted the Earldom of Arran, and in 1584 become governor of Stirling Castle and Lord Chancellor. His tyranny and insolence were so great that they provoked an outrush of opposition before which he fled in 1585. History says that it is questionable if he ever—now an obscure fugitive—really left Scotland, and it is certain that he was killed towards the end of 1595 near Symington in Lanarkshire by Sir James Douglas, nephew of the Earl of Morton whom he betrayed. His head was paraded on a spear through the country, his body being left to waste where it lay. The deed was the outcome of a vicious rivalry: Stewart, it is said, intended to extirpate the family of Douglas.

Scot, who calls him, "Captain James Stewart, thereafter styled Arran", says that being advanced to the highest favour by James, "he ruled all at his pleasure".[1, 2]

This noble, who claimed descent from Duke Murdo and sometimes publicly aired his royal origin, staged a pretty drama in the Session on an occasion when the King was present. Pulling a French silver piece from his pocket he threw it to the Clerk,

[1] "He took no man's advice but his own." Melville's *Diary*, p. 294.
[2] Note No. 96, p. 229.

213

therewith taking instrument that he claimed no right to the Crown, although, as he said, he was descended from Duke Murdo.[1]

This audacious action charmed James so greatly that—as Scot observes drily—"he was as well pleased as if he had received the greatest favour in the world".

The peculiar virtue of Scotstarvit's treatment of cases is that it throws a light on the inner and human side of characters who are imperfectly delineated by the conventional historians. In the Introduction to the Register of the Privy Council, 1578-1585 p. xxxii, Professor Masson makes a reference in point. When discussing Lennox he says that he made James Stewart one of his Gentlemen of the Bedchamber, and declares that the latter, "surpassed Lennox ten times in energy and ability". He then goes on to say: "And it is from this moment that there flashes into Scottish history, by the side of Lennox, this extraordinary and daring man, whose career, first in association with Lennox and afterwards more daringly by himself, has left such a track of lurid radiance in the records and traditions of his time". It is obvious that placed alongside such summaries as this the intimate etchings of Scot have their uses.

Scotstarvit gives us a good version of the famous story of the Master of Glamis, and James, in 1582.

"It was he", he says of Glamis,[2] "that at the raid of Stirling when King James was pressing to go out at the castle gate to the lords who came to take him, put his foot to the gate and held the King in. Who then, weeping for anger, got that answer from the Master: *Tis better bairns greet as bearded men.* Yet for all that, says Scot, "the King honoured him with that place", i.e. the place of Treasurer.[3]

Of Walter Stewart, Commendator of Blantyre, he reports that when he was riding up the High Street of Edinburgh his horse fell and the nobleman's leg was broken, which caused a witty courtier to observe: "That it was no marvel the horse couldn't bear him, seeing he had so many offices engrossed in his person, for besides being Commendator he was a Lord of Session, of Council, and Exchequer."[4]

As a scholar Sir John is inclined to make fun of high officials

---

[1] *History of Scotland*, Burton V, pp. 227-228.
[2] Sir Thomas Lyon.
[3] *The Staggering State*, p. 31.
[4] *Ibid.*, p. 32.

who were unlettered. Of a certain Chancellor he says that he was "altogether void of learning" and no more than a figurehead in office. So notorious were his deficiencies that someone dared to write on the wall of the Council chamber the line *Et Bibulo memini consule nil fieri*, knowing that the Chancellor would not understand what it meant.[1] Much the same comment was made on a Lord Privy Seal, to whom all official writs were directed in Latin, which he did not understand.

Sir John's love of a joke awakens also when he is offering his notes about Sir William Maitland of Lethington. Having praised his parts and called him "The firebrand of all the conjurations betwixt the Scots Queen and the Lord Norfolk against Queen Elizabeth", he illustrates his domination at Court by saying that when he had gout the Queen's ministers flocked to him so submissively that his chamber was called "the School", and those who consulted him "his scholars".[2]

There is also a good but rather mischievous witticism about his fellow-statesman, the Secretary, Sir William Alexander, "respected", he says, "for his poesy and the edition of his four tragedies, and *Doomsday*". The joke is that the King among his favours gave him liberty to coin money, which liberty he used by minting large numbers of a small copper coin called a "turner". These were originally worth a farthing but the new coin was given an increased value and on this account the Secretary was considerably enriched.[3] His fortune may be said therefore to have been made by his cultivation of poetry on the one hand and his use of the mint on the other. It happened, relates Sir John, that he then "built his great lodging in Stirling and put on the gate the motto, *Per mare per terras*", a reference perhaps to his colonising interests in distant Nova Scotia. But, reads our narrative, a witty man remembering his other activities proposed to change the motto into, "*Per metre per turners*".[4]

Here we may interject one of his personal recollections of which some occur in the book. He has been praising Sir Gideon Murray, "Treasurer Depute under his cousin the ill-fated Earl of Somerset, but full Treasurer in effect", and having recounted his excellent services relates the following pleasant anecdote:

[1] Note No. 97, p. 229.
[2] *The Staggering State*, p. 55.
[3] Reg. P.C. 1629-1630, p. 139, p. 204.
[4] *The Staggering State*, p. 73.

"He was so beloved by King James VI that when he went to the Court of England, there being none in the royal bedchamber but the King, Sir Gideon, and myself, Sir Gideon by chance letting fall his glove, the King although both stiff and old, stooped down and gave him his glove, saying, 'My predecessor Queen Elizabeth thought she did any man a favour when she let fall her glove that he might take it up. But, sir, you may say that a King lifted up your glove.'"[1]

Readers of seventeenth-century annals have noticed how general was the love of curious occurrences and the belief in portents and wonders. Calderwood, for example, reports: "Upon the 27th of Januar (1616) about five efternoone there was a great fierie starre, in form of a dragon with a taile, running through the firmament, and giving light and spouting fyre: which continued a prettie space before it vanished". As it passed from sight he says, it gave "two great cracks". Also of a flood-tide at Leith he says: "The people took this extraordinary tyde to be a forewarning of some evil to come".[2] Balfour in his *Annals* reports: "Tuesday, the 3rd day of June this yeire, 1650, it rained from the heavens drops of blood in Easdale, which was certified by divers gentlemen of good crydit, inhabitants ther."[3] There is an assortment of these credulous matters served up by the author of *The Staggering State*.

He repeats for example the public story that Montrose "ate a toad whilst he was a sucking child". Observing that, "Often what is most pleasant to a man is his overthrow", and that the Earl of Mar's chief delight was hunting, he says of him that, "while walking in his own hall a dog cast him off his feet and lamed him, of which he died", and that at his funeral a hare ran through the company and "caused his chamberlain to fall off his horse and break his neck".[4]

In connection with his succession to the Chancery Office he was baulked for some time by the loss of a bond which he alleged had been put in the fire by Sir William Scott's servant that it might never come to light: "But God, the protector of orphans, revenged the injury in a strange way, for the said servant when he was sickly and left alone in his sister's house fell in the fire and burnt his head and his hands before any came near him".[5]

---

[1] *The Staggering State*, p. 51.
[2] *History of the Kirk of Scotland*, VII, p. 210.
[3] The *Annals* IV, p. 79. A natural phenomenon repeated lately.
[4] *The Staggering State*, p. 38.
[5] *Ibid.*, p. 123.

To a man capable of this literal belief in judgment, the retributive character of the loss of family estates which had been doubtfully or greedily won was an inevitable conclusion.

Of the current belief in witches and warlocks there is a good deal. We hear of people in high station getting a "response", and he relates that in some great houses witches were retained as "familiars". The outstanding case of a warlock occurs in connection with a Justice Clerk: "Sir Lewis Ballantyne by curiosity dealt with a warlock called Richard Graham to raise the Devil: who, having raised him in his yard in the Canongate, Sir Lewis was thereby so terrified that he took sickness and died".[1] Superstitious credulity was rife all classes.

There is a quaint element introduced by the author's liking for oddity of incident, thus he reports on the eldest son of Walter Stewart, Lord Blantyre, "a gallant youth of great hopes", how that having quarrelled with the young Lord Wharton, "they went out to single combat a mile from London and at the first thrust killed each other and fell dead in one another's arms".[2] Carlyle in his *Cromwell* mentions this tragedy, Wharton being of the Cromwell faction, and says that it became a popular item with ballad-writers and was sung all over the country.[3]

Of Robert, Earl of Roxburgh, he remembers best that he made "his first voyage on horseback in the year 1585 in the raid of Stirling. At which time he had on a jack,[4] being about fifteen years of age."

On Robert Crichton, the Lord Advocate, the paper is highly incidental. He says his son had no success after killing the Laird of Moncoffer at the Chapel of Eglismaly.[5] He then refers to his brother James, a prodigy of learning, and quotes Aldus Manutius as saying that, "He was a miracle of Nature, seeing he could forget nothing". The person briefly described in this negative way was by contemporary report the wonder of his age. In his twenty-first year he had perfect skill in ten languages, and excelled in philosophy, mathematics, divinity, and *belles-lettres*. He was a perfect athlete and an Adonis in looks. The account of his death in Mantua depicts him as slain while he wandered playing

[1] *The Staggering State*, p. 131.
[2] *Ibid.*, p. 32.
[3] *The Letters and Speeches* (1850), II, p. 53.
[4] Note No. 98, p. 229.
[5] Note No. 99, p. 229.

his guitar in the streets at a Carnival. His fame is thought to have been exaggerated by the flattering sentiments of Manutius.[1]

Other odd comments are these: "The Estate of Ratho belonging to Thomas Marjoribanks, Clerk of Register, was sold by his grandson to the Queen's taylor, Mr Duncan". Sir Archibald Napier is son "to that learned Merchiston who wrote a logarithmy and a commentary upon the Revelation". The only son of the Good Wife of Humbie, "running his horse at full speed on the sands near Aberdeen, sank, horse and all, and was never seen again". James Hay of Fingask, Comptroller from 1610 to 1615, married Lord Denny's daughter, "who being in a coach at night in the streets of London got her ear rent by a rogue who pulled the diamond forth thereof, and with fright the lady died".[2]

Twice we get glimpses of popular tumult in Scotland's capital. The first was in a rising against the Octavians. Scot gives the day: 17th December 1596.

He says: "Their councils and strict dealings were so hateful that the Commonalty of the town of Edinburgh rose in arms to have killed the Secretary and the rest in the King's presence. But by his Majesty's presence they were saved and the tumult pacified."[3] The other note tells us how Sir John Hay, Provost of Edinburgh, "undertook stoutly to cause ministers to accept the Service Book", but was forced to fly to England, "there being a mutiny, and the bishops chased down the streets for attempting this rash enterprise".[4]

There is a constant presumption throughout these papers that Sir John is a man whose moral standing is above suspicion. We see it reflectively in the observations he makes about dishonesty and immorality. When he describes a certain Lord as "A noble spendthrift, exquisite in all manner of debauchery", we know that he is not approving of these vicious accomplishments. Thus also he refers obviously with aversion to two young men who were "greatly subject to drunkenness and companionry". He occasionally calls attention to infidelity and licence in marital relationships and invariably appends a grave rebuke, often

---

[1] *Life of the Admirable Crichton.* Tytler, pp. 36-38, pp. 43-44.

[2] *The Staggering State*, p. 151. For the state of the London streets at that time, see Trevelyan's *England Under the Stuarts*, I, p. 23. Penguin Books.

[3] *Ibid.*, p. 57. The tumult in which Andrew Hart the publisher was involved.

[4] *Ibid.*, p. 124.

with an air of shocked regret. The incident of moral discipline already reported, where he brought his man-servant before the Privy Council for telling a lie, seems to indicate an unusually acute conviction of the serious principle involved in simple truth.

Sir John may in fact be something new in Scottish history: a Reformation figure, a kind of prototype of the serious Church layman or influential elder of later days who stands forth as a champion of honesty in public office and virtue in private character. The reader must judge from the story whether or not his life was consistent with these professions.

The annotator who stands behind all these pages has been summed up with rare skill by Professor Masson in his *Life of William Drummond*. He says of Scot:

"A shrewd sagacious Scottish lawyer and judge of his peculiar generation, very orthodox in his morals and beliefs, but with a dash of the eccentric and humorist in his ways, and something crabbed and cynical in his temper; systematically acquisitive of lands and gear, and not more scrupulous as to the means than most Scottish officials of his time, but thrifty in his use of what he had acquired, and with a rough sense of honour and responsibility in him after all. His liking for learning and literature amounted to a passion, and for this object he was munificent to an extent that shamed his contemporaries among the Scottish nobility. . . . So we would picture for ourselves the Sir John Scot of Scotstarvit, whose figure in his judicial robes, or in his ordinary town garb, was familiar to all Edinburgh; while Fife knew him best in his old suit and top-boots, plodding about his farms."[1]

This summary, fair for the most part in what it says, and graphically suggestive, possibly errs, although with an indulgent tone, when it says that he was "not more scrupulous than most Scottish officials of his time". No doubt Sir John could drive a hard bargain, but his condemnation of fraud and illegal practices in the conduct of official affairs and in the acquirement of wealth and land is too pronounced and spirited to admit of his participation in them. In his attitude and words there is a testimony of sincerity which we are inclined to accept.

He is also worthy of special praise as a great patriot: he was intensely a Scot both in name and character, and towers as such above many of his compatriots in his generation: a positive and

[1] *Drummond of Hawthornden* (1873), pp. 224-226.

self-reliant personality, proud and careful of place and quick to oppose any who wronged him or challenged his right.

Professor Masson asserts that he makes "most of the people" he mentions in his catalogue "to be dubious characters". If this statement were modified to "many people" it would be true, but there are cases of individuals who appear as unfortunate men, almost the playthings of fate, and there are also a number of favourable presentations where he sees the just life followed by a corresponding benefit.

When Alexander Montgomery, the poet, eulogised Scot's estimable grandfather he concluded his praise in the following terms: "Good Robert Scot, who while thou liv'dst for honesty was odd, as writ bears witness of thy worthy works:

> So faithful, formal, and so frank and free
> Shall never use that office after thee".

But the unexpected seems to have happened, the grandson also being odd for honesty, and being worthy of his grandsire, and holding office as commendably and as long. "Faithful, formal, frank, free", seem terms not unfitted to describe this old patriot, statesman, lawyer, scholar, churchman, and benefactor. His life and history shine with the clear light of patriotic zeal and duty well performed, and his enlightened public services in an age disturbed by faction and selfishness give him an honoured place in the annals of his native country.

NOTES

1. Now preserved in Tarvit House, close at hand.
2. Scot is said to have been related to the Inglis family, and to have treated the owner with marked generosity, exchanging with him his own estate of Knightspottie in Perthshire. Nisbet's *Heraldry* 1722, II, Appendix, p. 293.
3. MacGibbon and Ross say of the fire-place referred to: "a style of fire-place altogether different from the earlier buildings." *Castellated and Domestic Architecture*, II, p. 42.
4. Major-General Scott's daughters married: Henrietta, the Marquis of Titchfield (Duke of Portland), Lucy, Lord Doune (9th Earl of Moray), Joan, George Canning, later becoming Viscountess Canning. Millar's *Fife* I, p. 266.
5. In 1578 he received the special thanks of the Regent and the Lords of Secret Council for his care of the Register Books of Session. Reg. P.C. 1567-1578, p. 138.
6. His name is not in the list compiled by Sir Francis J. Grant, but there is evidence of his appearance before the Privy Council as procurator. Reg. P.C. 1610-1613, p. 532.
7. Internal evidence suggests that the poem was written at a later date. Drummond was abroad for the most part of 1625-1630, but was home in 1627. In that year he patented a military machine and made his gift of books to Edinburgh University.
8. "Stank dyke": Scot had certain rights to seaweed in Kingsmure and Carrailmure as the owner of the lands at Thirdpart: the estate of Barns intervened.
9. The Presbytery on 18th May of the same year possibly allude to the above decision. They say: "Anent buriall in the kirk of Kinghorn, the brethren according to ane act of the Assemblie of Glasgow inhibiting kirk burials, inhibits any kirk buriall in the kirk of Kinghorn heirafter, that is to say within the bodie of the kirk: as for the aisles it leaves that for further consideratioun." *The Presbytrie Booke of Kirkcaldie*, Stevenson, p. 233.
10. Sir Walter states that on the death of the last of the male Scotstarvit line, namely General John Scott, the chiefship reverted to Scott of Harden, from which branch of the family Sir Walter himself derived.
11. In 1655 he petitioned against the fine of £15,000 on the Buccleuch estate. Cromwell's Council reduced it to £7,000. Calendar of State Papers, Domestic 1655, p. 71.
12. Gordon of Rothiemay says of the Committee: "A mixed multitude: Parliament epitomised: many heads but few statesmen." *Hist. of Scottish Affairs*, 1637-1641. Spalding Club, III, p. 182.
13. A covenant subscribed by Montrose and a few other noblemen in opposition to Argyll.

14. A reference to the Whiggamore Raid. When news of the defeat at Preston arrived in Scotland the Kirk party rose to arms in the west.

15. *Index to the Acts of the General Assembly*, 1646, No. 79. "Act concerning the Lord Scottistarbit's deliverie of the authentick Confession of Faith subscribed by King James and his household, with an order for thanks to him therefore." The Covenant was "allowed" by the General Assembly in April 1581. Melville's *Diary* (Wodrow Soc.), p. 87.

16. This would carry back his interest in Pont's maps to approximately 1632. John Blaeu in a petition to Parliament in March 1647 reports that his father and himself had been exercised about printing the maps of Scotland for seventeen years. This shows that their interest was first engaged in 1630. In the above Parliament Blaeu asked that, as his Majesty had already given warrant prohibiting any others from printing the maps in Scotland, they would assist him to procure a like Licence in England, which the Estates agreed to do. Acts Parl. Scot., VI, p. 736.

17. Clarendon describes him as "a proud gloomy man", who for private reasons had contracted an implacable displeasure against both the Court and the Church. *Hist. of the Rebellion*, III, p. 32.

18. When he was pardoned Lord Sinclair suggested that he be appointed to the parish of Dysart. Archbishop Sharp's response was: "That one Metropolitan was enough for Scotland and two would be too many for the province of Fife." *Dict. Nat. Biog.*, VII, p. 1242.

19. In his Autobiography he tells the story of George Gillespie at the Assembly of Divines, and although speaking both of the father of Gillespie and of George makes no mention of Patrick. *Select Biographies* (Wodrow Soc.) I, p. 330.

20. Henceforth to be done with political engrossments and yet to write *Paradise Lost* and *Samson Agonistes*. Charles forbore to pursue him: "Was he not old, blind, destitute?"

21. Joseph Scaliger called Buchanan "The greatest Latin poet in Europe." Dr Johnson praised not only his Latinity but his genius. Boswell's *Life* (1804), IV, p. 199.

22. Bacon's contemporary poem on *Life* is noticeably similar and closes with almost the same lines.

> "What then remains, but that we still should cry
> For being born, or, being born, to die."
> *Palgrave's Golden Treasury*, Bk. I, No. LVII.

Dean Inge claims that this is an imitation from a well-known chorus of Sophocles. Aubrey in his *"Brief Lives"* prints it in full.

23. Hart's shop was in the "Heich buith" on the north side of the High Street a little beneath the Cross. Due perhaps to the similarity of names and to Sir John Scot's editorship, *Hodaeporicon* has sometimes been wrongly attributed to him. In the *Delitiae Poetarum* the above poem is attributed to John Scot simply, and is followed by the poems of John Scot of Scotstarvit.

24. In March 1784 Dr Johnson wrote to Boswell: "If you procure heads of Hector Boece, the historian, and Arthur Johnston, the poet, I will put them in my room." Boswell's *Life of Johnson* (Napier, 1884), III, p. 360.

25. This distinguished jurist, who at his own will was never a Lord of Session, refused a knighthood, but by command of King James he was styled a knight. *Dict. Nat. Biog.*, IV, p. 1373.

26. John Lindsay, 17th Earl of Crawford, (*c.* 1596-1678). He lived at Struthers Castle not far from Scotstarvit Tower in the parish of Ceres. *Dict. Nat. Biog.*, XXXIII, p. 304.

27. His map of "Clydesdale" bears the date 1596. There is an exceptional instance of publication in the year 1608. This is Pont's map of the "Shyres of Lothian and Linlitquo". "It appears to have been published by Andrew Hart (d. 1621) and engraved by Judocus Hondius (d. 1611) whose names appear on it." *The Early Maps of Scotland*, Scot. Geog. Soc. (1934), p. 26, p. 74.

28. This is based on his reckoning of time when applying for a printing licence from Cromwell, and is supported by John Blaeu's statement made to Parliament in 1647.

29. Robert Pont had remarkable versatility. He was associated with John Craig, minister of St Magdalen's Chapel, Edinburgh, in producing the metrical version of the Psalms for the Scottish Psalter (the first) in 1564. *Dict. Nat. Biog.*, XVI, pp. 90-92.

30. Originally published in 1683, Sibbald's work was historical and topographical, and was done at the request of Charles II. James Gordon was responsible for the excellent map of Fife, and it is shown that his father supplied topographical matter, and probably did so for other regions also.

31. Blaeu the publishers at Amsterdam were William and John, father and son. William died in 1638 and thereafter John was the principal. The plan to produce maps of the world, *Theatrum Mundi*, was begun in 1634. *Biographie Universelle*, IV, p. 396.

32. On 29th January 1630, the Convention of Burghs answering an appeal for a Pastor by the Scottish people at Campvere, appointed William Spang, Student of Divinity, taking him bound to assume office by 1st July of the same year. It was remitted to certain burghs to deal with the Archbishop of St Andrews to receive and admit him. *The Scottish Staple at Veere*, Davidson and Gray, p. 278. In October 1652 Mr Spang was called to the English church at Middelburg and left Campvere in May 1653. His flock at Veere testified that he had exercised "a comfortable and powerful ministry". *Ibid.*, p. 299. Campvere, or Veere, on the island of Walcheren was the ancient capital of Zeeland, and the port for the entry of Scottish goods.

33. *Cunningham Topographized* by Pont. There is a manuscript copy in the Nat. Lib. This is not the original but a transcription in the handwriting of Sir James Balfour. Mr James Dobie of Crummock edited it in 1853 and it was issued with a Continuation in 1876.

34. This letter which dedicated the whole work to Scotstarvit was printed in the early chapters of the Atlas. The reference to Sir John's action does not warrant any inference that he urged James VI to have the maps published. After quoting the King's action Gordon says the papers remained in darkness until the time that Scot took them up.

35. When working in Sutherland Pont scribbled on his survey: "Extreme wilderness." "Many woolfs in this place."

36. The ancient pier of the ferry still exists. The Celtic name may mean the steading or place of the boat, *curach*. This ferry was in use at least until the middle of the nineteenth century. Sir Walter Scott after visiting Wemyss Castle on 18th June 1827, says "We reached Pettycur about half-past one, crossed to Edinburgh, and so ended our little excursion". *The Journal*, I, p. 406.

37. In 1662 a charter granted Inchkeirie to Margaret Rigg, wife of George Scot, with "the newly built house on the west side of the close of Piteadie". In view of Scot's claim to a seat which had belonged to the laird of Piteadie it may be that Inchkeirie was part of that estate and the present ruined castle may be the house "newly built". Reg. Gt. Seal, XI, 925.

38. Despite this decision the Presbytery is seen acting contrariwise two years later: "Dysart, 23rd August, 1643. Sir James Melvill of Hallhill presented ane presentatioun from the King's Majestie in favour of Mr John Smith (Minister at Leslie) to the kirk of Burntisland, whereof the Presbytrie accepts". *The Presbytrie Booke of Kircaldie*, p. 255.

39. When the Committee of Estates was captured by the English at Alyth in September 1651, Law, with some other clergy, was taken with them. An appeal was made to Lt. General Monk for their release but Law died a prisoner in England in 1660. *Ecc. Records*, Presbytery of St. Andrews, 1641-1698. (Abbotsford Club), p. 63. *The Synod of Fife* (Abbotsford Club), p. 229.

40. The Lord Advocate, Hope, prepared two books on Minor and Major Practicks. These are forms of pleading which may have been intended for the use of his sons, of whom three were lawyers.

41. There is a short independent account of the affair in the Mar and Kellie MSS. *Hist. Manuscripts Commission* (1904), pp. 139-144.

42. Thomas Hamilton. Scot says he was "very learned but of a cholerick constitution". At this time he was State Secretary and President of the Court of Session.

43. The Act is printed in the Introduction to Brunton and Haig. pp. xxxi-xxxii. No principle of appointment is stated. The rules and statutes are such "as sall pleise the King's Grace".

44. The Earl of Winton, temporary Vice Chancellor and President of the Council, writes to the King that "The aucht auld Ordinaris has quate thair plaices and sax of the seven new intrants are ressaved and admittit". He says he writes "in simplicitie and waiknes". Reg. P.C. 1625-1627, Footnote, p. 224.

45. He was re-appointed to the Privy Council, but it was 1629 when he was made Lord Extraordinary, which after a short period was withdrawn. In 1632 he became a Lord Ordinary.

46. The practice to-day is that Judges are not sworn in afresh on the accession of a new Sovereign. This hinges on the doctrine contained in the maxim that "The King never dies". Halsbury says "The sovereign is regarded as legally immortal". Death in this case is legally termed "demise" (dimissio) implying "transfer of the kingdom to the successor". Halsbury's *Laws of England*, edited by Lord Simonds, VII, p. 224.

47. Napier was appointed a Lord Extraordinary in February 1626, and was raised to the Peerage in May 1627.

48. Napier accuses the King's advisers of seriously abusing his confidence. Napier's *Diary*.

49. Baillie says Hope's "idle curiositie put us all to infinite difficulty", when an effort was being made to settle schools and churches in 1641. *The Journal*, I, p. 395.

50. Scot took his seat as a Lord Ordinary in July 1632, as did also Sir John Hope of Craighall the Advocate's eldest son. Of the Advocate's other sons, Sir Thomas Hope of Kerse became a Lord of Session, and in 1641, Lord Chief Justice; and the sixth son, Sir James Hope, was admitted to the Session as Lord Hopetoun in 1649.

51. Colin, Lord Mackenzie, was created Earl of Seaforth in 1623 (d. 1633).

52. Tytler in his *History of Scotland* says no ground appears for the assertion that it was a male fief, and suggests that the recall may have been affected by James's general policy of breaking the power of the nobles. In 1427 in a Parliament held at Inverness he arrested many turbulent chiefs. *Hist. of Scot.* (3rd edit.), III, pp. 96-97, pp. 137-140.

53. In May 1633 Sir John wrote to Morton: "I have sent you herein the doubill of the Chartour of the erledome of Stratherne grantit by King James the First to his uncle Walter, erle of Atholl, efter the death of David, whereby it is evident that it was then in his Majesteis hands and at his disposition". *Earldoms of Strathearn, etc.*, Appendix lxxxvii.

54. Professor Masson in his *Life of Drummond* alludes to various whisperings of sedition at this time and mentions the above case of Hamilton as one where the King's suspicions had been aroused. He says that for eighty years there were persistent doubts as to the true line of royal descent. *Drummond of Hawthornden*, p. 188.

55. Sir Archibald Gibson of Durie in Fife, a Lord of Session and later Lord President: compiler of *Durie's Decisions*.

56. Clarendon calls Traquair, "A man of great parts, without doubt not inferior to any of that nation in wisdom and dexterity"; but his history is marked with craft and opportunism. *Dict. Nat. Biog.*, XVIII, pp. 1213-1215.

57. The text of Drummond's paper is given in *The Lives and Reigns of the Jameses* (1680), pp. 221-223, and in *The Works of Drummond* (1711), pp. 129-131. It is dated December 1632. Professor Masson, in spite of the evidence of the *True Relation*, makes the statement that it may never have been submitted to the King.

58. Sir Harris Nicolas quotes it and speaks of "The known and acknowledged falsehood of the above statement, upon which allegation the Earl's status and rights were denied".

59. "The King had full power of disposal by grant of the crown lands, which were increased from time to time by confiscation, escheat, forfeiture, etc. The history of these lands to the reign of William III was one of continuous alienation to favourites. In the reign of Queen Anne an Act was passed limiting the right of alienation to a period of not more than thirty-one years. The revenue was also made to constitute

part of the civil list. At the beginning of his reign George III surrendered his interest in crown lands in return for a fixed civil list." *Ency. Brit.*, 11th edition, VII, p. 519.

60. "Dominating every line of action was the determination to retain land and to increase it, to gain vassals and subordinate allies, and to dispossess those who supported a rival family." *Scotland under Charles I*, Mathew, p. 141.

The nobles knew how to hold with a strong hand the lands and goods which they had acquired." *The Personal Government of Charles I*, Gardiner, I, p. 330.

61. By this action holders of Crown land were to be compelled to come into court and prove their titles or have them declared null. Professor Masson discusses this fully in a footnote. Reg. P.C. 1625-1627, pp. 397-398.

62. "In its final shape the arrangement thus made is worthy of memory as the one successful action of Charles's reign." *The Personal Government of Charles I*, Gardiner, I, p. 351.

63. This Hall still stands in the Cowgate, being the back building of an original court or quadrangle; at present it is occupied as a brewery. It was the scene of the Convention immediately preceding the signing of the National Covenant and was used as a Court House for Cromwell's Commission on forfeited estates. In the eighteenth century it was a theatre. The hall upstairs was probably the scene of the larger gatherings.

64. In 1648 Lord Stair delivered his oration, the spirit and terms of which seem to be echoed in the Gentry's Petition. The oration is printed in full: *Scot. Hist. Review*, XIII, pp. 380-392.

65. Sir James Lumsden of Innergellie, Kilrenny, a soldier, and brother of Robert who as Governor defended Dundee when it was besieged by General Monk in 1651.

66. In discussing the growth and functions of the English Council in Tudor times, particularly under Henry VII, Professor T. F. Bindoff reports that this advisory body came to discharge an almost unlimited range of duties, "legislative, judicial, executive". He instances a number of features strikingly similar to the characteristic marks of the Scottish Council during the fifteenth and sixteenth centuries. *Tudor England*. Pelican Hist. of England, vol. 5. pp. 59-62.

67. A remarkable example occurred at the burning of Dunfermline in May 1624. The Council's concern and the practical steps taken to bring relief are marked with a deep sense of responsibility and sympathy. Reg. P.C. 1622-1625, p. xxxi, p. lxv, pp. 510-512. Calderwood's *Hist.*, VII, p. 607.

68. At St Andrews in 1617 he emphasised that in Church policy his will was to have the force of law.

69. On the occasion of the Coronation George Hay, Viscount of Dupplin, was created Earl of Kinnoull, and in the following year Spottiswoode became Chancellor.

70. Court of High Commission: "That institution abhorred and dreaded both in England and Scotland". Burton's *Hist.*, VII, p. 436.

71. Letter of Horning. A letter issued from his Majesty's Signet by messenger, requiring a debtor to pay a debt for which he is prosecuted,

or to perform the obligation within a limited time under pain of rebellion. Erskine quoted in Jamieson's *Dictionary*.

72. It will be seen that Charles neglected this order when he named Archbishop Spottiswoode first in re-appointing the Council, and in wishing to place him in front of the Chancellor at the Coronation procession.

73. His attitude was consistent with the stand taken by the Scottish Church since the twelfth century. When William the Lion acknowledged Henry II as his feudal superior, the Scottish bishops, having then no Archbishops, yet refused (1176) to make submission to the Archiepiscopal English Church. In 1192 the Scottish Church was pronounced to be a "special daughter" to the Roman See. "Never since then has any English Archbishop had jurisdiction over Scottish bishops." *Scotland: Church and Nation*, p. 25. Gordon Donaldson, D. Litt.

74. "Hasp and Staple." A mode of entry in Scotland, in burghs, by which a bailie declared a person heir, delivering the property over to the heir by the hasp and staple of the door, of which the heir laid hold. Bell's *Law Directory*, 1890, p. 499.

75. Prince Frederick, son of Frederick, Elector Palatine, King of Bohemia, whose wife was a daughter of James VI and ancestress of the present Royal family.

76. Scotstarvit was added to the Commission when it was enlarged at a later date.

77. It was forbidden to hunt deer or roe, hares or wildfowl, within eight miles of any of the palaces.

78. There are five Bishops in this sederunt.

79. The Lord Lyon, commissioned on 8th August 1620, was Sir Gerome Lindsay of Annatland and Dunino, who died in December 1642. He appears for some unexplained reason to have demitted office early in 1630, for in March of that year a Privy Council minute shows that Sir James Balfour had been appointed. *Court of the Lord Lyon*, p. 22. Scot. Rec. Soc. Edited by Sir Francis Grant, Albany Herald.

Sir Gerome Lindsay was a son of David Lindsay, first Protestant minister of Leith and afterwards Bishop of Ross (d. 1613). He married a daughter of Sir David Lindsay of the Mount, nephew of the poet, and succeeded his father-in-law as Lord Lyon.

80. On 13th June 1633, the King when in Edinburgh named Edward Kellie with reference to certain books of music required for royal use in his chapel. Reg. P.C. 1633-1635, pp. 114-115.

81. "Nicholas Briot was chief engraver for the English mint at the beginning of the Civil War." Carlyle, *Cromwell's Letters and Speeches*, (1850), Vol. III, p. 339.

82. The Chancellor, George Hay, Viscount of Dupplin, was accustomed in conference to interrupt the speech of anyone, even the King.

83. Seaforth, son of Lord Mackenzie of Kintail, was noticeably present at Privy Council meetings during the Coronation negotiations. It was he who passed to Sir John Scot the paper which originally discussed the implications of Menteith's transaction in the Strathearn affair. He was succeeded by George, the second Earl, in 1634.

84. "Estates" and "Convention" are interchangeable terms as used in the minutes. The "public meeting" was the general meeting of the Estates.

85. The expression "every Estait" refers to the various groups on the Commission which had a proportionate representation of the three classes, nobles, gentry, and burghs.

86. It is well within the bounds of possibility that Scot, who was a stickler for order, and from whose office the warrant had to be issued, called attention to the national character of the superscription on the Great Seal and secured the framing of the commission in the above terms.

87. In 1605 when King James was promoting the Union of the Kingdoms by personal mandate and had sanctioned a new Union flag, the Scottish mariners made protest, saying, "That the Scottis Cross, callit the Sanctandrois Cross, is twice dividit; and the Inglische Cross, callit St. George, is halden haill and drawn through the Scottis Cross, which is thereby obscurit, and no token nor mark to be seene of the Scottis Armes". The Council wrote to the King about this and furnished two new and unobjectionable patterns. Reg. P.C. 1604-1607, p. 498.

88. Clarendon comments upon "the new style of address" on the part of the Scots, particularly during the troubles of 1638-1639. He says "They reproached the actions of his Majesty and then made the greatest professions of duty that could be invented". *Hist. of the Rebellion*, (1826), p. 215.

89. On this occasion Sir John Scot was absent. It was in this same month of September that Robin Dalzell carried south to the King the Reasons explaining the dangers of the Strathearn transaction.

90. The Charter so dated was submitted to the Scottish Council on 7th September. In the month of July Scot had been appointed an Ordinary Lord of Session.

91. Professor G. S. Pryde referring to the scheme of 1632 and the later scheme of 1661 comments: "The Royal Burghs, sensing a threat to their monopoly of trade, resisted these ventures and rejoiced in their complete collapse". *Scotland from 1603 to the Present Day*, II, p. 29.

92. Hume Brown comments on the hardness and violence of expression which marked the polemics of the late sixteenth century and was not inconsistent with self-respect and refinement in the contestants. *John Knox*, I, p. 160.

One writer says that Scot attacked Balmerino "with his usual malignancy", and yet Scot calls the Secretary "a man of notable spirit and great gifts", and supports the view that he was made a scapegoat for the King in his indiscretion in communicating with Pope Clement VIII. *The Staggering State*, p. 59.

93. Calderwood, speaking of the Earl of Dunbar, almost echoes Sir John's observation: "None of his posteritie enjoyeth a foot-breadth of land this day of his conqueist in Scotland". *Hist. of the Kirk of Scotland*, VII, p. 153.

94. Baillie made the same charge and so did the Earl of Haddington: but Baillie stood for Presbytery and Hamilton had personal interests.

95. The date is usually given as February 1591-92.

96. Scot says significantly that he was "styled Arran". When the Hamiltons were prosecuted and under forfeiture in 1579, James, Earl of Arran, being invalid, was placed under the guardianship of Stewart who quickly acquired the Earldom of his ward. Stewart was disgraced and deprived of the title in 1586.

97. The line as quoted by Suetonius runs: *Nam Bibulo fieri consule nil memini.* Bibulus was a nephew of Cato and Caesar's colleague in the consulship. "For in the consulship of Bibulus I remember nothing being done."

98. A defensive coat of mail or leather.

99. Near Kirkcaldy and referred to in connection with Scot's lands of Inchkeirie. Wm. Meldrum of "Moncoffer" is denounced as a rebel. Reg. P.C. 1585-1592, p. 191.

100. G. M. Trevelyan offers an interesting account of 'Child Marriage' in England in the fifteenth and sixteenth centuries. *Social Hist. of England* (illus.), I, pp. 132-138. Penguin Books.

INDEX

231